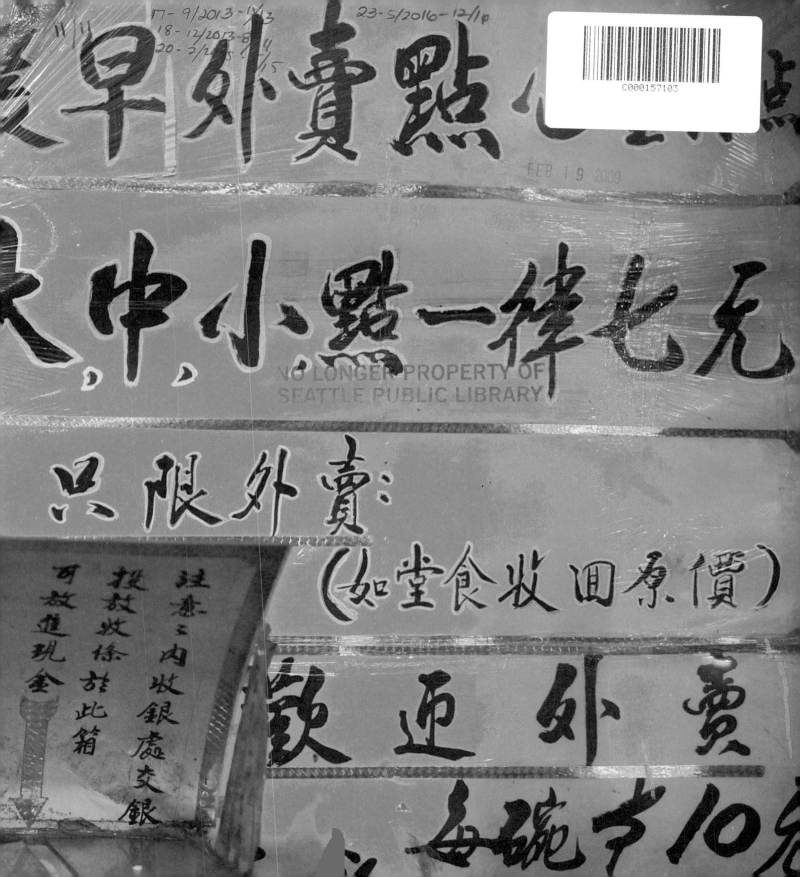

早外賣點心

中小點一樣七元

只限外賣

(如堂食收回原價)

歡迎外賣

每碗十10

Published by Periplus Editions (HK) Ltd.,
with editorial offices at 130 Joo Seng Road
#06-01, Singapore 368357

First published in 2006 by Hardie Grant Books
85 High Street, Prahran, Vic 3181, Australia
www.hardiegrant.com.au

ISBN-10: 0-7946-0492-7
ISBN-13: 978-0-7946-0492-9

The publishers are grateful to villa & hut for their
generous assistance and the loan of props.

Design by 21-19 (Ryan Guppy)
Photography by Greg Elms
Styling by Sara Backhouse

Distributed by

North America
Tuttle Publishing
364 Innovation Drive, North Clarendon,
VT 05759-9436 U.S.A.
Tel: 1 (802) 773-8930; Fax: 1 (802) 773-6993
info@tuttlepublishing.com
www.tuttlepublishing.com

Japan
Tuttle Publishing
Yaekari Building, 3rd Floor, 5-4-12 Osaki,
Shinagawa-ku, Tokyo 141 0032
Tel: (81) 3 5437-0171; Fax: (81) 3 5437-0755
tuttle-sales@gol.com

Asia Pacific
Berkeley Books Pte. Ltd.
130 Joo Seng Road
#06-01, Singapore 368357
Tel: (65) 6280-1330; Fax: (65) 6280-6290
inquiries@periplus.com.sg;
www.periplus.com

Printed in Singapore

10 09 08 07
6 5 4 3 2 1

Lotus
Asian Flavors
Teage Ezard

Contents

Introduction

Running ezard, **my restaurant, never ceases to excite me. I love the food we create, the focus on flavor and texture, heavily influenced by Asian techniques, in particular Thai, Indonesian and Chinese. I believe that at** ezard **we "taste outside the square", presenting unusual combinations where flavor is paramount.**

In the 22 years I've been cooking professionally, I've worked with many styles, including classical French, modern Greek, Italian, Chinese, Thai, Indian and Malaysian. All of these cuisines share one important characteristic—when at their best they have natural balance. While one ingredient may be the main focus in a dish, each individual flavor plays an important role, no matter how small or subtle.

I choose to cook mostly Asian food because it is what I like eating. The dishes rely on texture as much as they do on flavor, and this provides endless opportunity for creativity and experimentation. The versatility of Asian ingredients allows you to break the rules and to push boundaries, and to constantly come up with new dishes.

While at **ezard** we've adapted Asian-inspired food for an elegant restaurant setting, it's by no means the only way to enjoy it. I am just as easily seduced by the street food found in every Asian city, and by Chinese dim sum. I first discovered street food while trekking in Thailand, and was hooked. Along the streets and on the beach, itinerant food vendors whipped up fragrant curries and fried soft-shell crab from the backs of their carts, setting up shop wherever there were hungry people. One of my most memorable Thai takeaway experiences is black sticky rice served in the simple length of split bamboo in which it had been cooked, which goes to show that you don't need a kitchen or expensive equipment to eat well.

As well as the markets and street food, there are lush and lavish restaurants in every Asian city, where the emphasis is noticeably global. Chefs from Europe, America, Australia and New Zealand can be found working alongside their Asian counterparts, creating food that is often a fusion of Asian and international cuisines.

Lotus contains recipes for humble classics and also more contemporary Asian dishes with an **ezard** twist. This is the sort of food that I eat every day; it has flavor and variety, and is food for all occasions, ideal to share around a large table with a group of family and friends. The dishes should be served generously in big bowls or platters, and eaten with chopsticks, forks or fingers. Casual, communal dining is the way of Asia.

The lotus flower plays an integral part in Eastern philosophy, religion, medicine and mythology. While the flower is exquisite, the seeds, roots and leaves also have their own unique uses. Each part contributes to the harmony of the whole, which is the perfect symbol of what I aim for in my food.

Basics

Curry pastes

Of the three main kinds of Southeast Asian curry—green, red and yellow—green curries, based on green chilies, are often slightly hotter than red curries, based on red chilies. Yellow curries are heavily flavored and colored with fresh turmeric, an ingredient found all over Southeast Asia. Curry pastes are best used immediately as the flavors and fragrance tend to deteriorate, and they can go sour, but they will stay close to their peak in the refrigerator for a few days and you can keep them for a much longer period if frozen (although be sure to label them!) Making curry pastes with a mortar and pestle is the recommended method; however, breaking down the ingredients with a mortar and pestle first and finishing with a food processor or grinder also brings good results.

Roasted shrimp paste

Roasting dried shrimp paste makes it dry and crumbly, and easier to work with. It also gives it a distinctive, slightly nutty, salty and toasted aroma.

½ cup (100 g) firm dried shrimp paste

Preheat the oven to 350°F (180°C). Wrap the shrimp paste in foil and roast for 5 minutes or until fragrant. Set aside to cool. It is best to roast shrimp paste as you need it as it soon loses its vitality and roasted aroma, although it will keep in an airtight container for 2 days.

Makes ½ cup (100 g)

Green curry paste

1 cinnamon stick, broken
½ tablespoon coriander seeds
½ tablespoon cumin seeds
1 teaspoon sea salt
8 Asian shallots, coarsely chopped
6 cloves garlic, coarsely chopped
1 in (2½ cm) peeled ginger, coarsely chopped
1 in (2½ cm) peeled galangal root, coarsely chopped
¾ in (2 cm) peeled fresh turmeric root, coarsely chopped
2 stalks lemongrass, tender inner part of bottom third only, finely sliced
5 kaffir lime leaves, finely sliced
5 green finger-length chilies, deseeded and coarsely chopped
6 coriander (cilantro) roots, washed and coarsely chopped
1 teaspoon Roasted Shrimp Paste (see other recipe on this page)

Dry-roast the cinnamon, coriander, cumin and salt in a wok over medium heat until fragrant (1–2 minutes), stirring constantly to avoid burning. Remove from the heat and grind the spices to a fine powder with a mortar and pestle or spice grinder.

Using a mortar and pestle, pound the spices with the remaining ingredients until you have a smooth paste. Alternatively, pound to a coarse paste in a mortar and pestle and finish with a food processor. Store in the refrigerator.

Makes 1 cup

Red curry paste

½ tablespoon coriander seeds
3 star anise pods
½ teaspoon white peppercorns
1 teaspoon sea salt
8 Asian shallots, coarsely chopped
6 cloves garlic, coarsely chopped
1½ in (4 cm) peeled ginger,
    coarsely chopped
1 in (2½ cm) peeled galangal root,
    coarsely chopped
1 stalk lemongrass, tender inner part of bot-
    tom third only, finely sliced
4 kaffir lime leaves, finely sliced
8 dried red finger-length chilies, deseeded
    and softened in warm water for 30 minutes
5 coriander (cilantro) roots, washed and
    coarsely chopped
1 tablespoon Roasted Shrimp Paste
    (page 9)

Dry-roast the coriander, star anise, peppercorns and salt in a wok over medium heat until fragrant (1–2 minutes), stirring constantly to avoid burning. Remove from the heat and grind the spices to a fine powder with a mortar and pestle or spice grinder.

Using a mortar and pestle, pound the spices with the remaining ingredients until you have a smooth paste. Alternatively, pound to a coarse paste in a mortar and pestle and finish with a food processor. Store in the refrigerator.

Makes 1 cup

Yellow curry paste

10 candlenuts or macadamia nuts (or 15
    raw cashews), lightly dry-roasted
10 Asian shallots, coarsely chopped
5 cloves garlic, coarsely chopped
1¾ in (4½ cm) peeled ginger,
    coarsely chopped
1½ in (4 cm) peeled galangal root,
    coarsely chopped
1½ in (4 cm) peeled fresh turmeric root,
    coarsely chopped
3 red bird's-eye chilies, deseeded and
    coarsely chopped
5 kaffir lime leaves, finely sliced
5 coriander (cilantro) roots, washed
    and coarsely chopped
1 tablespoon coriander seeds,
    lightly dry-roasted
1 teaspoon sea salt
2 tablespoons Roasted Shrimp Paste
    (page 9)

Pound the ingredients to a smooth paste using a mortar and pestle. Alternatively, pound to a coarse paste in a mortar and pestle and finish with a food processor. Store in the refrigerator.

Makes 1 cup

Curry powder

2 tablespoons coriander seeds
1 tablespoon fennel seeds
½ tablespoon cumin seeds
2 star anise pods
5 cardamom pods
1 teaspoon cloves
1 teaspoon black peppercorns
½ teaspoon yellow mustard seeds
1 tablespoon ground red pepper
1 tablespoon garlic powder
1 tablespoon ground turmeric

Dry-roast the coriander, fennel, cumin, star anise, cardamom, cloves and peppercorns in a wok over medium heat until fragrant (1–2 minutes), stirring constantly to avoid burning. Remove from the heat and grind the roasted spices and mustard seeds to a fine powder with a mortar and pestle or spice grinder. Combine with the ground red pepper, garlic and ground turmeric and store in an airtight container for up to 2 weeks.

Makes ½ cup

Salt and sugar mixes

Sichuan pepper-salt powder

This pepper-salt has a light ash color and is prickly on the tongue. It is essential in many Chinese dishes.

2 tablespoons Sichuan peppercorns
4 tablespoons sea salt

Dry roast the peppercorns and salt in a wok over medium heat until fragrant (1–2 minutes), stirring constantly to avoid burning. Remove from the heat and grind to a fine powder with a mortar and pestle or spice grinder. Sift the powder and store in an airtight container. Use within a week as the pepper loses its fragrance quickly.

Makes ½ cup

Spiced chili salt

½ cinnamon stick, broken
1 tablespoon Sichuan peppercorns
1 tablespoon coriander seeds
2 star anise pods
1 teaspoon dried chili flakes
1 cardamom pod
4 tablespoons sea salt

Dry-roast the ingredients in a wok over medium heat until fragrant (1–2 minutes), stirring constantly to avoid burning. Remove from the heat and grind the mixture to a fine powder using a mortar and pestle or spice grinder. Sift the powder and store in an airtight container for up to 2 weeks.

Makes ½ cup

Salt and pepper mix

This is my version of the classic salt and pepper blend used in deep-fried dishes.

1 tablespoon Sichuan peppercorns
1 tablespoon white peppercorns
1 tablespoon black peppercorns
6 tablespoons sea salt

Dry-roast the ingredients in a wok over medium heat until fragrant (1–2 minutes), stirring constantly to avoid burning. Remove from the heat and grind the mixture to a fine powder using a mortar and pestle or spice grinder. Sift the powder and store in an airtight container for up to 2 weeks.

Makes ½ cup

Chili rock sugar

½ cup (120 g) raw rock sugar crystals
½ tablespoon dried red chili flakes

Pound the rock sugar and chili flakes to a fine powder using a mortar and pestle. Store in an airtight container for up to 3 weeks.

Makes ½ cup

Soup stocks

Asian brown chicken stock

4 lbs (2 kgs) chicken carcasses
1 tablespoon peanut oil
2 medium brown onions, diced
6 cloves garlic, bruised
1 in (2½ cm) peeled ginger, bruised
2 large carrots, coarsely chopped
½ bunch celery, coarsely chopped
1 leek, coarsely chopped
1 tablespoon Sichuan peppercorns
1 cup (250 ml) Shao Xing rice wine
3 liters (12 cups) water

Preheat the oven to 350°F (180°C). Rinse the chicken carcasses to remove any blood or innards. Place them on a tray and roast them for around 1 hour until dark brown.

Heat the oil in a large pot and brown the onion, garlic, ginger, carrots, celery and leek. Add the Sichuan pepper and Shao Xing rice wine and simmer until reduced by half. Add the roasted chicken carcasses and water and bring to a boil. Skim off any residue that rises to the surface then gently simmer the stock for 4–6 hours. Top up with fresh water from time to time to keep the liquid at its original level.

Strain the stock into another pot and set aside to cool. Once cool, skim any fat from the surface and return the stock to a boil. Reduce it by a third. Allow to cool, then pour into a container and refrigerate or freeze.

Makes 8 cups (2 liters)

Brown chicken stock

4 lbs (2 kgs) chicken carcasses
1 tablespoon olive oil
2 medium brown onions, diced
6 cloves garlic, bruised
2 large carrots, coarsely chopped
½ bunch celery, coarsely chopped
1 leek, coarsely chopped
1 sprig thyme
1 bay leaf
1 teaspoon black peppercorns
3 liters (12 cups) water

Preheat the oven to 350°F (180°C). Rinse the chicken carcasses to remove any blood or innards. Place them on a tray and roast for around 1 hour, or until dark brown.

Heat the oil in a large pot and brown the onion, garlic, carrots, celery and leek. Add the roasted chicken carcasses, thyme, bay leaf, pepper and water and bring to a boil. Skim off any residue that rises to the surface and gently simmer the stock for 4–6 hours. Top up with fresh water from time to time to keep the liquid at its original level.

Strain the stock into another pot and set aside to cool. Once cool, skim any fat from the surface and return the stock to a boil. Reduce it by a third. Allow to cool, then pour into a container and refrigerate or freeze.

Makes 8 cups (2 liters)

Master stock

This is the key ingredient in Chinese red-cooking. Meats braised in Master Stock take on a deep red color and a sweet, aromatic flavor. The stock can live forever if you treat it correctly, and it will become richer over time as it takes on the flavors of what has been cooked in it. After braising meat, usually poultry or pork, bring the master stock back to a boil, skim away any impurities and strain into a clean container. Cool and then refrigerate or freeze. When you use the stock again, top it up with water to maintain the volume and refresh with a small quantity of each of the ingredients.

3 liters (12 cups) water
1 cup (250 ml) soy sauce
2 cups (500 ml) Shao Xing rice wine
¾ cup (200 g) raw rock sugar crystals
1¾ in (4½ cm) peeled ginger, bruised
5 cloves garlic, bruised
4 star anise pods
2 cinnamon sticks
3 cardamom pods, cracked
4 whole cloves
1 teaspoon Sichuan peppercorns
2 pieces dried mandarin orange peel
2 pieces dried liquorice root
1 teaspoon fennel seeds

Place the ingredients in a large pot and bring to a boil. Simmer gently for 15 minutes then remove from the heat. Allow the stock to cool completely (overnight is ideal) before straining out the aromatics and refrigerating or freezing.

Makes 16 cups (4 liters)

Veal stock

6 lbs (3 kgs) veal knuckle bones
1 tablespoon olive oil
2 medium brown onions, diced
6 cloves garlic, bruised
2 large carrots, coarsely chopped
½ bunch celery, coarsely chopped
1 leek, coarsely chopped
1 sprig thyme
1 bay leaf
1 teaspoon black peppercorns
1 cup (250 ml) red wine
3 liters (12 cups) water

Preheat the oven to 350°F (180°C) degrees. Roast the veal bones for 1½ hours or until dark brown.

Heat the oil in a large pot and brown the onion, garlic, carrots, celery and leek. Add the thyme, bay leaf, peppercorns and wine and simmer until reduced by half. Add the roasted veal bones and water and bring to a boil. Skim off any residue that rises to the surface and then gently simmer the stock for 4–6 hours. Top up with fresh water from time to time to keep the liquid at its original level.

Strain the stock into another pot and set aside to cool. Once cool, skim any fat from the surface and return the stock to a boil. Reduce it by a third. Allow to cool, then pour into a container and refrigerate or freeze.

Makes 8 cups (2 liters)

Fish stock

3 lbs (1½ kgs) fish heads and bones (from fish such as blue eye tuna or snapper)
4 medium brown onions, diced
4 large carrots, coarsely chopped
½ bunch celery, coarsely chopped
6 stalks dill, coarsely chopped
1 tablespoon black peppercorns
2 tablespoons white vinegar
3 liters (12 cups) water

Rinse the fish bones to remove any blood or innards. Place them in a large pot with the remaining ingredients and bring to a boil. Skim off any residue that rises to the surface then simmer for 20 minutes. Strain the hot stock and cool before refrigerating or freezing.

Makes 8 cups (2 liters)

Sauces and sambals

Chili jam

⅓ cup (80 ml) peanut oil
15 red finger-length chilies, deseeded and finely chopped
8 dried red finger-length chilies, deseeded and soaked in warm water for 30 minutes, finely chopped
10 Asian shallots, finely chopped
10 cloves garlic, finely chopped
1 in (2½ cm) peeled galangal root, finely chopped
½ tablespoon Roasted Shrimp Paste (page 9)
1 tablespoon Roasted Dried Shrimp (page 21)
10 cherry tomatoes, diced
3 tablespoons Tamarind Paste (page 18)
¾ cup (150 g) shaved palm sugar
1½ tablespoons fish sauce

Heat the peanut oil in a large saucepan over medium heat and fry the chilies, shallots, garlic and galangal until fragrant and beginning to brown (around 10 minutes). Place in a food processor with the Roasted Shrimp Paste and Roasted Dried Shrimp and blend.

   Place the mixture back in the saucepan and add the tomatoes, Tamarind Paste and palm sugar. Simmer until the mixture reaches a thick, jam-like consistency (20–30 minutes). Add the fish sauce and cook for a further minute. Taste for a balance of flavors, adjusting if necessary. Cool and store in the refrigerator for up to 2 weeks.

Makes 2 cups (500 ml)

Chili caramel sauce

2 cups (400 g) shaved palm sugar
¾ cup (200 ml) water
2 red bird's-eye chilies, deseeded and finely sliced
2 green bird's-eye chilies, deseeded and finely sliced
2 red finger-length chilies, deseeded and finely sliced
2 green finger-length chilies, deseeded and finely sliced
2 tablespoons fish sauce
3 tablespoons freshly-squeezed lime juice

Place the palm sugar and water in a saucepan and bring to a boil. Simmer until it begins to turn into a light brown caramel (around 10 minutes), then watch it closely and take it off the heat just before it becomes dark brown. (You will need to brush or scrape the sides of the saucepan occasionally to stop crystals from forming.) Stir through the chilies and set the caramel aside to cool. Add the fish sauce and lime juice and taste for a balance of flavors, adjusting if necessary. Store in an airtight container for up to 3 days.

Makes 2 cups (500 ml)

Candied chilies

These are a great addition to salads.

10 red finger-length chilies, finely sliced into
    rings
½ cup (100 g) white sugar
2½ tablespoons rice wine vinegar
⅓ cup + 1 tablespoon (100 ml) water

Place the sliced chilies in a bowl of water to wash out the inner seeds. Drain and dry thoroughly—if possible, use a salad spinner, which also helps to get rid of any remaining seeds.

Place the sugar, vinegar and water in a saucepan and bring to a boil. Simmer until the liquid has reduced by around a third and is syrupy but not yet beginning to brown, then add the chilies. Simmer for 15–20 minutes, or until the chilies are tender. Remove from the heat and set aside to cool.

Spoon the chilies into a container (they will be in a thick syrup) and store in a cool, dry place for up to a week (if kept for a longer period they may crystallise). To serve, remove them from the syrup.

Makes 1 cup

Roasted tomato sambal

8 plum tomatoes, halved
¾ cup (200 ml) Pat Chun sweetened vin-
    egar (page 234)
2½ tablespoons peanut oil
3 Asian shallots, finely sliced
4 cloves garlic, finely sliced
1 in (2½ cm) peeled ginger, sliced into thin
    shreds
3 red finger-length chilies, deseeded and
    finely sliced
1 stalk lemongrass, tender inner part of bot-
    tom third only, finely sliced
3 kaffir lime leaves, finely sliced
1 teaspoon Roasted Shrimp Paste (page 9)
⅓ cup (80 ml) freshly-squeezed lime juice
3 tablespoons fish sauce
1 tablespoon shaved palm sugar

Preheat the oven to 325°F (160°C). Place the tomato halves on a tray facing up and pour over the Pat Chun. Roast until soft and caramelized (around 30 minutes).

Heat the peanut oil in a saucepan and fry the shallots, garlic, ginger, chilies, lemongrass and kaffir lime leaves until fragrant and beginning to brown (3–4 minutes). Add the Roasted Shrimp Paste and fry for 1 minute, then add the tomatoes and their roasting juices. Simmer for 5 minutes then remove from the heat and set aside to cool.

Pound the mixture to a smooth paste with a mortar and pestle or blend in a food processor. Add the lime juice, fish sauce and palm sugar and taste for a balance of flavors, adjusting if necessary. Cool and store in the refrigerator for up to 5 days.

Makes 2 cups (500 ml)

Sweet fish sauce dip

This is a dipping sauce for spring rolls and is also great with deep-fried shrimp and other seafood.

⅓ cup (75 ml) water
1 cup (200 g) shaved palm sugar
1 stalk lemongrass, tender inner part of
    bottom third only, bruised and quartered
2 kaffir lime leaves, torn
1 red bird's-eye chili, split
2½ tablespoons fish sauce
2 tablespoons Tamarind Paste (page 18)
1 tablespoon freshly-squeezed lime juice

Place the water, palm sugar, lemongrass, kaffir lime leaves and chili in a saucepan and bring to a boil. Simmer until it begins to turn into a light brown caramel (around 10 minutes). You will need to brush or scrape the sides of the saucepan occasionally to stop crystals from forming. Remove from the heat and add the fish sauce. Set the mixture aside to cool and then strain. Add the Tamarind Paste and lime juice and taste for a balance of flavors, adjusting if required. Store in the refrigerator for up to 1 week.

Makes 1 cup (250 ml)

XO sauce

XO sauce originated in Hong Kong in the 1970s and is referred to as the "caviar of the Orient". Its creators considered it the equivalent in quality of XO (extra old) brandy, the best brandy on the market, hence the name. The sauce is a spicy combination of dried seafood and pork, and while you can buy it in jars, I prefer to make my own. Use it with meat dishes, stir-fries, tofu and vegetable dishes.

1 piece pork belly weighing 5 oz (150 g)
7 oz (200 g) dried scallops, soaked overnight
¾ cup (200 ml) peanut oil
15 Asian shallots, finely chopped
15 cloves garlic, finely chopped
½ cup (50 g) dried shrimp, soaked for 30 minutes
¼ cup (50 g) shaved palm sugar
12 dried red finger-length chilies, deseeded and soaked in warm water for 30 minutes, finely chopped
1 teaspoon ground white pepper
½ tablespoon fish sauce

Heat the oven to 400°F (200°C) and roast the pork belly for around 30 minutes or until the juices run clear when tested with a skewer. Let the pork cool completely then cut away the skin and finely chop the meat (including any fat).

Place the soaked scallops in a heatproof dish and insert into a steamer. Steam until tender (around 2 hours). Remove the scallops from the steamer and set aside to cool. Reserve any juices that have pooled in the dish. Coarsely chop the scallops.

Heat the peanut oil in a saucepan and fry the shallots, garlic, shrimp and palm sugar until the sugar starts to caramelize. Add the chilies, pork, scallops and their reserved steaming juices and simmer for 1 hour, topping up with water from time to time if the mixture begins to stick on the bottom of the pan. Remove from the heat and add the pepper and fish sauce. Cool and store in the refrigerator for up to 2 weeks.

Makes 2 cups (500 ml)

Dressings, oils, syrups and waters

Hot and sour dressing

This dressing is used in many salads and seafood dishes at my restaurant.

⅓ cup + 1 tablespoon (100 ml) freshly-squeezed lime juice
2 tablespoons fish sauce
2 red bird's-eye chilies, deseeded and finely chopped
1 teaspoon dried red chili flakes
¼ teaspoon dried shrimp powder (made by processing several dried shrimp in a blender or food processor)

Combine the ingredients and taste for a balance of flavors, adjusting if required. This is best used immediately, although it can be refrigerated for up to 24 hours.

Makes ⅔ cup (150 ml)

Toasted sesame oil

Toasted sesame oil is simply sesame oil that has been heated until it smokes. This makes it more fragrant and also reduces bitterness.

⅓ cup (80 ml) sesame oil

Heat the oil in a wok or saucepan until smoking, then remove from the heat. Cool and store in a jar or container. It is best to toast sesame oil as you need it as it dulls in fragrance and flavor over time.

Makes ⅓ cup (80 ml)

Chili shrimp oil

Roasted shrimp shells add a wonderful flavor and fragrance to oil. This is a great oil for drizzling over dishes before serving or for using as a base for salad dressings. For a simple dressing, combine it with rice wine vinegar and sugar. This recipe uses more oil than it makes as the shrimp shells soak up some oil.

¼ cup (50 g) shrimp shells and heads
⅔ cup (150 ml) olive oil
1 teaspoon tomato paste
3 red bird's-eye chilies, split

Preheat the oven to 350°F (180°C). Wash the shrimp shells, making sure there are no innards left in the heads. Dry them as well as you can then roast them in the oven for 20 minutes or until fragrant and lightly colored. Coarsely pound the shells with a mortar and pestle.

Place the oil, tomato paste and chilies in a saucepan and when the chilies begin to fry, add the crushed shrimp shells and continue to cook for 2–3 minutes. The oil should be a deep red color.

Set aside to cool then strain into a jar or container. Store in a dark, cool place for several days, or in the refrigerator for up to 1 week.

Makes ⅓ cup + 1 tablespoon (100 ml)

Palm sugar syrup

I use this syrup in many recipes, often together with lime juice and fish sauce as its palm sugar sweetness is the perfect match for sour and salty flavors and also for chili heat. I also use it in desserts.

1½ cups (300 g) shaved dark palm sugar
1¼ cups (300 ml) water
2 pieces dried mandarin orange peel
1 cinnamon stick, broken

Place the ingredients in a saucepan and bring to a boil. Simmer until reduced by around a half and the consistency is syrupy. It will thicken more as it cools. Remove from the heat and cool. Pour into a jar or container (mandarin orange peel and cinnamon included, as their flavors will continue to infuse) and store in the refrigerator for up to 2 weeks.

Makes 1¼ cups (300 ml)

Tamarind paste

Tamarind Paste is used when a strong, sour tamarind flavor is required. For a lighter flavor, use Tamarind Juice.

1¼ cups (375 g) tamarind pulp
¾ cup (190 ml) warm water

Place the tamarind pulp in a bowl and add the water. Use your fingers to work the pulp into a smooth paste, then push it through a sieve to remove the fibers and seeds. The paste will keep in the refrigerator for a few days.

Makes scant 1 cup (250 g)

Tamarind Juice

¼ cup (100 g) tamarind pulp
1⅔ cups (350 ml) warm water

Place the tamarind pulp in a bowl and add the water. Use your hands to break up the lumps of pulp and thoroughly incorporate the water. Strain to remove the fibers and seeds. This will keep in the refrigerator for a few days.

Makes 1⅔ cups (350 ml)

Maltose liquid

This is used as a coating for Chinese roast duck. It is the secret to the crisp, golden-brown skin.

½ cup (125 ml) maltose syrup
½ cup (125 ml) water
3 tablespoons rice wine vinegar

Combine the ingredients in a saucepan and bring to a boil. Simmer for 1–2 minutes then remove from the heat and cool. Store in a container in the refrigerator for up to 4 weeks.

Makes 1 cup (250 ml)

Garnishes and accompaniments

Fried shallots

At **ezard** we include garlic, ginger and chilies in this classic Southeast Asian garnish. It is similar to an Indonesian fried sambal.

2 cups (500 ml) vegetable oil
12 Asian shallots, finely sliced into discs
10 cloves garlic, finely sliced into discs
1¾ in (4½ cm) peeled ginger, finely sliced into discs
4 red finger-length chilies, finely sliced diagonally into rings
Sea salt
Superfine (caster) sugar

Heat the oil in a wok to 350°F (180°C). Fry the shallots, garlic, ginger and chilies separately until crisp and golden. Remove from the oil with a slotted spoon and drain on paper towels. Cool and combine, and season to taste with salt and sugar. Store in an airtight container for up to 1 week.

Makes 2 cups (400 g)

Fried chili peanuts

2 cups (500 ml) peanut oil
1⅓ cups (200 g) raw peanuts, coarsely chopped
8 Asian shallots, finely chopped
6 cloves garlic, finely chopped
¾ in (1½ cm) peeled ginger, finely chopped
5 red bird's-eye chilies, deseeded and finely chopped
1 tablespoon sea salt

Heat the oil in a wok to 350°F (180°C). Add the peanuts, shallots, garlic, ginger and chilies and fry until just golden (once removed from the oil the peanuts will continue to cook and deepen in color). Remove the mixture from the oil with a slotted spoon and drain on paper towels. Set aside to cool.

Toss the mixture in salt and store in the refrigerator for up to a week. The cooking oil can be strained and reused the next time you fry peanuts, or used when a stronger flavored oil is required in salads or other dishes.

Makes 2 cups (300 g)

Fried garlic

10 cloves garlic, finely sliced
1 cup (250 ml) milk
1 cup (250 ml) vegetable oil
Sea salt
Superfine (caster) sugar

Soak the garlic slices in milk for 10 minutes then drain, discarding the milk.

Heat the oil in a wok to 350°F (180°C) and fry the garlic until crisp and golden. Remove from the oil with a slotted spoon and drain on paper towels. Toss with salt and sugar to taste and store in an airtight container for up to 3 days.

Makes ⅓ cup (65 g)

Crispy fish floss

This recipe requires a non-oily fish, as oily fish does not become crispy when fried. This is a fantastic garnish for Thai salads.

10 oz (300 g) non-oily white fish fillets such as catfish, skinned and deboned
1⅔ cups (400 ml) vegetable oil

Preheat the oven to 250°F (120°C). Use your fingers to break the fish into bite-sized chunks. Line a tray with greaseproof paper and spread the fish on top. Place in the oven to dry out for 6–8 hours or overnight.

When the fish is cool, place it in a food processor and pulse until it resembles breadcrumbs.

Heat the oil in a wok to 350°F (180°C) and add the crumbled fish. Fry until crisp and golden. Remove from the oil with a slotted spoon and drain on paper towels. Cool and store in an airtight container for up to 2 days.

Makes 1 cup (300 g)

Roasted dried shrimp

Tiny Roasted Dried Shrimp add character and complexity to Thai relishes and salads.

1 cup (120 g) dried shrimp

Preheat the oven to 350°F (180°C). Place the dried shrimp on a tray and roast for 5 minutes or until lightly colored and fragrant. Cool the shrimp and store in an airtight container for up to 1 week.

Makes 1 cup (120 g)

Toasted coconut

When buying mature coconuts, find a supplier that has a high turnover and choose coconuts that feel heavy (the ones that are light are old and dried out). While this recipe calls for thin slices, you can also grate the coconut for a different texture in salads and desserts.

1 coconut

Split the coconut with a hammer and discard any water inside. Prise out the flesh in large chunks with a screwdriver or a small, sharp knife (an oyster knife is ideal).

Toast the outside surface of the coconut by holding the pieces with tongs and moving them over an open flame until the surface turns dark brown. Let the pieces cool, then peel into fine slices with a vegetable peeler. It is best to use the coconut immediately, but it can be stored in an airtight container for up to 3 days.

Makes 1 cup

Roasted rice powder

Ground roasted rice gives a nutty flavor to salads and other dishes.

½ cup (100 g) uncooked Jasmine rice
2 tablespoons sea salt

Preheat the oven to 350°F (180°C). Spread the rice out on a tray and roast until it turns golden brown and has a nutty aroma (around 20 minutes).

Use a spice grinder or mortar and pestle to grind the rice and salt to a fine powder. Sift the powder and store in an airtight container for up to 3 weeks.

Makes ½ cup

Lettuce cups

1 head iceberg lettuce

Discard the old outer leaves of the lettuce. Hold the lettuce with the stem facing down and gently tap it on the bench a few times. (This helps to loosen the core.) Flip it over and twist out the core with your hands.

Fill a sink with cold water and soak the lettuce for a few minutes. Carefully peel off the leaves one at a time, placing them in a colander as you go.

With scissors, cut the leaves into neat cups by trimming off the ragged edges.

Makes around 12 cups

Peanut brittle

I use peanut brittle in desserts, but also to add a sweet nutty crunch to chili-hot dishes—particularly salads.

1 cup (150 g) raw peanuts
¾ cup (200 ml) water
1½ cups (300 g) white sugar

Preheat the oven to 325°F (160°C). Spread the peanuts out on a large tray and roast for around 8 minutes or until golden brown. Tip the peanuts onto a smaller tray (around 8 x 12 in/20 x 30 cm) lined with greaseproof paper.

Place the water and sugar in a saucepan and simmer until it begins to turn into a light brown caramel (around 10 minutes). Watch it closely and take it off the heat just before it becomes dark brown. (You will need to brush or scrape the sides of the saucepan occasionally to stop crystals from forming.) Carefully pour the caramel over the peanuts and set aside to cool and harden. Once cool, break the brittle into large shards and store in a container in the freezer.

Makes around 1¾ cups (400 g)

Preserves

Pickled cucumber

2 cucumbers, peeled, deseeded and
   cut into sticks
2 tablespoons sea salt
4 cloves garlic, bruised
1 in (2½ cm) peeled ginger, bruised
1 red finger-length chili, split and deseeded
1 green finger-length chili, split and deseeded
1 tablespoon sesame oil
2½ tablespoons peanut oil
¾ cup (150 g) white sugar
¾ cup (200 ml) rice wine vinegar

Combine the cucumbers and salt in a
bowl and leave for 2 minutes. Add the
garlic, ginger, chilies, sesame oil and
peanut oil.

   Place the sugar and vinegar in a
saucepan and heat, stirring, until the
sugar dissolves. Pour the liquid over
the cucumbers and set aside to cool.
Place the cucumbers and liquid in a
container and store in the refrigerator
for 5 days before using. The pickle will
keep for 2 months.

Makes 2 cups

Pickled bean sprouts

These are a lovely crunchy addition to
Thai salads.

1¼ cups (300 ml) mirin
1¼ cups (300 ml) rice wine vinegar
⅔ cup (150 ml) soy sauce
2 tablespoons shaved palm sugar
2 cups (100 g) bean sprouts

Combine the mirin, vinegar, soy and
palm sugar in a bowl and stir until the
sugar dissolves. Add the bean sprouts
and marinate in the refrigerator for at
least 30 minutes. Use within 2 hours
so they retain their crunchiness.

Makes 2 cups (100 g)

Salted duck eggs

These salt-cured eggs are a delicacy
in China. They turn a grey color and
are served fried or raw in salads and
other dishes, and are eaten as a snack.
A fantastic salty, dry accompaniment
to curries.

4 cups (1 liter) water
¾ cup (150 g) sea salt
6 duck eggs

Place the water and salt in a pot and
bring to a boil. Simmer for 5 minutes
then remove from the heat and cool.

   Wipe the eggs clean and place them in
a large jar. Pour over the salted water.
Seal the jar and refrigerate for 2 weeks
before peeling and using the eggs. Use
within 6 weeks or they will become
too salty.

Makes 6 eggs

Salted shrimp

Salted shrimp are a great match with
curries or salads.

4 cups (1 liter) water
8 tablespoons sea salt
1½ lbs (750 g) raw jumbo shrimp, shelled
   and deveined (about 18 shrimp)
2 red finger-length chilies, split and deseeded
2 green finger-length chilies, split and
   deseeded
2 stalks lemongrass, tender inner part of
   bottom third only, bruised and quartered
2 coriander (cilantro) roots, washed

Place the water and salt in a saucepan
and bring to a boil. Add the shrimp,
chilies, lemongrass and coriander
root and when the liquid comes back
the boil, turn off the heat. Cool and
transfer the shrimp and liquid to a
container and store in the refrigerator
for 5 days before using. Use within
2 weeks.

Makes about 18 Salted Shrimp

Batters, dough and pancakes

Tempura batter

2 cups (225 g) tempura flour
1¼ cups (300 ml) chilled soda water
1 lime, juiced
1 egg
1 cup ice cubes

Sift the flour into a mixing bowl and gently whisk in the soda water and lime juice. Break up any lumps with your fingers if necessary. Whisk in the egg. The mixture should be the consistency of pancake batter. Add the ice cubes and use the batter before they melt.

Makes 2 cups (500 ml)

Beer batter

1⅔ cups (250 g) self-raising flour
1 cup (250 ml) Tiger beer (or other lager or pilsener)

Sift the flour into a mixing bowl and pour in half the beer. Whisk to a smooth paste; if there are lumps, use your fingers to break them up. Gradually whisk in the remaining beer. Leave the batter to stand for 20 minutes before using.

Makes 2 cups (500 ml)

Bun dough

1½ tablespoons superfine (caster) sugar
1 cup (250 ml) lukewarm water
1½ teaspoons dried yeast
1 tablespoon vegetable oil
1½ teaspoons baking soda
2⅔ cups (400 g) all-purpose (plain) flour

Place the sugar and water in a mixing bowl and stir until the sugar dissolves. Add the yeast and leave to rest for 10 minutes or until frothy.

Add the oil and baking soda and sift in the flour. Stir the mixture with your hands until it comes together as a smooth, slightly wet dough. Cover the bowl with a damp cloth and allow the dough to rise.

When the dough has doubled in size, knock it back and scrape it out of the bowl. Use immediately or cover with plastic wrap and refrigerate (use within 12 hours).

Makes 12 buns

Mandarin pancakes

These are traditionally served with Peking duck. They are cooked as double pancakes, sandwiched together with oil. To serve, reheat in a steamer then pull them apart and roll up with the desired filling, the blistered side of the pancake on the outside.

2⅔ cups (400 g) all-purpose (plain) flour
1 cup (250 ml) warm water
1 tablespoon Toasted Sesame Oil (page 17)

Sift the flour into a mixing bowl and make a well in the center. Pour in the water and mix it with your hands until it forms a firm dough. Cover the bowl with a damp cloth and rest the dough for 20 minutes.

Place the dough on a lightly floured bench and knead for 5 minutes or until smooth, then flatten the dough into a rectangle with your hands and roll it into a tight cylinder. Stretch the cylinder a little and cut it into thirds. Cut each third into six pieces—you should end up with 18 slices.

With a rolling pin, roll each piece into a pancake around 4 in (10 cm) in diameter. Brush half of the pancakes with a little Toasted Sesame Oil and place the unoiled pancakes on top. Roll each double pancake into a larger pancake around 6 in (15 cm) in diameter. Cover the finished pancakes with a damp cloth as you go to stop them drying out.

To cook, heat a pan or skillet over medium heat and dry-fry the pancakes until they are slightly brown and blistered on both sides.

Makes 18 pancakes (9 double pancakes)

Meat

Char siu pork

Char siu, or barbecued pork, is used in everything from steamed buns to fried rice. It is also a good substitute for duck in the Peking duck recipe (page 172–3) or simply wrapped up in Chinese cabbage leaves.

1 pork loin fillet weighing around 10 oz (300 g), trimmed of fat and sinew
1 in (2½ cm) peeled ginger, finely chopped
2 cloves garlic, finely chopped
1 tablespoon hoisin sauce
1 tablespoon soy sauce
1 tablespoon tomato sauce
1 tablespoon Shao Xing rice wine
½ tablespoon shaved palm sugar
1 tablespoon honey

With a sharp knife make shallow diagonal slits across the surface of the pork at ¾-in (2-cm) intervals. Combine the ginger, garlic, hoisin, soy, tomato sauce, Shao Xing rice wine and palm sugar in a bowl and add the pork. Marinate in the refrigerator for at least 2 hours (or overnight).

Heat a broiler grill or barbecue to medium heat and add the pork. Cook, turning and basting with leftover marinade, for 15 minutes or until the juices run clear when tested with a skewer. By this stage the surface should be nicely charred. Brush the pork with honey just before taking it off the heat.

Makes 10 oz (300 g)

Rice

Jasmine rice

To increase or decrease the quantity, simple follow the ratio of 1 cup of rice to 1½ cups of water.

3 cups (600 g) uncooked Jasmine rice
4½ cups water

Place the rice in a sieve or fine colander and rinse until the water runs clear. Drain. Combine with the water in an electric rice cooker and cook according to the manufacturer's instructions. Alternatively, combine in a large saucepan and cook by the absorption method: cover with a lid and bring to a boil, then turn down the heat to a gentle simmer and cook until the water has been absorbed and the rice has begun to stick on the bottom of the pan just slightly (15–20 minutes). Serve immediately.

Makes 9 cups (enough to serve 6 people generously)

Coconut rice

For pure coconut rice, omit the ginger, green onions and coriander roots.

1¼ cups (300 ml) coconut cream
1 teaspoon sea salt
½ teaspoon white sugar
6 cups (600 g) freshly cooked Jasmine Rice (see left)
1 in (2½ cm) peeled ginger, finely chopped
5 green onions (scallions), finely sliced
5 coriander (cilantro) roots, washed and finely chopped

Place the coconut cream, salt and sugar in a large saucepan or small pot and bring to a boil. Simmer for 5 minutes or until slightly reduced. Add the hot rice, ginger, green onions and coriander and combine. Serve immediately.

Makes 6 cups (600 g)

Sticky rice

1 cup (200 g) uncooked white glutinous rice

Place the rice in a large bowl and cover with cold water. Soak for 4 hours (or overnight).

Rinse the soaked rice under cold running water until the water runs clear (this removes the excess starch). Drain. Place into a steamer lined with muslin cloth and steam for 30 minutes or until tender. If not serving immediately, spread the rice out on a tray or dish (or on the muslin cloth) to stop it from becoming soggy.

Makes 3 cups (300 g)

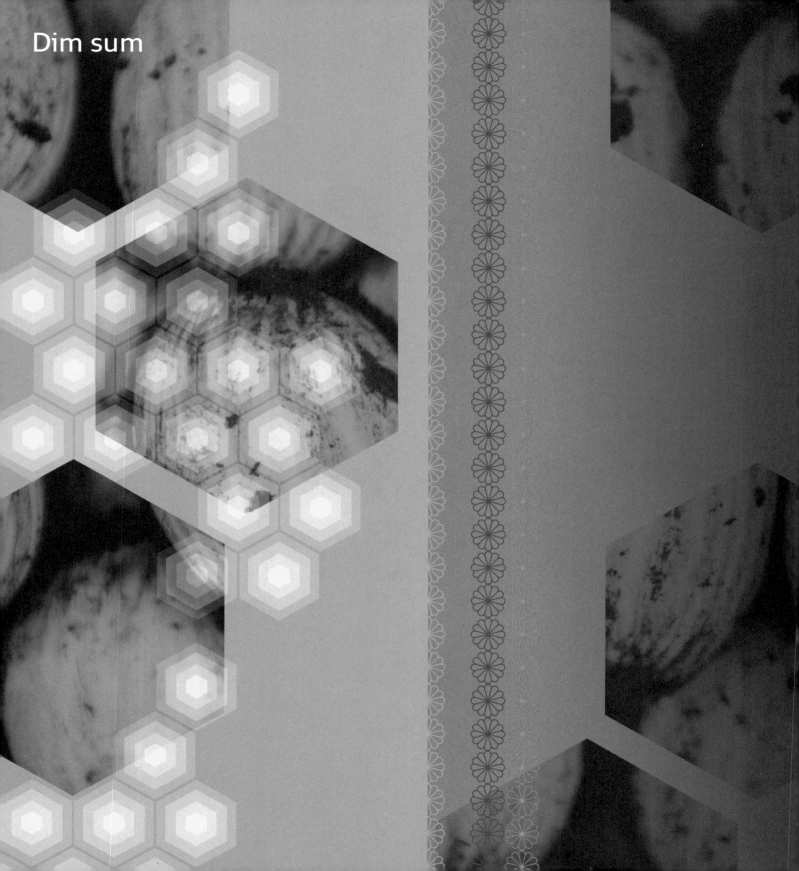

Dim sum

Dim sum is served throughout China, but the most impressive meals I've experienced have been in the cities of Shanghai and Hong Kong, where chefs push the boundaries of dim sum as a culinary art form, constantly experimenting with new flavors, ingredients and combinations.

Originally a Cantonese custom similar to the Western idea of "brunch," dim sum evolved along the roads in rural areas where farmers and travelers needed to stop, rest and refuel. From a simple concept, dim sum has blossomed into a discipline practiced at the highest level by specialist chefs.

Dim sum is served in small portions made to share so you can try many different dishes at once. It is eaten in the morning or around midday and served banquet style, which is one of the reasons I love it. An important part of the dim sum ritual is the flow: lighter, steamed dishes are served first, building up to heavier, fried pieces—also making it easier on the digestive system. The dim sum staples of *siu mai* (pork and shrimp dumplings), *char siu bao* (steamed barbecued pork buns) and *har gao* (shrimp dumplings) feature among different soups, meat, rice and tofu dishes, and countless rolls and parcels. Egg custard tarts are traditionally served at the end of the meal, and everything is washed down with plenty of Chinese tea.

Today, especially in Hong Kong, restaurants are breaking the mold by serving dishes with non-traditional ingredients such as fish roe, dashi, seaweed and different kinds of seafood. In these restaurants dim sum is a creative expression.

Making dim sum at home is a lot simpler than you might expect. Many dishes can be prepared and assembled in advance and cooked as required.

I've included a range of recipes in this chapter—some traditional and some twists on the traditional.

Fried tofu
with spiced chili salt

3 cups (750ml) vegetable oil

2 large cakes (1⅓ lbs/600 g) soft tofu

⅔ cup (75 g) cornstarch

½ cup (75 g) all-purpose (plain) flour

6 cloves garlic, finely chopped

2 tablespoons Spiced Chili Salt
   (page 11)

Serves 6

I've had fried tofu at a dim sum restaurant in Hong Kong, where it was served as an appetizer. I was amazed—so simple and so tasty. Soft tofu has a beautiful texture when deep-fried.

Make the Spiced Chili Salt by following the recipe on page 11.

Heat the oil in a wok to 350°F (180°C). Use a sharp knife to cut the tofu into small squares (about ½ in/1 cm). Combine the two flours in a bowl and roll the tofu in the flour, then place in a sieve and gently shake off any excess.

Fry the tofu in batches until crisp and golden (3–5 minutes). Drain on paper towels. While the tofu is draining, add the garlic to the hot oil—it will float on the surface. Once it has browned remove it from the oil using a fine sieve or "spider." (Alternatively, fry the garlic in a little oil in a pan.) Drain on paper towels. Toss the tofu in a bowl with the garlic and Spiced Chili Salt, and serve.

Crisp sticky rice balls
stuffed with pineapple chili jam

1 tablespoon rice flour

1 cup (250 ml) warm water

1 egg, lightly beaten

1 tablespoon sugar

½ teaspoon sea salt

3 cups (300 g) cooked Sticky Rice (page 24)

2 tablespoons (30 g) Peanut Brittle (page 21)

½ small pineapple, peeled, cored and finely diced

½ cup (125 ml) Chili Jam (page 13)

2 kaffir lime leaves, finely sliced

½ cup (20 g) mint leaves, finely chopped

½ cup (25 g) coriander leaves (cilantro), finely chopped

¾ cup (100 g) sesame seeds

3 cups (750ml) vegetable oil

Serves 6

This isn't a traditional dim sum dish, but it works well as part of a dim sum meal. It's my version of the popular fried glutinous rice ball snacks found in Southeast Asia. The peanut brittle adds a nutty crunch.

Make the Chili Jam, Peanut Brittle and Sticky Rice by following the recipes on pages 13, 21 and 24.

Combine the rice flour and water in a bowl and whisk to get rid of any lumps. Add the egg, sugar and salt and continue whisking. Add the Sticky Rice. Using wet hands, mix until it forms a smooth, firm ball. Divide into 18 small balls and set aside.

To make the stuffing, pound the Peanut Brittle into small pieces using a mortar and pestle. Combine with the pineapple, Chili Jam, kaffir lime leaves, mint and coriander leaves.

With a wet finger, poke a hole in the center of each rice ball. Fill the cavities with a teaspoon of stuffing and close them up. Roll the balls in sesame seeds.

Heat the oil in a wok to 350°F (180°C) and fry the balls in batches until crisp and golden. Drain on paper towels and serve.

Vietnamese spring rolls

1 tablespoon peanut oil

10 oz (300 g) ground pork

2½ tablespoons Shao Xing rice wine

1⅓ lbs (600 g) fresh shrimp, peeled and deveined, then finely chopped

2 coriander (cilantro) roots, washed and finely chopped

4 green onions (scallions), finely sliced

4 cloves garlic, finely chopped

½ tablespoon fish sauce

Pinch of ground white pepper

18 spring roll wrappers

3 cups (750ml) vegetable oil

1 head iceberg lettuce, washed and sliced into quarters, core removed

1 cup (40 g) Vietnamese mint leaves

1 cup (250 ml) Sweet Fish Sauce Dip (page 16)

Serves 6

Spring rolls are a dim sum classic and I like them best served the Vietnamese way, with mint and lettuce and dipped in fish sauce.

Make the Sweet Fish Sauce Dip by following the recipe on page 16.

Heat the peanut oil in a wok and add the pork. Fry for 1 minute then add the Shao Xing rice wine and continue frying until it evaporates (this will help separate the pieces of pork). Take off the heat and allow to cool.

In a bowl combine the shrimp, coriander roots, green onions, garlic, fish sauce and pepper. Add the pork and set aside.

Lay a spring roll wrapper on a floured surface with one corner facing you. (Keep the remaining pastry under a damp cloth to stop it drying out.) Brush the sheet with a little water and place a heaped tablespoon of the filling about a quarter of the way up the pastry. Fold the corner over and gently press the filling to make a sausage roll shape. Fold the sides into the center and brush the top with more water. Roll the pastry up to form a firm but not too tight roll. Repeat this with the remaining wrappers and filling. Refrigerate until ready to fry.

Heat the oil in a wok to 350°F (180°C) and fry the spring rolls in batches until crisp and golden. Drain on paper towels. Serve with lettuce, mint and Sweet Fish Sauce Dip.

Siu mai with chili soy dip

7 oz (200 g) ground pork

14 oz (400 g) fresh shrimp, peeled and deveined, then finely chopped

¾ in (1½ cm) peeled ginger, finely chopped

3 green onions (scallions), finely sliced

3 coriander (cilantro) roots, washed and finely chopped

2 tablespoons finely chopped garlic chives

1 red bird's-eye chili, deseeded and minced

½ tablespoon soy sauce

½ tablespoon fish sauce

¼ teaspoon ground white pepper

18 wonton skins

Chili soy dip

⅓ cup + 1 tablespoon (100 ml) soy sauce

1 tablespoon lemon juice

2 red bird's-eye chilies, deseeded and minced

Serves 6

One of the most popular dishes at the dim sum table, these dumplings are called *siu mai*, which means "cook and sell", and they are sometimes made with just pork. Dim sum master chefs are trained to get the right shape using the palm of their hand, but you can also use an egg cup.

In a large mixing bowl, work the pork with your hands for several minutes until it becomes slightly elastic (this will help the filling to hold together). Add the shrimp, ginger, green onions, coriander roots, garlic chives, chili, soy sauce, fish sauce and pepper and mix thoroughly.

Place a wonton skin in the palm of your hand (or in an egg cup) and lightly brush with water. Place two teaspoons of filling in the center, then carefully gather the edges together to form a basket shape (the top is not supposed to be sealed). Make sure that the filling is firmly packed and flatten the base of the dumpling by pressing it down on the palm of your hand. Using a wet knife, scrape the top of the filling to flatten the top. Repeat this process with the remaining wonton skins and filling, then refrigerate until ready to steam.

Combine the ingredients for the Chili Soy Dip.

To serve, stand the dumplings upright in a steamer and steam for 7 minutes. Serve with the Chili Soy Dip.

Scallop dumpling soup

1 bunch (1 oz/30 g) enoki mushrooms, trimmed at the base
2½ tablespoons fish sauce
¼ cup (12 g) coriander leaves (cilantro)
2 teaspoons Fried Shallots (page 19)

Soup
6 large dried scallops, soaked overnight
4 cups (1 liter) Fish Stock (page 13)
2½ tablespoons sweet soy sauce
3 cloves garlic, bruised
5 green onions (scallions), coarsely chopped
2 red bird's-eye chilies, coarsely chopped

Dumplings
4 oz (100 g) ground pork
7 oz (200 g) fresh shucked scallops (roe attached), coarsely chopped
3 cloves garlic, finely chopped
¾ in (1½ cm) peeled ginger, finely chopped
2 tablespoons finely chopped garlic chives
4 green onions (scallions), finely sliced
1 coriander (cilantro) root, washed and finely chopped
1 tablespoon soy sauce
¼ teaspoon ground white pepper
1 teaspoon sea salt
18 wonton skins

Serves 6

I like to use a combination of fresh and dried produce in my cooking—whether mushrooms, shrimp, seaweed, chilies or, in this recipe, scallops—as this creates a fuller and more authentic flavor.

Make the Fish Stock and Fried Shallots by following the recipes on pages 13 and 19.

Soup
Place the dried soaked scallops in a heatproof dish and place into a steamer. Steam until tender (around 2 hours). Remove the scallops from the steamer and set aside to cool. Reserve any juices that have pooled in the dish.

In a medium-sized pot combine the Fish Stock, sweet soy sauce, garlic, green onions and chilies and simmer for 30 minutes or until reduced by a quarter. Strain and reserve.

Dumplings
In a large mixing bowl, work the ground pork with your hands for several minutes until it becomes slightly elastic (this will help the filling to hold together). Add the fresh scallops, garlic, ginger, garlic chives, green onions, coriander root, soy sauce, pepper and salt and mix thoroughly.

Lay a wonton skin out on a floured surface and place two teaspoons of filling in the center. Brush around the edges with water. Bring the four corners of the skin together at the top and pinch them shut. Do the same until all the wonton skins and filling are used up. Refrigerate the dumplings until needed.

To serve
Bring the stock back to a simmer, adding the reserved scallop juices. Add the Dumplings and gently poach for 3–4 minutes. Add the steamed scallops and enoki mushrooms until just heated through, then add the fish sauce and remove from the heat. Ladle the Soup into six serving bowls with three Dumplings and one scallop in each bowl. Garnish with coriander leaves and Fried Shallots.

Crab claw balls with XO sauce

9 fresh crabs, roughly equal in size

7 oz (200 g) ground pork

3 cloves garlic, finely chopped

1 in (2½ cm) peeled ginger, finely chopped

1 coriander (cilantro) root, washed and
   finely chopped

2 green onions (scallions), finely sliced

2½ tablespoons soy sauce

¼ teaspoon ground white pepper

4 eggs

2½ tablespoons Shao Xing rice wine

⅓ cup (50 g) rice flour

1⅔ cups (100 g) fine breadcrumbs

3 cups (750 ml) vegetable oil

½ cup (125 ml) XO Sauce (page 17)

Serves 6

This traditional dim sum dish also makes great finger food. A mixture of crab meat and pork is shaped into balls, with a crab claw inserted into each one. The balls are fried and the claws used like toothpicks to pick them up.

Make the XO Sauce by following the recipe on page 17.

Bring a large pot of water to a boil. Calculate the cooking time for the crabs, allowing 7–8 minutes for each pound (500 g) of whole crab.

Add the crabs to the pot and simmer for the correct time. The shells will turn red when cooked. Remove the crabs from the pot and plunge them in a sink of iced water to stop the cooking process. Allow them to cool in the sink for 10 minutes, then drain.

Twist off the claws and trim them so you have just the claws—set them aside. Use your fingers to pull the top shells away from the bodies. Discard the gills and rinse the crabs. Twist off the legs. Use a mallet or the flat side of a cleaver to crack the legs and the remainder of the claws. Use a crab pick or metal skewer to extract the meat. Measure out 2 cups (250 g) of meat and refrigerate or freeze the remainder for another use.

Combine the crab meat, pork, garlic, ginger, coriander root, green onion, soy sauce and pepper in a bowl. Roll the mixture into 18 balls. Insert a crab claw (claw end out) three-quarters of the way into each ball, and mold the ball around the claw a little so it will hold in place. Refrigerate the balls for 1–2 hours to set.

Lightly beat the eggs in a bowl and add the Shao Xing rice wine. Dredge each ball in rice flour, dusting off any excess. Dip the balls in the egg mix then in the breadcrumbs, then in the egg and breadcrumbs again to build up a coating.

Heat the oil in a wok to 350°F (180°C). Fry the balls in batches until crisp and golden. Drain on paper towels and serve with XO Sauce.

Quail san choi bao lettuce cups

4 large quail
½ tablespoon peanut oil
4 Asian shallots, finely chopped
¾ in (1½ cm) peeled ginger, finely chopped
3 cloves garlic, finely chopped
7 oz (200 g) ground pork
⅔ cup (150 ml) Shao Xing rice wine
7 fresh shiitake mushrooms, stems
  trimmed, finely sliced
3 dried Chinese sausages (*lup cheong*),
  finely sliced
½ cup (120 g) diced peeled water chestnuts
3 green onions (scallions), finely sliced
4 coriander (cilantro) roots, washed and
  finely chopped
⅓ cup (80 ml) oyster sauce
12 Lettuce Cups (page 21)
2 tablespoons sesame seeds, dry-roasted
  (optional)

Serves 6

There are many versions of this Chinese classic—meat, seafood and vegetarian. I like to use quail as it provides a delicate texture and sweetness. Some butchers may debone the quail for you.

Make the Lettuce Cups by following the recipe on page 21.

Cut off the quail wings and discard. Hold a bird in the palm of your hand and using a pair of kitchen scissors, cut along either side of the backbone. Remove the backbone and open the bird up.

Use your fingertips to carefully peel the breast meat from the bones, feeling your way across the carcass. For the legs, make a slit to the bone and scrape the meat away.

Check the meat for any hidden bones. Leave the skin on. Repeat this process with the remaining quail, then finely chop the meat and set aside.

Heat the peanut oil in a wok and add the shallots, ginger and garlic. Fry until beginning to brown. Add the pork and half of the Shao Xing rice wine and cook until it evaporates (this will help separate the pieces of pork).

Turn up the heat and add the quail. Once the meat begins to color add the shiitake mushrooms, dried Chinese sausage, water chestnuts, green onions and coriander roots and fry for a further 2 minutes. Add the remaining Shao Xing rice wine and oyster sauce and cook until the liquid has reduced by half. Remove from the heat and allow the mixture to cool a little.

Spoon the warm mixture into Lettuce Cups and sprinkle with sesame seeds, if using.

Oxtail pot sticker dumplings with black vinegar dip

1 tablespoon peanut oil
2/3 cup (150 ml) Shao Xing rice wine

Dumplings
2 tablespoons peanut oil
2 lbs (1 kg) oxtail pieces (to yield about
   1 lb/500 g cooked meat)
6 cups (1½ liters) Veal Stock (page 12)
2 dried Chinese sausages (*lup cheong*),
   finely sliced
6 fresh shiitake mushrooms, stems trimmed,
   finely diced
5 green onions (scallions), finely sliced
¾ in (1½ cm) peeled ginger, finely chopped
3 cloves garlic, finely chopped
½ tablespoon Palm Sugar Syrup (page 18)
1 teaspoon sesame oil
½ tablespoon soy sauce
1 teaspoon sea salt
18 round wonton skins

Black vinegar dip
2/3 cup (150 ml) black Chinese vinegar
¾ in (1½ cm) peeled ginger, sliced into thin
   shreds
1 tablespoon sugar

Serves 6

Pot sticker dumplings originate from China although they're also popular in Japan where they're known as *gyoza*. The dumplings are first fried then steamed, all in the same pan. To steam, you just add a little liquid and cook until it evaporates—be mindful of the dumplings sticking to the pan.

Make the Veal Stock and Palm Sugar Syrup by following the recipes on pages 12 and 18.

Dumplings
Preheat the oven to 325°F (160°C). Heat the peanut oil in a large pan or skillet and brown the oxtail. Transfer to a casserole dish. Bring the Veal Stock to a boil and pour it over the oxtail pieces. Cover the dish with a tight-fitting lid or foil and place in the oven for 2–3 hours, until the meat is falling off the bone.

When cool enough to handle, remove the oxtail from the stock and pick off the meat. Break it into small pieces. Discard the bones, and refrigerate or freeze the cooking stock for another use.

Combine the dried Chinese sausage, shiitake mushrooms, green onions, ginger, garlic, Palm Sugar Syrup, sesame oil, soy sauce and salt in a large bowl. Carefully fold in the oxtail.

Lay the wonton skins out on a floured surface. Place two teaspoons of filling in the center of each skin and lightly brush around the edges with water. Fold one side of the skin over to meet the other and press the edges shut as shown. The Dumplings should look like half moons. Press the base of each Dumpling down on the work surface to create a flat bottom (so the Dumplings can sit upright). Using your fingers, mold the rim of each Dumpling so it has a fluted appearance. Cover the Dumplings with a damp cloth until you're ready to serve.

Black vinegar dip
Place the vinegar, ginger and sugar in a non-reactive saucepan and bring to a boil. Simmer, stirring, for 2 minutes, then set aside to cool.

To serve
Heat the peanut oil in a large non-stick skillet. Gently fry the Dumplings until crisp on the bottom, then add the Shao Xing rice wine. Cover the Dumplings and steam for 1–2 minutes, or until the liquid has just evaporated. Remove from the pan and serve immediately, with the Black Vinegar Dip.

Chili turnip cakes with black mushrooms and sweet sausage

6 dried black Chinese mushrooms

2 lbs (1 kg) daikon radish

1 large brown onion

1 tablespoon peanut oil

3 dried Chinese sausages (*lup cheong*), finely diced

8 fresh shiitake mushrooms, stems trimmed, finely chopped

3 red bird's-eye chilies, deseeded and finely chopped

10 coriander (cilantro) roots, washed and finely chopped

12 green onions (scallions), green ends only, finely sliced

1 tablespoon Palm Sugar Syrup (page 18)

1 tablespoon black Chinese vinegar

¼ teaspoon ground white pepper

1 teaspoon sea salt

1 tablespoon sesame seeds, dry-roasted

2 cups (250 g) rice flour

½ cup (125 ml) XO Sauce (page 17)

Serves 6

These cakes are traditionally made during Chinese New Year as a symbol of prosperity and rising fortunes. During the first ten days of the festivities, slices of the different New Year cakes are fried for breakfast each morning. Chinese turnip (*lo bak*) is a type of Japanese daikon or white radish.

Make the XO Sauce and Palm Sugar Syrup by following the recipes on pages 17 and 18.

Place the dried mushrooms in a bowl and cover with boiling water. Let them soften for 30 minutes. Squeeze them dry and dice into small pieces.

Meanwhile, lay a piece of muslin cloth into a large mixing bowl so that it reaches over the sides. Peel the daikon and onion and grate them into the cloth. Cover the mixture with boiling water and set aside to cool for a few hours. Once cool, lift the sides of the cloth out of the water and form a ball around the turnip and onion. Squeeze all the liquid out of the ball. Reserve both the liquid and the solids.

Heat the oil in a wok and add the dried Chinese sausage, fresh and dried mushrooms, chilies and coriander roots and stir-fry until the mixture begins to brown. Add the green onions and continue to fry until they soften. Add the Palm Sugar Syrup, black Chinese vinegar, pepper and salt and cook until the liquid has almost evaporated. Stir in the sesame seeds and remove from the heat.

In a bowl combine the daikon and onion with the rice flour. Add enough of the reserved daikon liquid to form a thick porridge consistency, then add the contents of the wok and mix thoroughly.

Find a rectangular heat-proof dish (preferably with a lid) that will fit inside a steamer. Line the dish with a muslin cloth or greaseproof paper. Scoop the mixture daikon onto the cloth or paper, then press down and smooth the top.

Place the dish in a steamer covered with a lid or foil that has been lightly oiled on the inside, and cook for around 2 hours, or until the cake becomes firm. Set aside to cool. Once cool, refrigerate the dish for a further 2 hours (it can be refrigerated for up to 3 days if you want to prepare it in advance).

To serve, turn the cake out and cut into 2½ in (6 cm) squares. Heat a little extra peanut oil in a skillet and fry the cakes in batches until they are crisp and golden. Serve with XO Sauce.

Fried green onion cakes

½ tablespoon peanut oil

10 green onions (scallions), green leaves only, finely chopped

1 cup (150 g) all-purpose (plain) flour

⅓ cup (80 ml) hot water

½ egg, lightly beaten

1 teaspoon sea salt

½ tablespoon sesame oil

2 cups (500 ml) vegetable oil

Serves 6

These traditional Chinese pancakes are at their best when freshly cooked. Eat them on their own or as an accompaniment to other dishes.

Heat the peanut oil in a wok or pan. Fry the green onions until soft then drain on paper towels.

Place the flour in a bowl and make a well in the center. Add the water, egg and salt and, using your hands, work the mixture into a smooth dough. Allow to rest for 30 minutes.

Divide the dough into six balls. On a floured surface roll a ball out into a circle around $1/16$ in (2 mm) thick. Brush with a little sesame oil and place a tablespoon of spring onions on top. Roll the circle up tightly to form a cylinder. Roll the cylinder up in the opposite direction to form a swirl. Using a rolling pin, flatten out the swirl to a thick pancake (around ¾ in/2 cm thick). Repeat with the remaining balls.

Heat the oil in a wok to 350°F (180°C) then fry the cakes in batches for around a minute on each side, or until golden. Drain on paper towels and serve.

Steamed barbecued pork buns

½ tablespoon peanut oil

1 teaspoon sesame oil

2 cloves garlic, finely chopped

¾ in (1½ cm) peeled ginger, finely chopped

4 fresh shiitake mushrooms, stems trimmed, caps diced

10 oz (300 g) Char Siu Pork (page 24, or bought from a restaurant), diced

2 green onions (scallions), finely sliced

1½ tablespoons Pat Chun sweetened vinegar

3½ tablespoons hoisin sauce

1 tablespoon soy sauce

1 portion Bun Dough (page 23)

Serves 6

In China these buns are called *char siu bao* and are a classic Cantonese comfort food. Steam the buns long enough for the dough to expand and open at the top, revealing the filling inside. Eat them straight from the steamer.

Make the Bun Dough and Char Siu Pork by following the recipes on pages 23 and 24.

Heat the peanut and sesame oils in a wok and add the garlic, ginger and mushrooms. Stir-fry until fragrant. Add the Char Siu Pork, green onions, Pat Chun sweetened vinegar, hoisin and soy sauce. Cook for 1–2 minutes or until the liquid has almost evaporated. Remove from the heat and set aside to cool.

Divide the Bun Dough into 12 balls. On a floured surface, roll each ball into a neat disc, about 3 in (8 cm) in diameter. Place a tablespoon of the pork mixture into the center of each disc. Bring the edges up around the filling and pinch them together at the top to seal.

Place the buns in a steamer lined with greaseproof paper, allowing space in between them for rising. Steam for 10–12 minutes, or until the tops have opened. Serve immediately.

Crispy scallop stuffed chicken wings with chili caramel sauce

18 large chicken wings

4 oz (100 g) ground pork

4 oz (100 g) fresh shucked scallops (roe attached), finely chopped

¾ in (1½ cm) peeled ginger, finely chopped

3 coriander (cilantro) roots, washed and finely chopped

2 green onions (scallions), finely sliced

½ tablespoon soy sauce

¼ teaspoon ground white pepper

Pinch of sea salt

18 toothpicks

4 cups (1 liter) Master Stock (page 12)

3 cups (750ml) vegetable oil

½ head iceberg lettuce, finely sliced into shreds

½ cup (125 ml) Chili Caramel Sauce (page 13)

½ cup (25 g) coriander leaves (cilantro)

2 limes, quartered

Serves 6

Stuffing chicken wings is a time-consuming job but well worth it. A tip: always work with warm chicken wings, as they are a lot easier to debone and stuff. For maximum flavor I simmer the stuffed wings in Master Stock before I fry them, but a simpler way is to marinate them in soy sauce.

Make the Master Stock and Chili Caramel Sauce by following the recipes on pages 12 and 13.

Using a sharp knife or cleaver, remove and discard the tips of the chicken wings by cutting through the first joint. Trim the knuckle from the base of the wings so that you expose the two small bones on either side.

Place the wings in a steamer and steam for 20 minutes. Remove from the steamer and set aside until they're cool enough to handle. Use your thumb and forefinger to gently slide the bones out through the opening at the base of the wings. Return them to the steamer (turned off the heat) to keep them warm while you prepare the stuffing.

In a large mixing bowl, work the ground pork with your fingers for several minutes until it becomes slightly elastic (this will help the stuffing to hold together). Add the scallops, ginger, coriander roots, green onions, soy sauce, pepper and salt and mix thoroughly.

Scoop the mixture into a piping bag fitted with a small nozzle and tightly fill each chicken wing. Use toothpicks to seal the ends of the wings.

Bring the Master Stock to a boil in a large pot then add the chicken wings. Simmer for 5 minutes. Remove from the heat and allow the wings to cool in the stock. Once cool, drain on paper towels and refrigerate until ready to fry.

Heat the vegetable oil in a wok to 350°F (180°C) and fry the wings in batches until crisp and golden. Drain on paper towels. Place the shredded lettuce on a platter and top with the wings. Drizzle them with the Chili Caramel Sauce and garnish with coriander leaves. Serve the lime wedges on the side.

Warm salad of pig's ears with soy, chili shrimp oil and herbs

6 pig's ears

4 cups (1 liter) Master Stock (page 12)

2 cups (500 ml) vegetable oil

4 cloves garlic, finely chopped

¾ in (1½ cm) peeled ginger, sliced into thin shreds

⅓ cup + 1 tablespoon (100 ml) soy sauce

2½ tablespoons Chili Shrimp Oil (page 18)

3 green onions (scallions), finely sliced

1 cup (50 g) coriander leaves (cilantro)

1 tablespoon Sichuan Pepper-Salt Powder (page 11)

Serves 6

Pig's ears are a Chinese delicacy that many Westerners shy away from. They're delicious, especially slow-cooked in Master Stock (red-cooked) and then fried and tossed in soy sauce, Chili Shrimp Oil and fresh herbs. Pig's ears can be purchased from most butchers. Choose ears from younger pigs, around the size of the palm of your hand. They should be intact and unblemished.

Make the Sichuan Pepper-Salt Powder, Master Stock and Chili Shrimp Oil by following the recipes on pages 11, 12 and 18.

Using the back of your knife, scrape the ears to remove any grit or bristles, then rinse thoroughly. Place the ears into a baking dish.

Preheat the oven to 275°F (140°C). Bring the Master Stock to a boil then pour over the ears. Cover the dish with a lid or foil and cook in the oven for 1½ –2 hours or until the ears are tender.

Allow the ears to cool in the stock. Once cool, remove and refrigerate for a few hours or overnight to firm up.

Slice the ears into fine strips. Heat the vegetable oil in a wok to 350°F (180°C) and fry the ears for a few minutes until they begin to crisp. Add the garlic and continue frying until the garlic is golden brown and the aroma is nutty. Remove the ears and garlic with a slotted spoon and drain on paper towels.

Place the ears and garlic in a bowl with the ginger, soy sauce, Chili Shrimp Oil, green onions, coriander leaves and Sichuan Pepper-Salt Powder and toss together. Serve immediately.

Chicken and okra curry puffs

2 coriander (cilantro) roots, washed and
    coarsely chopped

3 cloves garlic, coarsely chopped

6 white peppercorns

1 teaspoon sea salt

1 tablespoon peanut oil

1 tablespoon Curry Powder (page 10)

2 skinless chicken breasts, finely chopped

1 tablespoon Palm Sugar Syrup (page 18)

3 tablespoons water

½ tablespoon sweet soy sauce

4 Asian shallots, finely chopped

2 red bird's-eye chilies, deseeded and
    finely chopped

6 okra, finely sliced

½ cup (25 g) coriander leaves (cilantro),
    finely chopped

4 Thai basil leaves, finely chopped

3 cups (750ml) vegetable oil, for deep-frying

Pastry

2¾ cups (410 g) all-purpose (plain) flour

1 tablespoon cornstarch, plus
    1 teaspoon extra

Sea salt

1½ tablespoons (30 g) clarified butter or
    ghee, melted

¾ cup (190 ml) water

⅓ cup (80 ml) peanut oil

1 teaspoon sesame oil

Serves 6

Dumplings and little parcels of all descriptions are part of every dim sum meal. This recipe is an Indian take on traditional dim sum, with Thai flavors added as well. The pastry is quite complex: two doughs are folded together repeatedly, similar to traditional French puff pastry. The texture you get by doing this is sublime and I find the process a real labor of love.

Make the Curry Powder and Palm Sugar Syrup by following the recipes on pages 10 and 18.

    Using a mortar and pestle, pound the coriander roots, garlic, peppercorns and salt into a fine paste. Heat the peanut oil in a wok and fry the paste until fragrant. Add the Curry Powder and fry for a further 2 minutes. Add the chicken and Palm Sugar Syrup and fry until the chicken begins to brown, then add the water and let it evaporate. When the chicken looks slightly caramelized, add the soy sauce, shallots, chilies and okra and cook for 1–2 minutes. Stir through the coriander and Thai basil leaves and remove from the heat. Check the seasoning and set aside to cool.

Pastry

Combine 1¾ cups (260 g) of the flour, 1 tablespoon of cornstarch and a pinch of salt in a bowl, then stir in the butter or ghee. Add the water and work the mixture with your hands until the dough comes together. Knead the dough on a floured surface until it is smooth and shiny (5–10 minutes) then refrigerate covered in plastic wrap for 30 minutes.

    Meanwhile, place the remaining flour, 1 teaspoon of cornstarch and a pinch of salt in the bowl and add the peanut and sesame oil. Work the mixture with your hands until the dough comes together. Knead the dough on a floured surface until it is smooth and shiny (5–10 minutes) then refrigerate covered in plastic wrap for 30 minutes.

    Roll each dough into a long sausage shape and cut into 18 pieces. Roll the pieces into small balls. The first dough should make balls around double the size of the second dough. Take one of the larger balls and use your hands to flatten and stretch it into an oval shape. Press a smaller ball into the center of the oval. Roll the outer dough around the inner dough to form a cigar shape. Place the cigar on a floured surface and roll it flat into a rectangle with a rolling pin. Use your fingers to roll the rectangle up lengthwise into a cylinder. Roll it into a rectangle again and then roll up into a cylinder another four times, then shape the final cylinder into a ball. Do the same with the remaining dough, to make 18 balls.

    Roll the balls out into ovals around ¹⁄₁₆ in (2 mm) thick. Place a heaped tablespoon of the filling on one side of the oval. Fold the empty side over the filling to form a half-moon shape and press the edges together to seal. Refrigerate until ready to fry.

To serve

Heat the vegetable oil in a wok to 350°F (180°C) and fry the curry puffs in batches until puffy and golden. Drain on paper towels and serve.

Har gao shrimp dumplings

Filling

1½ lbs (750 g) fresh shrimp, peeled and deveined (to make 12 oz/350 g)

6 green onions (scallions), finely sliced

1 teaspoon shaved palm sugar

½ tablespoon soy sauce

1 teaspoon fish sauce

½ teaspoon Toasted Sesame Oil (page 17)

Dough

2½ cups (375 g) wheat gluten starch

½ tablespoon cornstarch

1 cup (250 ml) boiling water

Serves 6

These dumplings are known as *har gao* in Cantonese, which means "shrimp dumpling". The dough, made of wheat gluten starch, becomes translucent when steamed. The trick is to cook them immediately as the dough can dry out quickly and become tough. I like to serve them with XO or chili sauce.

Make the Toasted Sesame Oil by following the recipe on page 17.

Dice two-thirds of the shrimp until fine. Coarsely chop the remaining shrimp then combine both in a bowl with the green onions, palm sugar, soy sauce, fish sauce and Toasted Sesame Oil. Mix well and set aside.

Sift the wheat starch and cornstarch into a mixing bowl. Add the boiling water and stir the mixture with chopsticks until it is cool enough to touch. Mix it with your fingers until well combined—it should have the consistency of light dough. Add a little more wheat starch or water if necessary. Turn it out onto a floured surface and knead until soft and pliable. Let it stand, covered, for 10 minutes. Meanwhile, lightly grease a steamer and drain any excess liquid from the filling mixture.

Divide the dough into 18 equal balls. Take one ball and place it between two sheets of greaseproof paper. Using a rolling pin, roll it out into a thin disc. Remove the top sheet of paper and place two teaspoons of filling into the center of the disc. Dip a finger in water and run it around one side of the disc. Fold the other side over and pinch the edges together to seal (the dumpling should look like a half-moon). Flatten the bottom of the dumpling by gently pressing it down on a flat surface so it will stand upright in the steamer. Place it into the prepared steamer while you make the remaining dumplings.

Steam the dumplings for 5 minutes or until the skins are translucent.

Rice noodle rolls with jumbo shrimp in wine broth

Rice noodle rolls

18 fresh jumbo shrimp (about 1½ lbs/
    750 g), peeled and deveined, heads and tail
    tips removed
9 fresh rice noodle sheets (around
    6 in/15 cm square), or fresh pasta sheets
3 tablespoons plum sauce
9 green onions (scallions), white ends only
    halved lengthwise
1 tablespoon Chili Rock Sugar (page 11)

Broth

8 green onions (scallions), coarsely chopped
1½ in (4 cm) peeled ginger, bruised
Scant 1 cup (225 ml) Shao Xing rice wine
½ cup (120 g) raw rock sugar crystals
5 dried black Chinese mushrooms
⅓ cup (80 ml) soy sauce
2 tablespoons water

Garnishes

4 green onions (scallions), finely sliced
1 cup (50 g) coriander leaves (cilantro)
1½ tablespoons sesame oil

Serves 6

A simple dish popular at **ezard**. Fresh rice noodle sheets are available from Asian grocers—they are thicker than Vietnamese rice paper, and make rolls that are silky and smooth, and sturdy enough to serve in a broth (or you can eat them on their own with a dipping sauce). The Chinese name for the rolls is *cheung fun*.

Make the Chili Rock Sugar by following the recipe on page 11.

Rice noodle rolls

Make small incisions crosswise along the back of each shrimp to assist them to cook straight without curling.

Place the rice noodle sheets (most likely stuck together) in a steamer and steam for 3 minutes or until they are warm and pliable. Separate the sheets on an oiled work surface. Working as quickly as possible while the sheets are still warm, place a smear of plum sauce and a piece of green onion on each sheet, then place two shrimp on top followed by a sprinkle of Chili Rock Sugar. Roll the shrimp inside the sheet into a neat, tight roll. Tightly wrap the individual rolls in plastic wrap, sealing the ends. Refrigerate for an hour to firm.

Broth

Place all the ingredients in a saucepan and bring to a boil, stirring until the rock sugar dissolves. Remove from the heat and set aside to cool and allow the flavors to infuse.

To serve

Strain the Broth and reheat. Place the Rice Noodle Rolls, still wrapped in plastic wrap, in a steamer and steam for 3–4 minutes.

Remove the Rolls from the steamer, unwrap from the plastic wrap, and cut in half. Place three halves in each serving bowl and ladle a little Broth over them. Garnish with the additional green onions and coriander leaves. Heat the sesame oil in a wok or saucepan until smoking and drizzle over the top. Serve immediately.

Drunken chicken
with cucumber salad and XO sauce

½ cup (125 ml) XO Sauce (page 17)
2 lemons, quartered

Chicken
1 large organic free-range chicken weighing
   around 3½ lbs (1.8 kgs)
4 cups (1 liter) Shao Xing rice wine
2 cups (500 ml) mirin
2 cups (500 ml) water
⅓ cup (80 g) raw rock sugar crystals
¾ in (1½ cm) peeled ginger, bruised

Salad
1½ tablespoons soy sauce
1 tablespoon lemon juice
1 teaspoon Toasted Sesame Oil
   (page 17)
2 cloves garlic, bruised
1 teaspoon sugar
1 cucumber, peeled, deseeded and sliced
   into thin shreds
⅓ cup (80 g) wood ear mushrooms, torn
¾ in (1½ cm) peeled ginger, finely sliced
2 red finger-length chilies, deseeded and
   finely sliced lengthwise
¼ head iceberg lettuce, finely sliced into
   shreds
1 cup (50 g) coriander leaves (cilantro)
1 tablespoon sesame seeds, dry-roasted
   (optional)

Serves 6

Drunken chicken, *jiu ji* in Mandarin, is the name given to different ways of preparing chicken using alcohol. It is usually poached in Shao Xing rice wine and garnished with ginger, green onions and soy sauce, and served cold. Try to keep the skin intact as you're cooking and carving the chicken—the chilled natural jelly and juices underneath the skin are really worth waiting for. Begin this recipe a day in advance.

Make the XO Sauce and Toasted Sesame Oil by following the recipes on pages 17.

Chicken
Bring a large pot of water to a boil and blanch the chicken for 10 seconds. Remove from the water and plunge into a large basin of iced water to stop the cooking. Repeat this process three times. This will help tighten the skin and keep it intact.

Rinse the pot and add the Shao Xing rice wine, mirin, water, rock sugar and ginger. Bring to a boil then add the chicken and simmer for 45 minutes. Remove from the heat and allow the chicken to cool in the poaching liquid. Refrigerate in the liquid overnight.

The following day, remove the chicken from the liquid and use a sharp knife or cleaver to cut it in half lengthwise. Slice off the wings where they meet the breasts. Trim the knuckles from the base of the wings to expose the two small bones on either side, and pull them out. Slice off the legs and separate the thighs from the drumsticks by cutting through the joint. Leave the drumsticks whole and cut the remaining thigh into three pieces. Cut the breasts from the carcass (but leave them attached to the breastplate) and cut each into six pieces.

Salad
Make a dressing out of the soy sauce, lemon juice, Toasted Sesame Oil, garlic and sugar, stirring until the sugar has dissolved. Combine with the remaining ingredients.

To serve
Place the cold chicken on a serving dish and ladle over some of the poaching liquid—just enough to keep the chicken moist. Accompany with the Salad, XO Sauce and lemon wedges. Sprinkle with the roasted sesame seeds, if using.

Bean curd skin rolls
with duck, scallop and water chestnuts

3 duck legs (marylands)

2 tablespoons peanut oil

4 cups (1 liter) Master Stock (page 12)

5 oz (150 g) ground pork

8 oz (250 g) fresh shucked scallops (roe attached), coarsely chopped

5 water chestnuts, peeled and finely chopped

3 green onions (scallions), finely sliced

3 coriander (cilantro) roots, washed and finely chopped

2 red bird's-eye chilies, deseeded and finely chopped

2 tablespoons soy sauce

1½ tablespoons oyster sauce

¼ teaspoon ground white pepper

4 cloves garlic, finely chopped

¾ in (1½ cm) peeled ginger, finely chopped

2 dried Chinese sausages (*lup cheong*), finely sliced

12 sheets dried bean curd skin

2 eggs, lightly beaten with 1 tablespoon water

3 cups (750ml) vegetable oil

½ cup (125 ml) XO Sauce (page 17)

Serves 6

Bean curd skin rolls come in many different varieties. This combination filling of duck, scallop, pork, sweet dried Chinese sausage (*lup cheong*) and water chestnuts has an interesting texture. The duck is slowly cooked in Master Stock, which gives the dish a richness as well as an authentic Chinese flavor.

Make the Master Stock and XO Sauce by following the recipes on page 12 and 17.

Cut the tendons in the duck legs near the joint (this allows the meat to shrink while cooking, which helps it to cook evenly). Heat 1 tablespoon of the peanut oil in a pan and fry the legs until browned and crisp. Transfer to a deep baking dish.

Preheat the oven to 325°F (160°C). Bring the Master Stock to a boil and pour it over the duck. Cover the dish with a lid or foil then cook it in the oven for 1½ hours or until the meat is tender.

Remove from the oven and set aside to cool. Once cool, remove the duck legs from the stock and refrigerate for a few hours or overnight (to make the meat easier to shred).

In a large mixing bowl, work the ground pork with your hands for several minutes until it becomes slightly elastic (this will help the filling to hold together). Add the scallops, water chestnuts, green onions, coriander roots, chilies, soy sauce, oyster sauce and white pepper. Shred the meat from the duck legs with your fingers, then add it to the mixture.

Heat the remaining peanut oil in a wok and add the garlic, ginger and dried Chinese sausage. Stir-fry until fragrant (about 2 minutes). Cool and then fold it through the mixture.

Soak the bean curd skins in a large bowl of cold water until soft (about 3 minutes). Drain and blot off the excess water with paper towels. On a flat surface, lay out one sheet of bean curd skin at a time and trim into a rectangle about 6½ in x 8 in (16 cm x 20 cm). Place 3 tablespoons of the filling at one end, then brush the rest of the sheet with the egg mixture. Roll up, folding in the sides of the sheet as you go, to make a tight roll. Repeat the process with the remaining sheets and refrigerate the rolls until needed.

Heat the oil in a wok to 350°F (180°C) and fry the rolls in batches until crisp and golden. Drain on paper towels and serve with XO Sauce.

Barbecued spareribs with sesame salt

2 lbs (1 kg) boneless pork spareribs
3½ tablespoons soy sauce
3 tablespoons plum sauce
1½ tablespoons Shao Xing rice wine
5 cloves garlic, finely chopped
1 tablespoon shaved palm sugar
2 red finger-length chilies, finely sliced
2 green finger-length chilies, finely sliced

Sesame salt
4 tablespoons sesame seeds, dry-roasted
2 tablespoons sea salt

Serves 6

Instead of baking these ribs, they are also great to grill on a barbecue.

Rinse the ribs under cold running water. Bring a large pot of water to a boil and add the ribs. Simmer for 20 minutes (this helps to remove excess fat). Drain and rinse the ribs.

Combine the soy sauce, plum sauce, Shao Xing rice wine, garlic and palm sugar in a bowl. Add the ribs and toss lightly. Marinate in the refrigerator for at least 2 hours or overnight.

Preheat the oven to 350°F (180°C). Tip the ribs and marinade onto a large baking sheet lined with foil. Bake for 45 minutes, turning once, until caramelized.

Meanwhile, prepare the Sesame Salt by grinding the sesame seeds and salt into a fine powder using a mortar and pestle.

To serve, sprinkle the ribs with the Sesame Salt and sliced chilies.

Steamed lotus leaf rice parcels with chicken and sweet sausage

3 dried lotus leaves
2 skinless chicken breasts
1 tablespoon peanut oil
2 cloves garlic, finely chopped
¾ in (1½ cm) peeled ginger, finely chopped
3 dried Chinese sausages (*lup cheong*), finely sliced
6 fresh shiitake mushrooms, stems trimmed, caps diced
2½ tablespoons Shao Xing rice wine
2 cups (200 g) cooked Sticky Rice (page 24)
½ cup (20 g) finely chopped garlic chives
2 red bird's-eye chilies, deseeded and finely chopped
3 coriander (cilantro) roots, washed and finely chopped
2 green onions (scallions), finely sliced
8 water chestnuts, peeled and finely chopped
½ teaspoon ground Sichuan pepper
1½ tablespoons oyster sauce
2½ tablespoons soy sauce
½ cup (125 ml) XO Sauce (page 17)

Serves 6

In China there are many varieties of steamed lotus leaf parcels. I like the simplicity of them.

Make the XO Sauce and Sticky Rice by following the recipes on pages 17 and 24.

Soak the lotus leaves in warm water for 1 hour or until soft. Drain and then cut the leaves in half.

Coarsely chop the chicken breasts then grind them in a food processor. Heat the peanut oil in a wok and add the chicken, garlic, ginger, dried Chinese sausage and shiitake mushrooms and stir-fry until the chicken has browned. Add the Shao Xing rice wine and cook until it evaporates. Remove from the heat.

Place the Sticky Rice in a large bowl and add the garlic chives, chilies, coriander roots, green onions, water chestnuts, Sichuan pepper, oyster sauce and soy sauce. Combine, then add the chicken mixture. Taste for seasoning.

Lay out the lotus leaves on a work surface and place a sixth of the rice mixture on the bottom third of each one. Roll the leaves up, folding the edges to the middle as you go, to make tight rectangular parcels.

Steam the parcels for 3–4 minutes. To serve, slice the parcels open (the leaves are not eaten) and accompany with XO Sauce.

Pork and shrimp stuffed tofu in fragrant rice wine broth

This is a Chinese classic. The combination of pork and shrimp gives a crumbly and velvety texture inside the tofu. The broth is delicate and sweet and can be used in many other dishes, especially those including meat or seafood.

Broth

1¼ cups (320 ml) Shao Xing rice wine

½ orange, rind finely grated

4 star anise pods

4 cinnamon sticks

2 cloves garlic, bruised

¾ in (1½ cm) peeled ginger, bruised

2½ tablespoons (40 g) raw rock sugar crystals

¾ cup (180 ml) soy sauce

⅔ cup (160 ml) water

Stuffed tofu

5 oz (150 g) ground pork

14 oz (400 g) fresh shrimp, peeled and deveined (to make 7 oz/200 g), then finely chopped

¾ in (1½ cm) peeled ginger, finely chopped

2 coriander (cilantro) roots, washed and finely chopped

4 green onions (scallions), finely sliced

½ cup (20 g) finely chopped garlic chives

2½ tablespoons soy sauce

¼ teaspoon ground white pepper

1 lb (500 g) firm tofu

3 cups (750ml) vegetable oil

⅓ cup (50 g) rice flour

Serves 6

Broth

Place the Shao Xing rice wine in a saucepan and bring to a boil to evaporate the alcohol. Add the remaining Broth ingredients and simmer for a few minutes. Remove from the heat and allow the flavors to infuse while you prepare the stuffed tofu.

Stuffed tofu

Combine the pork, shrimp, ginger, coriander roots, green onions, garlic chives, soy sauce and white pepper in a bowl and set aside.

Cut the tofu cakes into 12 cubes (they should each measure around 1¼ in/3 cm across). Take one cube and, using a small knife, make an incision on one side. Use a teaspoon to carefully fill the cavity with the stuffing, then press the incision shut. Repeat with the remaining tofu and stuffing.

To serve

Strain the Broth (reserving the seasonings) and reheat. Heat the oil in a wok to 350°F (180°C). Dredge the Tofu cubes in the rice flour and dust off any excess. Fry the Tofu in batches until crisp and golden. Drain on paper towels.

Place two pieces of Tofu in each bowl and ladle a little Broth over them. Top with some of the reserved spices if desired.

Fried sticky rice
with eggs and chili jam

2 tablespoons peanut oil

2 skinless chicken breasts, diced

¾ in (1½ cm) peeled ginger, finely chopped

2 red bird's-eye chilies, deseeded and finely chopped

2 dried Chinese sausages (*lup cheong*), finely sliced

8 oz (250 g) Char Siu Pork (page 24, or bought from a restaurant), diced

4 fresh shiitake mushrooms, stems trimmed, diced

½ cup (75 g) fresh or frozen peas

4 green onions (scallions), finely sliced

¼ cup (12 g) coriander leaves (cilantro), coarsely chopped

3 cups (300 g) cooked Sticky Rice (page 24)

2 tablespoons soy sauce

½ tablespoon Toasted Sesame Oil (page 17)

12 quail eggs or 6 chicken eggs

½ cup (125 ml) Chili Jam (page 13)

Serves 6

I love eating sticky rice at dim sum. I also like Malaysian nasi goreng with a fried egg, and this is my combination of the two. Chicken eggs are fine to use also, but quail eggs, due to their tiny size, are perfectly suited to dim sum. Serve this the traditional way, steamed in individual bowls after being fried, which allows the rice to set. The Chili Jam is a wonderful complement to the dish.

Make the Chili Jam, Toasted Sesame Oil, Sticky Rice and Char Siu Pork by following the recipes on pages 13, 17 and 24.

Heat 1 tablespoon of the peanut oil in a wok and add the chicken. Stir-fry over high heat until it begins to brown, then add the ginger, chilies, dried Chinese sausage, Char Siu Pork, mushrooms, peas, green onions and coriander leaves and fry for 1 minute.

Add the Sticky Rice, soy sauce and Toasted Sesame Oil and stir until heated through and well combined. Divide the rice into six small bowls and insert into a steamer (or several steamers). Steam for 5–10 minutes over low heat.

Meanwhile, heat the remaining tablespoon of peanut oil in a pan and fry the quail eggs until the whites are set but the yolks are still runny. Invert the rice onto small serving plates or serve in the hot bowls. Top each serving with two fried quail eggs (or 1 chicken egg) followed by a spoonful of Chili Jam.

Five spice egg custard tarts

A favorite to be enjoyed at the end of every dim sum meal. Traditionally the tarts are filled with a simple egg custard, but I like the additional flavor of the spices. Eat them when they are still warm from the oven.

Pastry
7 oz (200 g) unsalted butter, softened
¾ cup (100 g) confectioner (icing) sugar
1 vanilla pod
2 egg yolks
1¾ cups (250 g) all-purpose (plain) flour
Pinch of salt

Custard
1¼ cups (300 ml) milk
1¼ cups (300 ml) heavy cream
1 cinnamon stick
6 cardamom pods, cracked
2 star anise pods
3 whole cloves
1 whole nutmeg, grated
3 eggs
2 egg yolks
⅓ cup (75 g) superfine (caster) sugar

Makes 18

Pastry

Cream the butter and sugar until pale and smooth. Split the vanilla pod in half lengthwise and scrape out the seeds with the tip of a knife. Add the seeds and the egg yolks to the butter and sugar and stir through. Sift in the flour and salt and combine until the pastry comes together in a ball. (Alternatively, you could follow this process using a food processor.) Knead the pastry for a few minutes until smooth. Wrap in plastic wrap and refrigerate for 30 minutes.

Preheat the oven to 325°F (160°C). Knead the pastry briefly on a floured surface to soften it. Shape it into a long sausage and divide into 18 even pieces. Roll each piece into a circle about 1/16 in (2 mm) thick. Press the pieces into a greased muffin tin or 2 in (5 cm) individual tart tins and trim the edges. Cover each tart case with foil or baking paper and fill with rice or baking weights. Bake for 10–12 minutes or until the pastry is golden, removing the foil and rice towards the end. Leave the oven on as you prepare the Custard.

Custard

Put the milk, cream, cinnamon, cardamom, star anise, cloves and nutmeg in a saucepan and bring to a simmer. Turn off the heat and leave to infuse for 20 minutes.

Whisk the eggs, yolks and sugar until pale. Gradually strain in the milk mixture and combine. Pour the Custard into the cases and bake in the oven for 10 minutes, or until the Custard has just set. Allow the tarts to cool a little before removing from the tins.

Crispy fried chicken feet with spiced chili salt and lime

18 large chicken feet

1 teaspoon sea salt

8 cups (2 liters) Master Stock (page 12)

3 cups (750ml) vegetable oil

2 tablespoons Spiced Chili Salt
  (page 11)

1 cup (50 g) coriander leaves (cilantro)

1 red finger-length chili, deseeded and finely
  sliced lengthwise

2 limes, quartered

Serves 6

Chicken feet are bland on their own, but the soy braised chicken feet served at dim sum are a real delicacy. In this recipe the chicken feet are cooked in Master Stock (red-cooking) then fried until crisp. The Spiced Chili Salt and lime make them very tasty.

Make the Spiced Chili Salt and Master Stock by following the recipes on pages 11 and 12.

Snip the claws from the chicken feet and wash the feet. Fill a large pot with cold water and add the feet and salt. Bring to a boil (to help remove any impurities) then plunge the feet in a large basin of iced water. This helps to tighten the skin to keep it intact. Transfer the feet to a deep baking dish.

Preheat the oven to 325°F (160°C). Bring the Master Stock to a boil and pour it over the chicken feet. Cover the dish with a lid or foil and cook for 1 hour, or until the meat is tender.

Allow the feet to cool in the stock. Once cool, remove from the stock and refrigerate for a few hours or overnight to firm up.

Heat the vegetable oil in a wok to 350°F (180°C) then fry the feet in batches until crisp and golden. Drain on paper towels. Toss the chicken feet in the Spiced Chili Salt and transfer to a serving dish. Garnish with coriander leaves and chili, and serve with lime wedges on the side.

Flaky taro dumplings
with shrimp, pork and water chestnuts

3 cups (750ml) vegetable oil, for deep-frying

Filling
½ tablespoon peanut oil
5 oz (150 g) ground pork
10 oz/300 g fresh shrimp, peeled
   and deveined (to make 150 g/5 oz),
   then finely chopped
1½ tablespoons Shao Xing rice wine
2 dried Chinese sausages (*lup cheong*),
   finely sliced
¾ in (1½ cm) peeled ginger, finely chopped
3 cloves garlic, finely chopped
3 green onions (scallions), finely sliced
3 coriander (cilantro) roots, washed and
   finely chopped
6 water chestnuts, peeled and finely
   chopped
1½ tablespoons oyster sauce
½ tablespoon soy sauce
1 teaspoon sesame oil
1 teaspoon sugar
¼ teaspoon ground white pepper

Dough
1¾ lbs (800 g) taro root
3 tablespoons (60 g) clarified butter or ghee
¾ cup (90 g) cornstarch
½ tablespoon superfine (caster) sugar
¼ teaspoon ground white pepper
½ tablespoon baking soda

Serves 6

I have these dumplings every time I visit Hong Kong. Their texture is just fantastic—the crisp, flaky taro pastry encloses a velvety filling.

Filling
Heat the peanut oil in a wok and add the pork and shrimp and stir-fry until well browned. Add the Shao Xing rice wine and let it evaporate (this will help separate the pieces of pork). Add the dried Chinese sausage, ginger, garlic, green onions, coriander roots, water chestnuts, oyster sauce, soy sauce, sesame oil, sugar and pepper. Cook until the liquids have evaporated then set aside to cool.

Dough
Peel the taro root and dice into 1¼ in (3 cm) pieces. Place on a heatproof dish and place in a steamer. Steam for 30 minutes or until tender.
   Mash the taro until smooth. Add the butter or ghee to the hot mash and combine. Add the cornstarch, sugar, pepper and baking soda and mix well to form a dough.
   Let the Dough cool slightly. It should have the consistency of soft mashed potato (add a little water if it seems too thick). Lift the Dough onto a floured surface and knead briefly. Roll into a long sausage shape, then divide into 18 balls.
   Hold a ball of Dough in one hand and flatten it with the palm of your other hand. Place a heaped teaspoon of the Filling in the center and then mold the Dough around the Filling to form a torpedo shape, ensuring that the ends are sealed. Repeat with the rest of the Dough and Filling. Refrigerate until ready to fry.

To serve
Heat the vegetable oil in a wok to 350°F (180°C). Fry the dumplings in batches until fluffy and golden. Drain on paper towels and serve.

Rice noodle rolls
with quail and sweet sausage

Rice noodle rolls

6 large quail (about 2 lbs/1 kg in total)

½ tablespoon peanut oil

3 cloves garlic, finely chopped

¾ in (1½ cm) peeled ginger, finely chopped

10 oz (300 g) lean ground pork

2½ tablespoons Shao Xing rice wine

2 dried Chinese sausages (*lup cheong*), finely sliced

8 water chestnuts, peeled and coarsely chopped

¼ cup (40 g) Fried Chili Peanuts (page 19) or roasted peanuts, coarsely chopped

¼ teaspoon ground white pepper

⅓ cup (80 ml) oyster sauce

1½ tablespoons soy sauce

2 green onions (scallions), finely sliced

3 coriander (cilantro) roots, washed and finely chopped

9 fresh rice noodle sheets (around 6 in/15 cm square), or fresh pasta sheets

Broth

2½ tablespoons soy sauce

½ cup (120 ml) mirin

⅓ cup (80 ml) water

2 tablespoons sugar

Garnish

1 cup (50 g) coriander leaves (cilantro)

Serves 6

Make the Fried Chili Peanuts by following the recipe on page 19.

Cut off the quail wings and discard. Hold a bird in the palm of your hand and using a pair of kitchen scissors, cut along either side of the backbone. Remove the backbone and open the bird up.

Use your fingertips to carefully peel the breast meat from the bones, feeling your way across the carcass. For the legs, make a slit to the bone and scrape the meat away.

Check the meat for any hidden bones. Leave the skin on. Repeat this process with the remaining quail, then finely chop the meat and set aside.

Heat the peanut oil in a wok and add the garlic and ginger and fry until beginning to brown. Add the pork and fry until no longer pink. Add the Shao Xing rice wine and cook until it evaporates (this will help separate the pieces of pork).

Add the quail. When the meat begins to color, add the dried Chinese sausage, water chestnuts, peanuts and pepper and fry for a further 2 minutes. Add the oyster sauce and soy sauce and reduce the liquid by half. Add the green onions and coriander roots. Remove the mixture from the heat and allow to cool.

Place the rice noodle sheets (most likely stuck together) in a steamer and steam for 3 minutes or until warm and pliable. Separate the sheets on an oiled work surface. Working as quickly as possible while the sheets are still warm, place 2 tablespoons of the quail mixture on each sheet. Roll the the sheet around the filling into a neat, tight roll. Tightly wrap the individual rolls in plastic wrap, sealing the ends. Refrigerate for an hour to firm.

Place the rolls, still wrapped in plastic wrap, into a steamer and steam for 3–4 minutes. Meanwhile, combine the Broth ingredients in a saucepan and bring to a boil, stirring until the sugar dissolves. Remove the rolls from the steamer, unwrap from the plastic wrap, and cut in half. Place three halves in each serving bowl and pour a little Broth over them. Garnish with the coriander leaves.

Street food

Whenever I think of street food I recall the colorful tarps, plastic chairs and tables, the smells of charcoal and food mingling, and the very modest people who cook everything right there in front of you. Makeshift kitchens and mobile carts are set up along the roadside near shopping centers, markets, offices and night-time precincts. The range of food they sell is endless, and includes snacks, curries, soups, stir-fries and sweetmeats.

The food you find on the streets of a city like Bangkok is not just Thai—often it draws influence from other parts of Southeast Asia, China or India, even as far away as the Middle East. Some vendors specialize in one dish, traditional to their family or village, which they might adapt a little. In every part of the city the food is different, and I look forward to each new trip to Asia wondering what I'm going to eat next.

The recipes in this chapter are my interpretations of street food I've eaten over the years, mostly in Thailand. I've added a sauce or a few extra ingredients here and there, and some dishes are my creations entirely, but they are all in the spirit of food that's fast, fresh, sustaining and full of flavor. Serve these dishes as snacks, Asian tapas or light meals. And if you ever have the chance to spend time in Asia, sample the street food—it's some of the tastiest and freshest food you'll find anywhere in the world.

Chicken satay
with sticky rice

18 large bamboo skewers, soaked

1⅓ lbs (600 g) skinless chicken breasts,
cut into strips

1½ tablespoons fish sauce

1 tablespoon Palm Sugar Syrup (page 18)

1 teaspoon Roasted Shrimp Paste
(page 9)

4 cloves garlic, finely chopped

1½ in (4 cm) peeled fresh turmeric root,
finely chopped

1 teaspoon sea salt

1 banana leaf cut into 6 squares of around
1 ft/30 cm (optional)

3 cups (300 g) cooked Sticky Rice (page 24)

½ cup (125 ml) coconut cream

Basting paste

½ tablespoon coriander seeds,
lightly dry-roasted

1 teaspoon cumin seeds, lightly dry-roasted

1 teaspoon cardamom seeds

½ teaspoon dried red chili flakes

10 Asian shallots, coarsely chopped

3 cloves garlic, coarsely chopped

½ cup (75 g) Fried Chili Peanuts (page 19)
or roasted peanuts

1 tablespoon soy sauce

1 teaspoon shaved palm sugar

Dipping Sauce

6 Asian shallots, coarsely chopped

1 coriander (cilantro) root, washed and
coarsely chopped

2 red finger-length chilies, deseeded and
coarsely chopped

1 tablespoon sugar

1 teaspoon sea salt

½ cup (125 ml) white vinegar

1½ tablespoons freshly-squeezed lime juice

Serves 6

Satay—skewers of meat traditionally grilled over coals and often served with peanut sauce—originated in Indonesia and is popular in many Southeast Asian countries. In Malaysia it is served for breakfast. In my version the meat gets its flavor from being marinated and later basted with a peanut paste as it cooks. The sauce I serve it with is fresh and tangy and doesn't use peanuts. Serve the satay on banana leaves if you desire.

Make the Roasted Shrimp Paste, Palm Sugar Syrup, Fried Chili Peanuts and Sticky Rice by following the recipes on pages 9, 18, 19 and 24.

Place the skewers in a bowl of water to soak—this will prevent them burning when on the grill. Combine the chicken in a bowl with the fish sauce, Palm Sugar Syrup, Roasted Shrimp Paste, garlic, turmeric and salt. Allow the chicken to marinate for 1 hour in the refrigerator. Drain the skewers and then thread two or three strips of chicken on each one. Refrigerate until needed.

Basting paste
Using a mortar and pestle pound the coriander, cumin, cardamom and chili flakes to a fine powder. Add the shallots, garlic and peanuts and continue pounding to make a fine paste (alternatively, blend the ingredients with the spice powder in a food processor). Add the soy sauce and palm sugar and set aside.

Dipping Sauce
Using a mortar and pestle pound the shallots, coriander root and chilies until smooth. Add the sugar, salt, vinegar and lime juice. Taste and add more sugar or lime juice if needed.

To serve
Heat a broiler grill or barbecue. Baste the chicken skewers with the Basting Paste and place them on the grill. Turn them every minute or so, brushing with more Paste. Remove the skewers from the grill when cooked through (6–8 minutes) and serve on banana leaves or plates with a mound of Sticky Rice and a little coconut cream. Serve the Dipping Sauce on the side.

Fried turmeric rice with shrimp and chili

2½ tablespoons peanut oil

4 cloves garlic, finely chopped

1 in (2½ cm) peeled fresh turmeric root, finely chopped

3 dried red finger-length chilies, deseeded and soaked for 30 minutes in warm water, then coarsely chopped

14 oz (400 g) fresh shrimp, peeled and deveined (to make 7 oz/200 g), then coarsely chopped

3 cups (300 g) cooked Jasmine Rice (page 24)

3 coriander (cilantro) roots, washed and finely chopped

½ cup (20 g) mint leaves

1 tablespoon fish sauce

2 tablespoons Fried Chili Peanuts (page 19)

2 red finger-length chilies, finely sliced

Serves 6

Fresh turmeric is used in many rice dishes in Southeast Asia—it adds a sweet and nutty flavor, much more delicate than when using the dried powder. To turn this into a simple meal, accompany it with fresh tomato, chopped herbs and even a little yogurt.

Make the Fried Chili Peanuts and Jasmine Rice by following the recipes on pages 19 and 24

Heat the peanut oil in a wok and add the garlic and turmeric. Fry until fragrant and the color of the turmeric has infused the oil (around 3 minutes). Add the dried chilies and shrimp and continue frying until the shrimp are halfway cooked. Add the Jasmine Rice and fry until it begins to char. To finish, toss through the coriander roots, mint leaves and fish sauce. Transfer to a serving dish and garnish with the Fried Chili Peanuts and fresh sliced chilies.

Tea eggs

6 eggs

1 teaspoon sea salt

⅔ cup (150 ml) Shao Xing rice wine

⅓ cup + 1 tablespoon (100 ml) soy sauce

½ cup (25 g) black tea leaves

2 star anise pods

1 piece liquorice root

¼ teaspoon Sichuan peppercorns

1 piece dried mandarin orange peel

Serves 6

Tea eggs are a popular food during Chinese New Year and they are also served at dim sum, but the Taiwanese enjoy them as a street food. The eggs are hardboiled, then their shells are gently cracked before they're simmered in tea and other seasonings. The eggs develop an attractive marbled appearance and can be eaten on their own or added to soups and salads or served alongside cold meats.

Place the eggs in a shallow bowl and cover with hot (but not boiling) water. Let them warm in the water for 3 minutes (this keeps them from cracking when cooking).

Bring a medium-sized pot of water to a boil and add the salt. When boiling, gently add the eggs and turn the heat down to a simmer. Simmer the eggs until hardboiled (10 minutes). Remove the eggs from the water and use the back of a spoon to gently tap the eggs all over so their shells crack evenly.

Refill the pot with 4 cups (1 liter) of fresh water and add the remaining ingredients. Bring the liquid to a boil and simmer for 2–3 minutes, then add the eggs. Simmer the eggs for 1 hour, adding more water if the eggs are no longer covered. Remove from the heat and allow the eggs to cool and steep in the liquid overnight.

Peel the eggs. Serve hot or cold, quartered or halved.

Pad Thai omelet
with lime and chili rock sugar

Large handful (2 oz/50 g) dried rice
   vermicelli noodles
4 eggs
1 tablespoon fish sauce
1 tablespoon soy sauce
½ cup (125 ml) peanut oil
10 oz (300 g) fresh shrimp, peeled and
   deveined (to make 5 oz/150 g),
   then coarsely chopped
2 tablespoons Fried Chili Peanuts
   (page 19) or roasted peanuts, coarsely
   chopped
2 green bird's-eye chilies, finely sliced
3 cloves garlic, finely chopped
1 cup (50 g) bean sprouts
½ bunch garlic chives, cut into lengths
1 tablespoon Chili Rock Sugar
   (page 11)
2 limes, quartered

Serves 6

Pad Thai is traditionally served with the eggs scrambled through it, but I like to cook them separately as an omelet, filling it with the noodles and other ingredients. It can be cut into small portions and shared between six, or cut in half and shared between two as a meal. You could also halve the quantities for a meal for one. The Chili Rock Sugar gives the dish a nice kick.

Make the Chili Rock Sugar and Fried Chili Peanuts, if using, by following the recipes on pages 11 and 19.

Soak the noodles in boiling water until soft (around 1 minute), then drain.

Lightly beat the eggs with the fish sauce and soy sauce.

Heat 1 tablespoon of the peanut oil in a wok and add the shrimp, peanuts, chili and garlic. Stir-fry until the shrimp are no longer translucent then add the bean sprouts, chives and noodles. Once the ingredients are heated through, remove everything from the wok and keep warm.

Return the wok to the heat and add the remaining peanut oil. When it starts to smoke, pour in the egg mixture. Gently move the wok over the heat in a circular motion to spread the egg out and make sure it cooks evenly. The omelet will bubble and float over the oil. When it is set and crisp around the edges, carefully lift the omelet out with two slotted spoons or other implements, drain off any excess oil, and transfer to a platter. Top one side with the noodle mixture and fold over the top of the omelet. Sprinkle with Chili Rock Sugar and serve with lime wedges on the side.

Thai fish cakes
with red nam jim sauce

Fish cakes
1½ lbs (750 g) white fish fillets (such as
   whiting, porgy or sea bream), skinned,
   deboned and coarsely chopped
⅓ cup (80 g) Red Curry Paste (page 10)
1 egg
1 tablespoon fish sauce
1 teaspoon sugar
4 kaffir lime leaves, finely sliced
½ cup (75 g) finely sliced green beans
3 cups (750ml) vegetable oil

Red nam jim sauce
6 red finger-length chilies, deseeded and
   coarsely chopped
1 red bird's-eye chili, deseeded and coarsely
   chopped
2 cloves garlic, coarsely chopped
1 coriander (cilantro) root, coarsely chopped
1 tablespoon shaved palm sugar
½ cup (125 ml) freshly-squeezed lime juice
1½ tablespoons fish sauce

Serves 6

Make the Red Curry Paste by following the recipe on page 10.

Fish cakes
Place the fish, Red Curry Paste, egg, fish sauce and sugar in a food processor and blend for around 3 minutes until the mixture becomes smooth and sticky (this helps the cakes to hold together). Scoop into a bowl and stir in the kaffir lime leaves and green beans. Roll the mixture into 18 equal balls. Flatten each ball into a patty and refrigerate until needed.

Red nam jim sauce
Using a mortar and pestle pound the chilies, garlic and coriander root into a fine paste. Add the palm sugar and combine. Add the lime juice a little at a time until the ingredients are well incorporated, then add the fish sauce. The consistency should be like a wet salsa. Taste for a balance of sweet, sour and salty flavors, adjusting if required.

To serve
Heat the oil in a wok to 350°F (180°C) and fry the Fish Cakes in batches until crisp and golden. Drain on paper towels. Serve the Fish Cakes with the Red Nam Jim Sauce.

Son-in-law eggs
with chili caramel sauce

6 eggs

1 teaspoon sea salt

2 cups (500 ml) vegetable oil

½ cup (125 ml) Chili Caramel Sauce (page 13)

½ cup (25 g) coriander leaves (cilantro)

½ cup (20 g) mint leaves

½ cup (20 g) Thai basil leaves

1 tablespoon Fried Shallots (page 19)

Serves 6

There are a few different tales about how this dish got its name. One is about a husband who mistreated his wife. His mother-in-law made these eggs for him to let him know that if he kept it up, he might see some of his own body parts served in the same way! Quail eggs are often used in this dish and traditionally the eggs are hardboiled, but I like them better when the yolk is still soft. The combination of rich, silky egg yolk and Chili Caramel Sauce is heavenly. This is a great snack at any time of the day. Delicious served with a crisp salad of finely sliced iceberg lettuce.

Make the Chili Caramel Sauce and Fried Shallots by following the recipes on pages 13 and 19.

Place the eggs in a shallow bowl and cover with hot (but not boiling) water. Let them warm in the water for 3 minutes (this keeps them from cracking when boiled).

Bring a medium-sized pot of water to a boil and add the salt. When boiling, gently add the eggs and reduce the heat to a simmer. Cook the eggs until soft-boiled (3–4 minutes) then remove from the heat. Place the pot in a sink and run cold water into it to cool the eggs. (The water will run over the rim of the pot but the eggs should stay inside.) When the water is cold, turn off the tap and let the eggs cool completely in the water. Peel the eggs while still in the water and place them on paper towels to drain.

Heat the oil in a wok to 350°F (180°C) then add the eggs and fry until crisp and golden (around 4 minutes). Drain on paper towels.

To serve, slice the eggs in half and place them, yolks up, on a serving platter. Drizzle with Chili Caramel Sauce and sprinkle with the herbs and Fried Shallots. Serve immediately.

Green papaya and herb salad with fried sticky rice balls

Rice balls

2 cups (200 g) cooked Sticky Rice (page 24), cooled

2 cups (500 ml) vegetable oil, for frying

Salad

1 tablespoon Fried Chili Peanuts (page 19) or roasted peanuts

1 teaspoon Roasted Dried Shrimp (page 21)

2 red bird's-eye chilies, deseeded and coarsely chopped

1 green bird's-eye chili, deseeded and coarsely chopped

3 cloves garlic, coarsely chopped

2 kaffir lime leaves, finely sliced into thin shreds

1 stalk lemongrass, tender inner part of bottom third only, finely sliced

6 cherry tomatoes, quartered

1 cup (150 g) thinly sliced green beans, blanched

2 cups (300 g) grated green papaya

1 cup (50 g) coriander leaves (cilantro)

1 cup (40 g) mint leaves

½ cup (20 g) Thai basil leaves, torn

2 tablespoons fish sauce

3 tablespoons freshly-squeezed lime juice

1½ tablespoons Tamarind Paste (page 18)

Serves 6

Green papaya salad—*som tum*—is a Thai classic. Use the best and freshest ingredients, and prepare the dish in the traditional way—by pounding and bruising the ingredients with a mortar and pestle. The bruising brings out the flavors of the ingredients and mixes them into a wonderful chunky slurry. The salad is great with fried sticky rice balls, but it's also good simply eaten on its own or served with grilled or fried chicken or fish.

Make the Tamarind Paste, Fried Chili Peanuts, Roasted Dried Shrimp and Sticky Rice by following the recipes on pages 18, 19, 21 and 24.

Using wet hands roll the Sticky Rice into bite-sized balls, about ¾ in (1½ cm) in diameter. Refrigerate until ready to fry.

Using a large mortar and pestle pound the peanuts, Roasted Dried Shrimp, chilies, garlic, kaffir lime leaves and lemongrass into a fine paste. Add the cherry tomatoes and beans and pound until they bruise, then add the papaya and pound a little more. Add the coriander leaves, mint and Thai basil and combine, then add the fish sauce, lime juice and Tamarind Paste. Taste for a good balance of flavors, adjusting if required. Transfer to a serving dish.

Heat the oil in a wok to 350°F (180°C) and fry the Rice Balls in batches until golden brown and with a nutty aroma. Drain on paper towels and serve with the Salad.

Coconut and herb ceviche with fried chili peanuts

⅔ cup (150 ml) coconut milk

2 tablespoons Green Curry Paste (page 9)

2 kaffir lime leaves, finely sliced into thin shreds

1 stalk lemongrass, tender inner part of bottom third only, finely sliced

1 green bird's-eye chili, finely sliced

4 Asian shallots, finely sliced

3 tablespoons freshly-squeezed lime juice

1½ tablespoons fish sauce

1 tablespoon shaved palm sugar

1⅓ lbs (600g) sashimi-grade tuna or salmon fillets, skinned

¼ cup (40 g) Fried Chili Peanuts (page 19)

1 tablespoon Chili Shrimp Oil (page 18)

1 cup (50 g) coriander leaves (cilantro)

¼ cup (50 g) Fried Shallots (page 19)

Serves 6

This is a kind of Asian ceviche—the South American dish of raw fish "cooked" in a marinade of lime juice and other ingredients. Dried fish is often used in street food dishes, and this recipe is a twist on this by curing the fish instead of cooking it, resulting in a lighter and more delicate dish. This dish goes well with Green Mango Salad (page 185) and Coconut Rice (page 24).

Make the Green Curry Paste, Chili Shrimp Oil, Fried Chili Peanuts and Fried Shallots by following the recipes on pages 9, 18 and 19.

Place the coconut milk and Green Curry Paste in a food processor and pulse 6–8 times until well blended. Strain the liquid into a mixing bowl. Add the kaffir lime leaves, lemongrass, chili, shallots, lime juice, fish sauce and palm sugar. Taste for a balance of sweet, sour and salty flavors and adjust if required.

With a sharp and preferably thin knife, slice the fish as thinly as possible. Lay the fish in one layer on a deep serving platter and pour over just enough marinade to coat. Gently massage the marinade into the fish with your fingertips.

Dress with the Fried Chili Peanuts, Chili Shrimp Oil, coriander leaves and Fried Shallots and serve.

Pork nam prik ong
with lettuce cups and herbs

8 dried red finger-length chilies, deseeded
   and soaked in warm water for 30 minutes,
   coarsely chopped

1¼ in (3 cm) peeled galangal root, coarsely
   chopped

3 Asian shallots, coarsely chopped

6 cloves garlic, coarsely chopped

1 teaspoon Roasted Shrimp Paste
   (page 9)

1 teaspoon sea salt

2½ tablespoons peanut oil

1 lb (500 g) ground pork

⅔ cup (150 ml) Shao Xing rice wine

10 cherry tomatoes, halved

6 coriander (cilantro) roots, washed and
   finely chopped

¼ cup (50 g) Fried Shallots (page 19)

3 teaspoons Fried Garlic (page 19)

12 Lettuce Cups (page 21)

1 cup (50 g) coriander sprigs (cilantro)

1 cup (40 g) mint sprigs

6 Thai basil sprigs

1 cup (50 g) bean sprouts

2 limes, quartered

Serves 6

This is a dish from northern Thailand. Its traditional accompaniment is fried pork skin and Sticky Rice, but I like to serve it with Lettuce Cups, similar to a *san choi bao*. It can be prepared in advance and served warm or at room temperature.

Make the Roasted Shrimp Paste, Fried Shallots, Fried Garlic and Lettuce Cups by following the recipes on pages 9, 19 and 21.

Using a mortar and pestle pound the chilies, galangal, shallots, garlic, Roasted Shrimp Paste and salt into a fine paste.

Heat the peanut oil in a wok over high heat. Add the pork and brown for 1–2 minutes, then add the Shao Xing rice wine and cook until it evaporates (this will help separate the pieces of pork). Add the paste and fry until fragrant (2–3 minutes). Add the tomatoes and coriander roots and cook until the tomatoes start to break down. Take the wok off the heat and stir through the Fried Shallots and Garlic. Taste for seasoning.

Serve the nam prik ong with the Lettuce Cups, herbs, bean sprouts and lime wedges on the side.

Crab cakes with chili mayonnaise

1 live crab weighing at least 3 lbs (1½ kgs)
(or several smaller crabs equalling the
same weight)
1 large red bell pepper
½ tablespoon olive oil
1⅓ lbs (600 g) white fish fillets (such as
whiting, porgy or sea bream), skinned,
deboned and coarsely chopped
1 egg
1 teaspoon sugar
½ large red onion, finely chopped
1 tablespoon lemon juice
½ tablespoon fish sauce
1 teaspoon Worcestershire sauce
3 cups (750ml) vegetable oil, for frying

Mayonnaise
½ tablespoon caraway seeds,
lightly dry-roasted
½ tablespoon coriander seeds,
lightly dry-roasted
7 green finger-length chilies, deseeded and
coarsely chopped
2 green bird's-eye chilies, deseeded and
coarsely chopped
1 cup (250 ml) vegetable oil
1 cup (75 g) baby spinach leaves, washed
and dried
1 egg yolk
1½ tablespoons white wine vinegar
1 teaspoon Dijon mustard
½ cup (25 g) coriander leaves (cilantro)
½ cup (20 g) mint leaves
1 cup (250 ml) olive oil

Serves 6

These are similar to the traditional fish cakes on page 64, but the crab meat adds a touch of luxury and sweetness. It's always best to cook crabs and pick the meat yourself rather than buy precooked crabs or picked crab meat— the result is so much fresher and tastier. Ask for female crabs as they have a better yield of meat.

Kill the crab quickly and humanely by turning it onto its back and inserting a large metal skewer in its middle where the flaps meet. Leave the skewer inside the crab for 3–4 minutes or until the crab has died. Alternatively, place the crab in a freezer for 1 hour, which will send it to sleep.

Bring a large pot of water to a boil. Calculate the cooking time—allow 7–8 minutes/lb of whole crab. (On this basis, a 3 lbs (1½ kgs) crab will need to be cooked for 20–22 minutes.) Add the crab to the pot and simmer for the correct time. The shell of the crab will turn a reddish brown when cooked. Remove the crab from the pot and plunge it in a basin of iced water to stop the cooking process. Leave the crab to cool in the basin for 10 minutes, then drain.

Use your fingers to pull the top shell away from the body. Discard the gills and rinse the crab. Twist off the legs and claws and use a mallet or the flat side of the cleaver to crack them. Use a crab pick or metal skewer to extract the meat from the legs, claws and body. Measure 2 cups (250 g) of meat and refrigerate or freeze the rest for another use.

Preheat the oven to 400°F (200°C). Brush the bell pepper with olive oil and roast until the skin starts to blister (10–15 minutes). When cool enough to handle, peel the skin and scrape out the seeds. Finely chop the flesh.

Place the fish fillets, egg and sugar in a food processor and blend until the mixture is firm and sticky (around 3 minutes). This helps the cakes to hold together. Scoop the mixture into a bowl and fold through the crab meat, bell pepper, onion, lemon juice, fish sauce and Worcestershire and roll the mix into 18 equal balls. Press the balls flat into patties and refrigerate until needed.

Mayonnaise
Grind the caraway and coriander seeds to a fine powder using a mortar and pestle. Sift to remove the husks. Pound the chilies to a paste. Set the spice powder and chili paste aside.

Heat 1 cup (250 ml) of the vegetable oil in a wok to 350°F (180°C) and fry the spinach until crisp. Drain on paper towels. (Frying removes the moisture.)

Place the spice powder, chili paste, spinach, egg yolk, vinegar, mustard, coriander and mint leaves in a food processor. Blend to a smooth puree. Slowly add the olive oil until the mixture emulsifies and thickens. Taste for seasoning.

To serve
Heat 3 cups (750 ml) of vegetable oil in a wok to 350°F (180°C). Fry the crab cakes in batches until crisp and golden. Drain on paper towels and serve the cakes with the Mayonnaise.

Stir-fried quail, green beans and Thai basil in lettuce cups

6 large quail (about 2 lbs/1 kg in total)

2½ tablespoons Pat Chun sweetened vinegar

3 tablespoons peanut oil

3 cloves garlic, finely chopped

2 red finger-length chilies, finely sliced

8 oz (250 g) ground pork

2½ tablespoons Shao Xing rice wine

½ cup (65 g) cashew nuts, coarsely chopped

1 cup (150 g) thinly sliced green beans

1 cup (50 g) bean sprouts

3 tablespoons oyster sauce

1½ tablespoons soy sauce

8 Thai basil leaves, torn

1 cup (50 g) coriander leaves (cilantro)

12 Lettuce Cups (page 21)

Serves 6

Stir-fries are a common street food in Asia and it's easy to guess why—they're so quick to cook and use just one wok. Ask your butcher to debone the quail for you to make the dish even quicker to prepare. Alternatively, you can substitute shrimp for the quail.

Make the Lettuce Cups by following the recipe on page 21.

Cut off the quail wings and discard. Hold a bird in the palm of your hand and using a pair of kitchen scissors, cut along either side of the backbone. Remove the backbone and open the bird up. Use your fingertips to carefully peel the breast meat from the bones, feeling your way across the carcass. For the legs, make a slit to the bone and scrape the meat away.

Check the meat for any hidden bones. Leave the skin on. Repeat this process with the remaining quail then coarsely chop the meat. Marinate in Pat Chun sweetened vinegar and 1 tablespoon of the peanut oil for 10 minutes.

Heat the remaining peanut oil in a wok until smoking, then add the garlic and chilies and fry until fragrant (1–2 minutes). Add the quail and pork and stir-fry until browned all over, then add the Shao Xing rice wine and cook until it evaporates (this will help separate the pieces of pork). Add the cashew nuts, green beans and bean sprouts and cook for a further 1 minute. Add the oyster sauce and cook until the liquid has almost completely reduced, then add the soy sauce and remove from the heat. Transfer to a serving dish.

Garnish with the Thai basil and coriander leaves and serve in the Lettuce Cups.

Fried calamari with spiced chili salt, watercress and green chili soy dip

3 fresh whole baby squid (combined weight of around 1½ lbs/750 g)

2 tablespoons fish sauce

3 cups (750ml) vegetable oil, for frying

¼ cup Spiced Chili Salt (page 11)

1 bunch watercress sprigs

2 limes, quartered

Green chili soy dip

⅓ cup (80 ml) soy sauce

2½ tablespoons sweet soy sauce

1 tablespoon lemon juice

4 green bird's-eye chilies, deseeded and finely chopped

½ teaspoon ground white pepper

Batter

2½ cups (300 g) rice flour

2 tablespoons all-purpose (plain) flour

1 teaspoon cornstarch

1⅔ cups (400 ml) chilled mineral water

Serves 6

Make the Spiced Chili Salt by following the recipe on page 11.

To prepare the squid, twist and pull the tentacles away from the body—the internal organs and head will come away too. Cut the tentacles just below the head, discarding the head. Draw out the piece of transparent cartilage from the body and discard. Carefully peel off the wings and strip the wings and body of the dark membrane. Rinse the wings and tube and pat dry. Repeat with the remaining squid.

Insert a knife into a tube and make a slit so it will open and lie flat as a rectangle. On the outer surface score the tube with the tip of a knife in a criss-cross pattern, then cut the tube into strips around 3 in long x ¾ in wide (8 cm x 2 cm). Repeat with the remaining tubes. Score the wings. Cut the tentacles into bite-size pieces. Toss the squid in the fish sauce and refrigerate until needed.

Combine the Green Chili Soy Dip ingredients and set aside.

For the Batter, sift the flours into a mixing bowl. Slowly whisk in the chilled mineral water to get a nice creamy consistency without lumps.

Heat the oil in a wok to 350°F (180°C). Dip the pieces of squid in the Batter and place in the hot oil. Fry until just golden. Drain on paper towels then season with the Spiced Chili Salt. Serve with the Green Chili Soy Dip, watercress and lime.

Crisp corn cakes with herbs and chili caramel sauce

3 fresh cobs of corns
4 Asian shallots, coarsely chopped
4 cloves garlic, coarsely chopped
4 coriander (cilantro) roots, washed and coarsely chopped
4 red bird's-eye chilies, deseeded and coarsely chopped
1 tablespoon shaved palm sugar
½ tablespoon sea salt
½ teaspoon ground white pepper
⅔ cup (100 g) self-raising flour, sifted
3 eggs, lightly beaten
3 cups (750ml) vegetable oil, for frying
½ cup (125 ml) Chili Caramel Sauce (page 13)
1 cup (50 g) coriander leaves (cilantro)
1 cup (40 g) mint leaves
1 cup (40 g) Thai basil leaves
4 green onions (scallions), finely sliced
5 red finger-length chilies, finely sliced
¼ cup (50 g) Fried Shallots (page 19)

Serves 6

This combination is one of my favorites, and the smell of the corn cakes cooking is simply fantastic.

Make the Chili Caramel Sauce and Fried Shallots by following the recipes on pages 13 and 19.

Trim the bases and tips from the corn cobs. Stand them on a chopping board and slice downwards with a sharp knife to cut the kernels off. Place half of the kernels in a food processor along with the shallots, garlic, coriander roots, bird's-eye chilies, palm sugar, salt and pepper and puree until smooth.

Scoop the mixture into a bowl and stir in the flour, then the eggs. Fold through the remaining corn kernels. Check the seasoning. The mixture should be the consistency of soft ice cream—add more flour if necessary. Allow it to rest for 10 minutes.

Heat the oil in a wok to 350°F (180°C). Using a tablespoon, spoon torpedo shapes of the mixture into the hot oil and fry in batches until crisp and golden (3–5 minutes). Drain on paper towels.

To serve, place the cakes on a large serving platter and drizzle with the Chili Caramel Sauce. Sprinkle with the herbs, green onions, finely sliced chilies and Fried Shallots.

Homemade spicy pork sausages

4 star anise pods

4 whole whole cloves

1 teaspoon Sichuan peppercorns

3 coriander (cilantro) roots, washed and
coarsely chopped

6 cloves garlic, coarsely chopped

1 teaspoon sea salt

8 fresh shiitake mushrooms, stems trimmed,
caps finely diced

1 tablespoon peanut oil

1⅓ lbs (600 g) ground pork

4 oz (100 g) pork fatback, ground (or
2 tablespoons lard)

1½ tablespoons shaved palm sugar

2 tablespoons fish sauce

1 tablespoon soy sauce

2 tablespoons Shao Xing rice wine

¼ cup (40 g) Fried Chili Peanuts (page 19)
or roasted peanuts, finely chopped

3 red bird's-eye chilies, deseeded and finely
chopped

Juice of half a lemon

1 teaspoon sea salt

3¼ ft (1 meter) sausage casing
(see note)

1 small Chinese or Napa cabbage, cored and
cut into wedges

Serves 6

These little homemade sausages are a great savory snack and can be made with almost any meat. They take a little time to make, but you can prepare them in advance and even freeze them if you need to. Then all you have to do is grill them and serve wrapped in Chinese cabbage leaves.

Make the Fried Chili Peanuts by following the recipe on page 19.

Dry-roast the star anise, cloves and peppercorns in a wok until fragrant (1–2 minutes), stirring constantly. Remove from the heat and pound into a fine powder using a mortar and pestle. Pass the powder through a fine sieve and set aside.

Using a mortar and pestle, pound the coriander roots, garlic and salt to a fine paste.

Lightly stir-fry the shiitake mushrooms in the peanut oil.

Place the ground pork and pork fatback in a mixing bowl and add the ground spice powder, coriander paste, mushrooms, palm sugar, fish sauce, soy sauce, Shao Xing rice wine, peanuts and chilies. Combine thoroughly.

Fill a large bowl with water and add the lemon juice and salt. Wash the sausage casing thoroughly to remove any grit, then drain. Tie a knot in one end.

Fit a piping bag with a nozzle smaller than the width of the casing. Fill the bag with the sausage mixture, pressing down to remove any air bubbles. Insert the nozzle into the open end of the casing. Carefully gather the casing over the nozzle until it reaches the knot and begin piping. Once all the mixture has been piped in, tie off the casing at the end of the mixture, discarding any excess casing. Twist the sausages into 2½ in (6 cm) lengths and refrigerate for 2 hours to allow the meat to set (or freeze for later use).

To serve, fry the sausages over medium heat for 5–6 minutes on each side. You can cut the sausages before you cook them, but I like to grill the length of sausage whole, coiled into a spiral. Transfer the sausages to a serving platter and serve with the Chinese cabbage leaves.

Note: Sausage casings are available from most good continental-style butchers. Some butchers may be willing to fill the casing for you.

Pot sticker dumplings with dried shrimp relish

14 oz (400 g) ground pork

7 oz (200 g) fresh shrimp, peeled and deveined (to make 4 oz (100 g), then finely chopped

1¼ in (3 cm) peeled ginger, finely chopped

2 cloves garlic, finely chopped

1 red bird's-eye chili, deseeded and finely chopped

4 coriander (cilantro) roots, washed and finely chopped

2 green onions (scallions), finely sliced

2½ tablespoons soy sauce

2½ tablespoons fish sauce

Pinch of ground white pepper

18 round wonton skins

2½ tablespoons peanut oil

2½ tablespoons Shao Xing rice wine

2½ tablespoons water

Dried shrimp relish

¼ cup (20 g) dried shrimp

2 red finger-length chilies, deseeded and coarsely chopped

1 red bird's-eye chili, deseeded and coarsely chopped

1 green bird's-eye chili, deseeded and coarsely chopped

2 cloves garlic, coarsely chopped

¼ cup (10 g) mint leaves, coarsely chopped

1 teaspoon sea salt

2 tablespoons sugar

⅓ cup + 1 tablespoon (100 ml) freshly-squeezed lime juice

1½ tablespoons fish sauce

Serves 6

Shanghai is the city of dumplings—fried, steamed and pot sticker dumplings are sold everywhere. These dumplings are combined with a tangy, spicy Thai relish made with chilies, mint and dried shrimp.

Place the pork in a bowl and beat and mix it with your hands until it is firm and sticky (this helps the filling to hold together). Add the shrimp, ginger, garlic, chili, coriander roots, green onions, soy sauce, fish sauce and pepper to the pork and combine thoroughly.

Lay the wonton skins out on a work surface. Place 2 teaspoons of filling in the center of each one and lightly brush around the edges with water. Fold one side of the skin over to meet the other and press the edges shut. The dumplings should look like half moons. Press the base of each dumpling down on the work surface to create a flat bottom (so the dumplings can sit upright). Using your fingers, mold the rim of each dumpling so it has a fluted appearance. Cover the dumplings with a damp cloth until you're ready to cook them.

Dried shrimp relish
Soak the dried shrimp in a little warm water until soft (around 5 minutes), then drain. Using a mortar and pestle pound the dried shrimp, chilies, garlic, mint and salt into a fine paste. Add the sugar, lime juice and fish sauce and taste for a balance of flavors, adjusting if necessary.

To serve
Heat the peanut oil in a large non-stick pan. Fry the dumplings until crisp and golden on the bottom, then add the Shao Xing rice wine and water. Cover the dumplings with a large upturned bowl (or lid) and steam for 1–2 minutes, or until the liquid has just evaporated. Remove from the pan and serve with the Dried Shrimp Relish.

Fried eggs with crab and sweet chinese sausage

1 live crab weighing at least 3 lbs (1½ kgs) (or several smaller crabs equalling the same weight)

2 cups (500 ml) vegetable oil, for frying

6 eggs

2 dried Chinese sausages (*lup cheong*), finely sliced

2 red bird's-eye chilies, finely sliced

3 green onions (scallions), finely sliced

1½ tablespoons oyster sauce

1 cup (50 g) coriander leaves (cilantro)

¼ cup (50 g) Fried Shallots (page 19)

1 teaspoon Sichuan Pepper-Salt Powder (page 11)

Serve 6

A luxurious snack for any time of the day—the egg is crisp on the outside and silky on the inside, and the crab meat is the ultimate accompaniment. You could make this dish even better by using duck eggs.

Make the Sichuan Pepper-Salt Powder and Fried Shallots by following the recipes on pages 11 and 19.

Kill the crab quickly and humanely by turning it onto its back and inserting a large metal skewer in its middle where the flaps meet. Leave the skewer inside the crab for 3–4 minutes or until the crab has died. Alternatively, place the crab in a freezer for 1 hour, which will send it to sleep.

Bring a large pot of water to a boil. Calculate the cooking time—allow 7–8 minutes/lb of whole crab. (On this basis, a 3 lbs (1½ kgs) crab will need to be cooked for 20–22 minutes.) Add the crab to the pot and simmer for the correct time. The shell of the crab will turn a reddish brown when cooked. Remove the crab from the pot and plunge it in a basin of iced water to stop the cooking process. Leave the crab to cool in the basin for 10 minutes, then drain.

Use your fingers to pull the top shell away from the body. Discard the gills and rinse the crab. Twist off the legs and claws and use a mallet or the flat side of the cleaver to crack them. Use a crab pick or metal skewer to extract the meat from the legs, claws and body. Measure 1¼ cups (150 g) of meat and refrigerate or freeze the rest for another use.

Heat the oil in a large, deep skillet to 350°F (180°C). Crack an egg into a ladle or small bowl and slide it into the oil. Quickly repeat with two more eggs. Gently shake the pan to settle the eggs into the oil (there should be enough oil to just cover the eggs). Use a metal spoon to ladle the hot oil over the eggs so the tops cook as well. When the eggs become crisp on the outside but are still soft in the middle (around 3 minutes), sprinkle each one with a little crab meat, dried Chinese sausage, chili and green onion (the toppings should balance on top). Fry until the topping has warmed through then carefully remove the eggs from the oil with a slotted spoon. Drain any excess oil and place on a warm serving dish while you fry the remaining eggs.

Sprinkle the eggs with oyster sauce, coriander leaves, Fried Shallots and Sichuan Pepper-Salt Powder and serve immediately.

Beef salad with crispy fish floss, salmon roe and hot and sour dressing

1 piece beef flank steak weighing
   1⅓ lbs (600 g)
⅓ cup + 1 tablespoon (100 ml) sweet soy
   sauce
2 cloves garlic, coarsely chopped
½ tablespoon ground white pepper
1 tablespoon peanut oil
½ tablespoon Roasted Shrimp Paste
   (page 9)
¾ in (1½ cm) peeled ginger, sliced into thin
   shreds
2 kaffir lime leaves, finely sliced
1 stalk lemongrass, tender inner part of
   bottom third only, finely sliced
2 red finger-length chilies, finely sliced
1 red onion, finely sliced into rings
1 cup (150 g) thinly sliced green beans,
   blanched
1 cucumber, deseeded and cut into sticks
2 green onions (scallions), finely sliced
½ cup (25 g) coriander leaves (cilantro)
½ cup (20 g) mint leaves
½ cup (20 g) watercress sprigs
½ cup (125 ml) Hot and Sour Dressing
   (page 17)
1 cup (300 g) Crispy Fish Floss (page 19)
3 tablespoons fresh salmon roe

Serves 6

This dish has a great mix of textures. The beef is marinated overnight then cooked to medium rare. It's combined with salad, Crispy Fish Floss and salmon roe—little explosions that add a bit of excitement in the mouth.

Make the Roasted Shrimp Paste, Hot and Sour Dressing and Crispy Fish Floss by following the recipes on pages 9, 17 and 19.

Using a sharp knife trim the beef of any fat or sinew. Place the beef in a bowl and add the sweet soy sauce, garlic and pepper. Massage the marinade into the meat with your fingers then cover with plastic wrap and refrigerate overnight.

Preheat the oven to 350°F (180°C). Blot off any excess marinade from the meat with paper towels. Heat the peanut oil in a pan and fry the beef until browned and sealed on all sides (but not cooked through). Transfer the beef to an oven tray and cook for 10 minutes for medium rare.

Let the beef stand for 1 hour to cool. In the meantime, mix together the Roasted Shrimp Paste, ginger, kaffir lime leaves and lemongrass until the Shrimp Paste has been thoroughly blended. Add the chilies, red onion, beans, cucumber, green onions, coriander leaves and mint leaves, and watercress and combine.

Finely slice the beef across the grain. Lay the slices in a wide serving bowl and pour over the Hot and Sour Dressing. Leave to marinate for 2 minutes. Top with the salad, Crispy Fish Floss and salmon roe and serve.

Egg nets with spicy pork, tomatoes and bean sprouts

4 eggs

1 stalk lemongrass, tender inner part of bottom third only, finely sliced

4 Asian shallots, coarsely chopped

6 cloves garlic, coarsely chopped

1¼ in (3 cm) peeled ginger, coarsely chopped

4 red finger-length chilies, deseeded and coarsely chopped

4 coriander (cilantro) roots, washed and coarsely chopped

1 teaspoon Roasted Shrimp Paste (page 9)

1 tablespoon peanut oil

14 oz (400 g) ground pork

⅔ cup (150 ml) Shao Xing rice wine

3 medium tomatoes, diced

1 cup (150 g) finely sliced green beans

1 cup (50 g) bean sprouts

6 peeled water chestnuts, coarsely chopped

½ cup (20 g) mint leaves, coarsely chopped

3 cups (750ml) vegetable oil, for deep-frying

Serves 6

There must be hundreds of versions of this snack in Thailand—popular fillings include beef, shrimp and chicken. The mint provides a refreshing flavor but you can also use other Asian herbs. The water chestnuts give the dish a delicious crunch. While I prefer the traditional method of making egg nets by deep-frying them, you can also use a lightly oiled non-stick pan.

Make the Roasted Shrimp Paste by following the recipe on page 9.

Break the eggs into a mixing bowl and gently whisk until combined. Let stand for 5 minutes then strain them through a fine sieve into a smaller bowl. Refrigerate the eggs overnight to help break down the protein.

To make the filling, pound the lemongrass, shallots, garlic, ginger, chilies, coriander roots and Roasted Shrimp Paste to a fine paste using a mortar and pestle. Heat the peanut oil in a wok over medium heat and add the paste. Fry until fragrant (around 5 minutes), then add the pork and cook until it is no longer pink. Turn up the heat, add the Shao Xing rice wine and stir-fry until it evaporates (this helps to separate the pieces of pork). Add the tomatoes and beans and stir-fry until the tomatoes begin to break down (around 3 minutes). Remove from the heat and set aside to cool. Once cool, add the bean sprouts, water chestnuts and mint. Keep the mixture at room temperature while you make the egg nets.

Heat the oil in the wok to 325°F (160°C). Holding the bowl of eggs close to the wok, place your fingers into the egg mixture and drizzle it over the oil in a criss-cross motion to form a dense circular web. You will need to dip into the egg several times to do this. The net should float on the surface. When it is set but not colored (around 1 minute) remove the net from the oil with a wok "spider" (a sieve with a handle) or two slotted spoons. Drain on paper towels while you make five more nets.

To serve, lay the warm nets on a clean work surface and divide the filling between each one. Roll the nets up, folding in the edges as you go. Serve immediately.

Sweet tamarind pork
with thai herbs

1 tablespoon peanut oil

8 Asian shallots, finely chopped

5 cloves garlic, finely chopped

¾ in (1½ cm) peeled ginger, finely chopped

1 stalk lemongrass, tender inner part of
   bottom third only, finely sliced

¼ cup (30 g) sesame seeds

1⅓ lbs (600 g) lean ground pork

⅔ cup (150 ml) Shao Xing rice wine

2 tablespoons fish sauce

1 tablespoon Tamarind Paste (page 18)

½ teaspoon dried shrimp powder (made
   by processing several dried shrimp in a
   blender or food processor)

¼ cup (50 g) shaved dark palm sugar

2 kaffir lime leaves, finely sliced

½ cup (75 g) Fried Chili Peanuts (page 19)
   or roasted peanuts, finely chopped

1 red bird's-eye chili, finely sliced

1 green bird's-eye chili, finely sliced

18 large betel leaves or Lettuce Cups (page 21)

½ cup (100 g) Fried Shallots (page 19)

½ cup (25 g) coriander leaves (cilantro)

½ cup (20 g) mint leaves

2 limes, quartered

Serves 6

I had this tasty snack on a recent trip to Thailand. The dark palm sugar gives the pork mixture an almost toffee-like taste and consistency, with crunch and spice from the peanuts and chilies. You can substitute iceberg Lettuce Cups or Chinese cabbage leaves if betel leaves are unavailable, and you can easily make this dish a few hours in advance.

Make the Tamarind Paste, Fried Chili Peanuts, Fried Shallots and Lettuce Cups by following the recipes on pages 18, 19 and 21.

Heat the peanut oil in a wok and fry the shallots, garlic, ginger, lemongrass and sesame seeds until they begin to change color. Add the pork and continue frying for 1 minute, then add the Shao Xing rice wine and cook until it evaporates (this will help separate the pieces of pork). Keep stirring to avoid any lumps.

Add the fish sauce, Tamarind Paste, dried shrimp powder and palm sugar and cook until the mixture starts to caramelize and the consistency is firm and sticky. If it doesn't caramelize, add more palm sugar. Be careful not to let the sugar catch on the bottom of the wok. Add the kaffir lime leaves, peanuts and chilies and remove from the heat. Set aside to cool to room temperature, which will make the mixture firm and easier to serve.

Place a small amount of the mixture on each betel leaf or Lettuce Cup, followed by a sprinkle of the herbs and Fried Shallots. Serve warm with wedges of lime on the side.

Soups

Creamy cauliflower soup
with scallop dumplings and curry oil

Curry oil

2 tablespoons grapeseed oil

1 teaspoon Curry Powder (page 10)

1 teaspoon sea salt

Scallop dumplings

1 tablespoon olive oil

6 fresh shiitake mushrooms, stems trimmed, caps finely diced

6 water chestnuts, peeled and finely chopped

1 in (2½ cm) peeled ginger, finely chopped

3 green onions (scallions), finely sliced

7 oz (200 g) ground pork

12 oz (350 g) fresh shucked scallops (roe attached), finely chopped

1 teaspoon sea salt

¼ teaspoon ground white pepper

18 wonton skins

Soup

1 tablespoon olive oil

5 shallots, finely chopped

5 cloves garlic, bruised

⅔ cup (150 ml) white wine

1 cauliflower cut into florets, stems removed (to make around 4 cups)

2½ cups (625 ml) Fish Stock (page 13))

4 tablespoons (80 g) unsalted butter, diced

½ cup (100 g) Fried Shallots (page 19)

¼ cup (10 g) chopped garlic chives

1 tablespoon salmon roe

Serves 6

At ezard we have this soup on the menu during the cooler months. It is Western in flavor with the addition of Asian dumplings. For it to be at its rich and creamy best, make it when cauliflower is in season over winter.

Make the Curry Powder, Fish Stock and Fried Shallots by following the recipes on pages 10, 13 and 19.

Curry oil

Heat the oil in a wok or pan and add the Curry Powder and salt. Gently fry for 2 minutes then remove from the heat and set aside to cool.

Scallop dumplings

Heat the oil in a wok or pan and lightly stir-fry the shiitake mushrooms, water chestnuts, ginger and green onions. Set aside to cool. Place the pork in a bowl and work the pork with your hands until it becomes slightly elastic (this will help the filling to hold together). Add the shiitake mixture, scallops, salt and pepper and combine.

   Lay the wonton skins out on a clean work surface and add 2 teaspoons of the filling on the corner of each one. Lightly brush around the edges with water, then fold the skins over to form triangles. Press the sides together to seal. Cover the Dumplings with plastic wrap and refrigerate until needed.

Soup

Heat the oil in a medium-sized pot over low heat and fry the shallots and garlic for 2 minutes without letting them color. Add the wine and when almost evaporated, add the cauliflower. Cook, stirring, for 1–2 minutes without coloring. Add the Fish Stock and simmer until the cauliflower is soft when tested with a knife and the liquid has reduced by a quarter. Remove from the heat and strain the Soup, reserving the liquids and solids.

   Place the solids and the butter in a food processor or blender and puree. Add enough liquid until the consistency is of a thick, creamy Soup. Taste for seasoning.

To serve

Place the Scallop Dumplings in a steamer and steam for 5 minutes. Reheat the Soup. Divide the Dumplings between serving bowls and ladle over just enough Soup to cover them. Garnish with the Fried Shallots, garlic chives and salmon roe and drizzle with a little of the Curry Oil.

Poached salmon soup
with rice and lemon

1 lb (500 g) fresh salmon fillets, skinned

1 tablespoon soy sauce

1 tablespoon Shao Xing rice wine

1 teaspoon sesame oil

1 cup (200 g) uncooked shortgrain rice

4 cups (1 liter) Fish Stock (page 13)

4 Asian shallots, finely sliced

6 cloves garlic, finely chopped

1½ in (4 cm) peeled ginger, finely chopped

8 coriander (cilantro) roots, washed and
  finely chopped

Juice of 2 lemons

1 cup (50 g) coriander leaves (cilantro)

6 green onions (scallions), finely sliced

Serves 6

In this soup the rice is cooked until it's soft but not falling apart, unlike the classic Asian rice soup, congee (page 97). Adding lemon juice to a soup is quite a Mediterranean thing to do, but it really lifts this dish. I love the richness and wonderful flaky texture of the salmon.

Make the Fish Stock by following the recipe on page 13.

With a pair of kitchen pliers (or tweezers) carefully remove the pin bones from the salmon. Cut the fish into large chunks and marinate it in the soy sauce, Shao Xing rice wine and sesame oil for 20 minutes.

Bring a medium-sized pot of water to a boil with a pinch of salt. Add the rice and simmer until almost tender (around 10 minutes). Drain.

Rinse the rice pot and add the Fish Stock. Bring it to a boil and then turn down the heat and add the salmon pieces. Poach them gently for 5 minutes or until cooked through. Gently remove them from the stock with a slotted spoon and when cool enough to touch, break the fish into flakes with your fingers. Set aside.

Add the cooked rice, shallots, garlic, ginger and coriander roots to the pot containing the Fish Stock. Bring it to a boil then reduce the heat and simmer for 10 minutes. Add the salmon to the soup and gently stir so it breaks up. Add the lemon juice. Season to taste and remove from the heat.

Ladle the soup into serving bowls and garnish with coriander leaves and green onions.

Chicken soup with coconut, lemongrass and mushrooms

2 stalks lemongrass, tender inner part of
  bottom third only, bruised and cut in half
6 kaffir lime leaves, torn
1½ in (4 cm) peeled ginger, bruised
5 cloves garlic, bruised
3 green bird's-eye chilies, coarsely chopped
2 red finger-length chilies, coarsely chopped
1 tablespoon Roasted Shrimp Paste (page
  13)
2¾ cups (700 ml) coconut milk
¾ cup (200 ml) water
7 oz (200 g) skinless chicken breast,
  finely sliced
½ cup (75 g) Fried Chili Peanuts (page 19)
2½ tablespoons shaved palm sugar
3 tablespoons freshly-squeezed lime juice
2 tablespoons fish sauce
1 bunch (2 oz/50 g) enoki mushrooms,
  bases trimmed

Serves 6

This is a really quick and easy soup and you can adapt it with many different ingredients. Instead of chicken I sometimes use water spinach, tofu or shrimp. Add more chili if you like the soup with some heat.

Make the Roasted Shrimp Paste and Fried Chili Peanuts by following the recipes on pages 13 and 19.

In a medium-sized pot combine the lemongrass, kaffir lime leaves, ginger, garlic, chilies, Roasted Shrimp Paste, coconut milk and water. Bring to a boil and simmer for 10 minutes. Set aside to cool and allow the flavors to infuse. Once cool, strain the liquid into a bowl, wipe the pot clean, and pour the liquid back into the pot.

Fill a separate pot with water and bring to a boil. Lower the heat and add the chicken, simmering until just cooked through (3–5 minutes). Drain and gently refresh the chicken under cold water.

Add the chicken and Fried Chili Peanuts to the soup and bring it back to a simmer. Simmer for a few minutes then add the palm sugar, lime juice and fish sauce. Check for a balance of flavors, adjusting if necessary, then stir through the enoki mushrooms and remove the soup from the heat. Serve immediately.

Shrimp dumpling soup
with mixed mushrooms

I use oyster and wood ear mushrooms in this soup, but you could use any fresh Asian mushrooms such as shiitake or enoki. The shredded lettuce has the texture of crunchy strands of noodles.

Make the Fish Stock, Fried Garlic and Fried Shallots by following the recipes on pages 13 and 19.

Shrimp dumplings

2 lbs (1 kg) fresh shrimp, shelled and deveined (to make 1 lb/500 g), then finely chopped

2 red bird's-eye chilies, deseeded and finely chopped

4 coriander (cilantro) roots, washed and finely chopped

2 green onions (scallions), finely sliced

1 teaspoon sesame oil

1 tablespoon soy sauce

½ teaspoon ground white pepper

18 wonton skins

Soup

6 cups (1½ liters) Fish Stock (page 13)

1½ in (4 cm) peeled ginger, bruised

4 green onions (scallions), coarsely chopped

6 dried black Chinese mushrooms

⅓ cup + 1 tablespoon (100 ml) sweet soy sauce

3 tablespoons fish sauce

¼ cup (50 g) oyster mushrooms, torn

¼ cup (50 g) wood ear mushrooms, torn

¼ head iceberg lettuce, finely shredded

½ cup (100 g) Fried Shallots (page 19)

⅓ cup (65 g) Fried Garlic (page 19)

1 cup (50 g) coriander leaves (cilantro)

Serves 6

Shrimp dumplings
Place all the ingredients apart from the wonton skins in a bowl and combine thoroughly.

Lay the wonton skins out on a clean work surface and place 2 teaspoons of filling on the corner of each one. Lightly brush around the edges with water and fold the skins over to form triangles. Press the edges together to seal. Cover the Dumplings with plastic wrap and refrigerate until needed.

Soup
Combine the Fish Stock, ginger, green onions and shiitake mushrooms in a medium-sized pot and bring to a boil. Boil until the Stock has reduced by a third, then remove from the heat and strain the Soup, discarding the solids. Add the soy sauce and fish sauce and taste for a balance of flavors, adjusting if required.

To serve
Steam the Dumplings for 5 minutes. Meanwhile, bring the Soup back to a simmer and add the oyster and wood ear mushrooms. Simmer for 2 minutes then remove from the heat.

Divide the shredded lettuce into serving bowls and top with the steamed Dumplings. Ladle the broth and mushrooms over them and garnish with the Fried Shallots, Fried Garlic and coriander leaves.

Fried snapper and tamarind soup with tomatoes and thai herbs

4 cups (1 liter) Fish Stock (page 13)

¾ cup (250 g) Tamarind Paste (page 18)

3 stalks lemongrass, tender inner part of bottom third only, bruised and cut in half

6 cloves garlic, bruised

1½ in (4 cm) peeled ginger, bruised

¾ in (1½ cm) peeled fresh turmeric root, bruised

4 dried red finger-length chilies

3 cups (750ml) vegetable oil, for frying

6 baby snapper fillets (skin on), weighing around 5 oz (150 g) each

6 egg whites, lightly beaten

2¾ cups (350 g) rice flour

8 Asian shallots, finely sliced

1 cup cherry tomatoes, halved

4 kaffir lime leaves, torn

1 cup (50 g) coriander leaves (cilantro)

¼ cup (50 g) Fried Garlic (page 19)

Serves 6

This sour and fragrant soup is very light and quick to make. The broth is poured over the crisp snapper fillets at the last moment.

Make the Fish Stock, Tamarind Paste and Fried Garlic by following the recipes on pages 13, 18 and 19.

Place the Fish Stock, Tamarind Paste, lemongrass, garlic, ginger, turmeric and dried chilies in a medium-sized pot and simmer for 20 minutes. Set aside to allow the flavors to infuse for a further 20 minutes (or ideally, until completely cooled).

Heat the oil in a wok to 350°F (180°C). Dip the snapper pieces in the egg whites and then in the rice flour, shaking off any excess, and fry the fish in batches until crisp (around 3 minutes). Drain on paper towels.

Strain the soup and bring it back to a simmer. Taste for seasoning then add the shallots, tomatoes and kaffir lime leaves and remove from the heat. Place a fried snapper fillet in each serving bowl and ladle the soup over it. Garnish with the coriander leaves and Fried Garlic.

Clear soup with roast duck, asparagus and black beans

1 whole Roast Duck (pages 177–8, or bought from a Chinese restaurant)

8 cups (2 liters) Asian Brown Chicken Stock (page 11)

3 red bird's-eye chilies, coarsely chopped

1 in (2½ cm) piece fresh ginger, bruised

3 cloves garlic, bruised

8 coriander (cilantro) roots, washed and coarsely chopped

½ teaspoon Sichuan peppercorns

4 star anise pods

2½ tablespoons soy sauce

4 oz (100 g) ground beef

6 egg whites

10 asparagus spears, bases trimmed, sliced diagonally into pieces

2 tablespoons dried salted black beans, gently rinsed

8 green onions (scallions), white ends only, finely sliced

½ cup (25 g) coriander leaves (cilantro)

Serves 6

At **ezard** we serve this soup with the duck meat still on the bone, which is the Chinese way. It makes quite a rustic dish, although the broth is refined—clarified with a "raft" of ground beef and egg whites. Reducing the chicken stock deepens its flavor so it can stand up to the richness of the duck. Cucumber is a great substitute for asparagus if the latter is out of season. Add noodles to this soup to make a heartier one-bowl meal.

Make the Asian Brown Chicken Stock by following the recipe on page 11.

Follow the instructions for roasting and carving the duck on pages 177–8, but cut the breasts and thighs into smaller, bite-sized pieces. You will not need the drumsticks for this recipe.

Pour the Chicken Stock into a large pot and boil it rapidly until it has reduced by half (around 30 minutes).

Add the chilies, ginger, garlic, coriander roots, Sichuan peppercorns, star anise and soy sauce and simmer for a further 25 minutes. Set aside to cool completely.

Strain the broth into a smaller pot. Combine the ground beef and egg whites in a bowl. Add this "raft" to the cooled stock and whisk it vigorously. Once you remove the whisk, the "raft" will sink to the bottom. Heat the broth—as the liquid warms, the "raft" will float to the surface and catch impurities. Gently simmer the "raft" for 10 minutes without allowing it to boil. Remove the pot from the heat and allow the broth to cool slightly.

Gently tilt the pot to one side and ladle out the broth, taking care not to break up the "raft". For the clearest broth, it is best to then strain the clarified broth through muslin, which will remove any remaining impurities.

Blanch the asparagus. Arrange the roast duck pieces on a tray and gently heat them under a broiler grill. Meanwhile, reheat the broth and taste for seasoning. Divide the pieces of duck between serving bowls and scatter with black beans, asparagus and green onions. Ladle the hot broth into each bowl and garnish with the coriander leaves.

Chinese wine broth
with scallop stuffed tofu

1 tablespoon peanut oil

6 baby fresh cobs of corns, halved
   lengthwise

6 oyster mushrooms, torn

2 red finger-length chilies, finely sliced

Small handful of snow pea shoots

¼ cup (50 g) Fried Garlic (page 19)

Broth

2¾ cups (700 ml) Fish Stock (page 13)

1 cup (250 ml)) Shao Xing rice wine

½ cup (125 ml) soy sauce

2 tablespoons rice wine vinegar

½ tablespoon sesame oil

4½ tablespoons (60 g) raw rock sugar
   crystals

1¼ in (3 cm) peeled ginger, bruised

4 dried black Chinese mushrooms

1 tablespoon instant dashi powder

Stuffed tofu

12 fresh shucked scallops (roe removed)

¾ in (1½ cm) peeled ginger, finely chopped

2 cloves garlic, finely chopped

1 tablespoon soy sauce

¼ teaspoon ground white pepper

1 tablespoon peanut oil

1 lb (500 g) firm tofu

3 cups (750ml) vegetable oil, for frying

1⅓ cups (175 g) rice flour

⅔ cup (75 g) cornstarch

Serves 6

This soup is inspired by one of my favorite dim sum dishes—Fried Tofu with Spiced Chili Salt (page 29). The soup has a sweet and slightly salty flavor—add more vinegar to help balance the flavors if you need to.

Make the Fish Stock and Fried Garlic by following the recipes on pages 13 and 19.

Broth
Place the ingredients in a medium-sized pot and bring to a boil. Cook for 5 minutes then remove from the heat. Set aside to cool and allow the flavors to infuse.

Stuffed tofu
Marinate the scallops in the ginger, garlic, soy sauce and pepper for 10 minutes. Heat the oil in a wok or pan and quickly sear the scallops on both sides. Set them aside until they're cool enough to handle then slice in half lengthwise.

  Cut the tofu into 12 cubes (they should each measure around 1¼ in /3 cm across). Take one cube and make an incision in the side without cutting all the way through. Using a small teaspoon or your fingers, carefully fill the cavity with two scallop halves and press the incision shut. Repeat this process with the remaining tofu and scallops.

  Heat the oil in a wok to 350°F (180°C). Combine the rice flour and cornstach in a bowl and dredge the pieces of tofu, dusting off any excess. Fry the Stuffed Tofu in batches until crisp and golden. Drain on paper towels.

To serve
Strain the Broth and reheat. Heat the peanut oil in a wok or pan over high heat and sear the corn, oyster mushrooms and chilies. Divide the Stuffed Tofu between six serving bowls and top with the corn and mushroom mixture. Ladle the Broth into each bowl and garnish with snow pea shoots and Fried Garlic.

Rice congee with homemade veal sausage, red dates and black mushrooms

Sausage

2 coriander (cilantro) roots, washed and coarsely chopped

4 cloves garlic, coarsely chopped

1 teaspoon sea salt

10 oz (300 g) ground veal topside

4 oz (100 g) pork fatback, ground (or 2 tablespoons lard)

½ cup (50 g) cooked Sticky Rice (page 24)

2 red bird's-eye chilies, deseeded and finely chopped

1½ tablespoons shaved palm sugar

1 tablespoon fish sauce

2 ft (60 cm) sausage casing (purchased from a butcher)

Juice of half a lemon

1 teaspoon sea salt

Congee

⅓ cup (70 g) uncooked shortgrain rice

2 tablespoons (35 g) uncooked glutinous rice

6 dried black Chinese mushrooms, softened in warm water and coarsely chopped

½ cup (60 g) dried red dates, coarsely chopped

4 cups (1 liter) Asian Brown Chicken Stock (page 11)

2 teaspoons sea salt

1 small Chinese or Napa cabbage, cored and cut into thin wedges

Serves 6

Congee is Asian comfort food—the rice is cooked until it becomes the texture of creamy porridge. It is sometimes eaten for breakfast and is served with accompaniments such as chicken, fish, shrimp, eggs, ginger, green onions and coriander leaves. Dried Chinese sausage, *lup cheong*, is another traditional accompaniment, or you can make your own sausage as in this recipe. The Chinese eat crunchy cabbage with congee to aid digestion.

Make the Asian Brown Chicken Stock and Sticky Rice by following the recipes on pages 11 and 24.

Sausage

Using a mortar and pestle pound the coriander roots, garlic and salt to a fine paste. Place it in a mixing bowl along with the veal, pork fatback, Sticky Rice, chilies, palm sugar and fish sauce and combine thoroughly. Set aside.

Fill a large bowl with water and add the lemon juice and salt. Wash the sausage casing thoroughly to remove any grit, then drain. Tie a knot in one end.

Fit a piping bag with a nozzle that is smaller than the width of the sausage casing. Fill the bag with the sausage mixture, pressing down to remove any air bubbles. Insert the nozzle into the open end of the casing. Carefully gather the casing over the nozzle until it reaches the knot and begin piping. Once all the mixture has been piped in, tie off the casing at the end of the mixture, discarding any excess casing. Refrigerate for 2 hours to allow the meat to set.

Congee

In a medium-sized pot combine the shortgrain and glutinous rice, black Chinese mushrooms, red dates, Chicken Stock and salt. Bring to a boil then turn down the heat, cover with a lid and simmer for around 2 hours, or until the rice has broken down and the texture is creamy. Taste for seasoning. Keep the Congee warm while you fry the Sausage.

To serve

Heat a broiler grill or barbecue and fry the Sausage over medium heat for 5–6 minutes on each side. Remove from the grill and slice diagonally into thin slices.

Ladle the Congee into serving bowls and top with slices of Sausage. Serve with the Chinese cabbage.

Sour fishball soup
with green papaya

6 cherry tomatoes, halved
½ cup (75 g) shredded green papaya
6 betel leaves, torn
2 red finger-length chilies, finely sliced

Spice paste
5 Asian shallots
6 cloves garlic
1½ in (4 cm) peeled ginger
1½ in (4 cm) peeled galangal root
2 red finger-length chilies, deseeded
4 coriander (cilantro) roots, washed
2 stalks lemongrass, tender inner part of
   bottom third only, finely sliced
6 kaffir lime leaves, finely sliced
1 teaspoon Roasted Shrimp Paste
   (page 9)
2 small ripe tomatoes, coarsely chopped
1 medium green apple, coarsely chopped
   (peel and core included)

Broth
3¼ cups (800 ml) Fish Stock (page 13)
⅔ cup (150 ml) Tamarind Juice (page 18)
½ cup (125 ml) freshly-squeezed lime juice
⅓ cup (80 ml) fish sauce

Fishballs
1⅓ lbs (600 g) ocean trout fillets, skinned
2 kaffir lime leaves, finely sliced
1 tablespoon fish sauce
1⅓ cups (175 g) rice flour
2 cups (500 ml) vegetable oil, for frying

Serves 6

In this soup the Spice Paste is infused with the liquid instead of being fried, which results in a clear, aromatic and vibrant broth.

Make the Roasted Shrimp Paste, Fish Stock and Tamarind Juice by following the recipes on pages 9, 13 and 18.

Spice paste
Coarsely chop the shallots, garlic, ginger, galangal, chilies and coriander roots. Using a mortar and pestle pound them to a coarse paste with the lemongrass, kaffir lime leaves and Roasted Shrimp Paste. Add the tomatoes and apple and continue pounding until you achieve a smooth paste. Alternatively, blend the initial paste with the tomatoes and apple in a food processor.

Broth
Transfer the Spice Paste to a medium-sized pot. Add the Fish Stock and bring to a boil, stirring to break the Paste up, then turn off the heat and let the Paste infuse for at least 20 minutes (or ideally, until completely cooled).

Fishballs
With a pair of kitchen pliers (or tweezers) carefully remove the pin bones from the trout. Coarsely chop the fish, place the trout in a food processor and blend until firm and sticky (this will help the balls to hold together). Transfer to a bowl and add the kaffir lime leaves and fish sauce and combine. Wet your hands and portion the mixture into small balls. Roll the balls in the rice flour, shaking off any excess.

Heat the oil in a wok to 350°F (180°C). Fry the balls in batches until crisp and golden (around 3 minutes). Drain on paper towels.

To serve
Strain the stock and bring it back to a gentle simmer. Add the Tamarind Juice, lime juice and fish sauce and check for a balance of flavors, adjusting if required. Remove from the heat.

Add three or four fishballs to each serving bowl. Ladle the Broth over them and garnish with the cherry tomatoes, papaya, betel leaves and chilies.

Lime infused miso soup
with fish dumplings

This simple Japanese miso soup base is so versatile—you can use most seafood and vegetables in place of the dumplings if you prefer.

Fish dumplings

12 oz (350 g) white fish fillets (such as whiting, porgy,sea bream or sole, skinned and deboned

1 egg white

¼ cup (65 ml) heavy cream

2 coriander (cilantro) roots, washed and finely chopped

2 kaffir lime leaves, finely sliced

2 cloves garlic, finely chopped

2 green onions (scallions), finely sliced

1 teaspoon soy sauce

18 wonton skins

Broth

2¾ cups (700 ml) water

15-cm (6-in) square sheet kombu (dried kelp)

1½ cups (15 g) bonito flakes

1 cup (250 g) white miso paste

Grated rind and juice of 3 limes

2 tablespoons dried wakame seaweed flakes

4 green onions (scallions), finely sliced

1 tablespoon shichimi pepper powder

Serves 6

Fish dumplings

Check over the fish and remove any lines of blood. Measure ½ cup (100 g) of fish and puree in a food processor. With the motor running, add the egg white. Push the mixture though a fine sieve into a mixing bowl and stir in the cream.

Finely dice the remaining fish and add to the pureed fish along with the coriander roots, kaffir lime leaves, garlic, green onions and soy sauce. Combine thoroughly.

Lay the wonton skins out on a clean work surface and place 2 teaspoons of filling on the corner of each one. Lightly brush the edges with water and fold the skins over to make triangles. Press the edges together to seal. Cover the Dumplings with plastic wrap and refrigerate for at least 30 minutes to firm.

Broth

Place the water and kombu in a medium-sized pot and bring to a gentle simmer, then take off the heat and add the bonito flakes. Allow the flakes to settle and infuse for several minutes. Add the miso and whisk to combine. Bring back to a simmer and add the lime rind. Remove from the heat and check the flavor—if it is too light, add a little more miso. Leave for 20 minutes then strain.

To serve

Place the Dumplings in a steamer and steam for 5 minutes. Bring the Broth back to a simmer, add the lime juice and immediately remove from the heat.

Divide the Dumplings between serving bowls. Add a little wakame seaweed to each one and ladle the Broth over it. Garnish with green onions and shichimi pepper powder.

Chicken meatball soup
with Asian herbs and lemon

Meatballs

10 oz (300 g) skinless chicken breasts

1 egg, lightly beaten

2 tablespoons rice flour

3 cloves garlic, finely chopped

2 green onions (scallions), finely sliced

3 coriander (cilantro) roots, washed and
finely chopped

¼ teaspoon ground black pepper

1 teaspoon soy sauce

Salad

¼ head iceberg lettuce, shredded

5 green onions (scallions), finely sliced

1 cup (40 g) Vietnamese mint leaves

2 lemons, quartered

1 cup (50 g) bean sprouts

2 red finger-length chilies, finely sliced

¼ cup (50 g) Fried Shallots (page 19)

Soup

4 cups (1 liter) Brown Chicken Stock
(page 12)

⅓ cup + 1 tablespoon (100 ml) soy sauce

1½ tablespoons fish sauce

¼ cup (50 g) fresh rice noodles

1½ in (4 cm) peeled ginger, sliced into thin
shreds

Serves 6

This is a Vietnamese-inspired soup that is really simple to prepare. *Pho*, the most common soup in Vietnam, is quite light and eaten at any time of day, accompanied by a crunchy and aromatic salad.

Make the Brown Chicken Stock and Fried Shallots by following the recipes on pages 12 and 19.

Coarsely chop the chicken breasts then place them in a food processor and blend until firm and sticky (this will help the balls to hold together). Scoop into a mixing bowl and combine with the remaining Meatballs ingredients. Shape the mixture into small balls and refrigerate for at least 2–3 hours to firm.

Arrange the Salad ingredients in separate piles or bowls on a serving platter.

For the Soup, combine the Chicken Stock, soy sauce and fish sauce in a medium-sized pot and bring to a simmer. Add the Meatballs and simmer until cooked through (around 2–3 minutes) then add the noodles and ginger. Once the noodles are heated through, remove the Soup from the heat.

Ladle the Soup into serving bowls. Serve the Salad ingredients on the side, for people to add to taste.

Coconut laksa with Chinese doughnuts

Chinese doughnuts are often served with soups and congees, and they are the perfect complement for milky, sweet Malaysian laksa.

Make the Roasted Shrimp Paste, Fried Chili Peanuts (if using) and Fried Shallots by following the recipes on pages 9 and 19.

Spice paste

6 Asian shallots, coarsely chopped

3 cloves garlic, coarsely chopped

2 in (5 cm) peeled ginger, coarsely chopped

2 in (5 cm) peeled galangal root, chopped

2 stalks lemongrass, tender inner part of bottom third only, finely sliced

4 kaffir lime leaves, finely sliced

2 red finger-length chilies, deseeded and coarsely chopped

5 coriander (cilantro) roots, washed and coarsely chopped

1 teaspoon coriander seeds, lightly dry-roasted

2 candlenuts or macadamia nuts

1 tablespoon Roasted Shrimp Paste (page 9)

Soup

1 tablespoon peanut oil

⅓ cup (80 ml) coconut cream

4 cups (1 liter) coconut milk

1½ tablespoons shaved palm sugar

1½ tablespoons fish sauce

3 tablespoons freshly-squeezed lime juice

7 oz (200 g) boneless chicken thighs, cubed

Handful (2 oz/50 g) dried rice noodles

Doughnuts

2 tablespoons dried yeast

⅓ cup (80 ml) warm water

1½ cups (375 ml) milk

4 tablespoons (75 g) unsalted butter, diced

4¼ cups (650 g) all-purpose (plain) flour

⅓ cup (75 g) superfine (caster) sugar, plus ¼ cup (50 g) extra

1 teaspoon sea salt

1 egg, lightly beaten

3 cups (750ml) vegetable oil, for frying

1 cup (50 g) coriander leaves (cilantro)

2 tablespoons Fried Shallots (page 19)

2 tablespoons Fried Chili Peanuts (page 19), optional

Serves 6

Spice paste
Pound the ingredients to a fine paste with a mortar and pestle. Alternatively, pound to a coarse paste with a mortar and pestle and finish off in a food processor.

Soup
Heat the peanut oil in a medium-sized pot and add the coconut cream. Fry until the coconut cream splits (when the oils and solids separate and it begins to smell nutty). Add the Spice Paste and fry until fragrant (around 5 minutes), stirring to make sure it doesn't catch. Add the coconut milk and simmer for 10 minutes. Add the palm sugar, fish sauce and lime juice and taste for a balance of flavors, adjusting if required. Remove from the heat and set aside while you prepare the Doughnuts.

Doughnuts
Combine the yeast and water in a large mixing bowl and leave until bubbles appear. Combine the milk and butter in a saucepan and heat until the butter just melts. Add this to the mixing bowl along with the flour, sugar, salt and egg. Stir the mixture until it comes together in a soft ball. Turn out onto a floured surface and knead gently until smooth. Place back in the bowl and cover with a cloth. Leave in a warm place and allow the dough to roughly double in size (this will take around 30 minutes). After the dough has proved, it can be refrigerated for a few hours if required.

Heat the oil in a wok to 350°F (180°C). Knock the dough back to its original size and roll the mixture into balls around the size of golf-balls. Stretch them a little as you place them in the oil, to make oval shapes. Fry the Doughnuts in batches until crisp and golden (around 3 minutes). Drain on paper towels, then toss them in the extra caster sugar, shaking off any excess.

To serve
Strain the Soup and bring back to a simmer. Add the chicken and cook for 5 minutes. Add the rice noodles and simmer until heated through.

Ladle the Soup into serving bowls and garnish with coriander leaves, Fried Shallots and Fried Chili Peanuts (if using). Serve with the warm Doughnuts for dipping.

Spicy tom yum soup with shrimp

Spice paste
5 Asian shallots, coarsely chopped
6 cloves garlic, coarsely chopped
2 in (5 cm) peeled ginger, coarsely chopped
1½ in (4 cm) peeled galangal root, coarsely chopped
4 red bird's-eye chilies, deseeded and coarsely chopped
3 stalks lemongrass, tender inner part of bottom third only, finely sliced
4 kaffir lime leaves, finely sliced
5 coriander (cilantro) roots, washed and coarsely chopped
2 large ripe tomatoes, coarsely chopped
1 cup (200 g) fresh pineapple, coarsely chopped
1 large green apple, coarsely chopped (peel and core included)

Soup
4 cups (1 liter) water
Handful (2 oz/50 g) dried rice vermicelli
⅓ cup (80 ml) freshly-squeezed lime juice
3 tablespoons fish sauce
2 tablespoons shaved palm sugar
18 fresh jumbo shrimp (about 1½ lbs/750 g), peeled and deveined
10 cherry tomatoes, halved
2 kaffir lime leaves, torn
1 red finger-length chili, finely sliced
1 cup (50 g) coriander leaves (cilantro)
¼ cup (50 g) Fried Shallots (page 19)

Serves 6

Tom yum is the most well-known and popular soup of Thailand, often sold and eaten on the street. It's a simple hot and sour broth, usually with shrimp or chicken. The amount of fish sauce and lime juice is a personal preference—I would suggest adding a little at a time until you are satisfied with the balance of flavors.

Make the Fried Shallots by following the recipe on page 19.

Spice paste
Using a mortar and pestle pound the shallots, garlic, ginger, galangal, chilies, lemongrass, kaffir lime leaves and coriander roots to a coarse paste. Add the tomatoes, pineapple and apple and continue pounding until you achieve a smooth paste. Alternatively, blend the initial paste with the tomatoes, pineapple and apple in a food processor.

Soup
Place the Spice Paste and water in a medium-sized pot and bring to a boil. Reduce the heat and simmer for 20 minutes, then remove from the heat and leave to cool for 20 minutes (or ideally, until completely cooled) to allow the flavors to develop.
   Cover the noodles with boiling water and leave for a minute or until tender. Drain and refresh under cold water.
   Strain the Soup and return to the heat adding the lime juice, fish sauce and palm sugar. Taste for a balance of flavors, adjusting if required. When simmering, add the shrimp and cook for 2–3 minutes. Stir through the noodles.
   To finish, stir through the cherry tomatoes, kaffir lime leaves, chili, coriander leaves and Fried Shallots and ladle into serving bowls.

Chicken dumpling soup
with Chinese broccoli

Chicken dumplings
10 oz (300 g) ground chicken
5 oz (150 g) ground pork
2 dried Chinese sausages (*lup cheong*),
    finely sliced
2 tablespoons finely chopped garlic chives
2 coriander (cilantro) roots, washed and
    finely chopped
2 red bird's-eye chilies, deseeded and
    finely chopped
3 green onions (scallions), finely sliced
1 teaspoon soy sauce
1 teaspoon sesame oil
1 teaspoon sea salt
¼ teaspoon ground white pepper
18 round dumpling skins

Soup
Handful (2 oz/50 g) dried rice vermicelli
4 cups (1 liter) Asian Brown Chicken Stock
    (page 11)
2½ tablespoons oyster sauce
1½ tablespoons soy sauce
½ bunch Chinese broccoli (*kailan*), stems
    peeled and finely sliced, leaves finely
    shredded
⅓ cup (80 g) wood ear mushrooms,
    coarsely chopped
½ teaspoon ground white pepper
1 tablespoon Fried Garlic (page 19)

Serves 6

Make the Asian Brown Chicken Stock and Fried Garlic by following the recipes on pages 11 and 19.

Chicken dumplings
Combine the chicken and pork in a mixing bowl and work the mixture with your hands for several minutes until it becomes slightly elastic (this will help the filling to hold together). Add the remaining ingredients apart from the dumpling skins and mix thoroughly.

Lay the dumpling skins out on a clean work surface. Place 2 teaspoons of filling in the center of each one and lightly brush the edges with water. Bring the sides together to create half-moon shapes and press the edges shut.

Soup
Cover the noodles with boiling water and leave for a minute or until tender. Drain and refresh under cold water.

Steam the Dumplings for 7 minutes. Meanwhile, bring the Chicken Stock, oyster sauce and soy sauce to a boil in a medium-sized pot. Taste for seasoning. When the stock boils add the rice noodles, Chinese broccoli and wood ear mushrooms, then remove from the heat. Divide the Dumplings and Soup between serving bowls and garnish with pepper and Fried Garlic.

Fried pork cheek soup with peanuts, yellow bean paste and lime

1⅓ lbs (600 g) pork cheeks
⅓ cup + 1 tablespoon (100 ml) sweet soy sauce
3 cups (750ml) vegetable oil, for frying
2 limes, quartered

Spice paste
4 star anise pods
10 white peppercorns
2 teaspoons sea salt
5 Asian shallots, coarsely chopped
6 cloves garlic, coarsely chopped
1 in (2½ cm) peeled ginger, coarsely chopped
¾ in (1½ cm) peeled galangal root, coarsely chopped
3 coriander (cilantro) roots, washed and coarsely chopped
½ cup (125 ml) yellow bean paste

Soup
1 tablespoon peanut oil
½ cup (75 g) Fried Chili Peanuts (page 19) or roasted peanuts
2 tablespoons shaved palm sugar
3 tablespoons soy sauce
3½ tablespoons Shao Xing rice wine
4 cups (1 liter) Asian Brown Chicken Stock (page 11)
1 cup (50 g) coriander leaves (cilantro)

Serves 6

This is a great winter soup—quite rich and full-flavored. The pieces of pork through the soup add a luxurious texture.

Make the Asian Brown Chicken Stock and Fried Chili Peanuts by following the recipes on pages 11 and 19.

Marinate the pork cheeks in the sweet soy sauce overnight. The following day, heat the oil in a wok to 350°F (180°C). Remove the pork cheeks from the marinade and pat dry with paper towels. Fry the cheeks in batches until dark and caramelized on the surface. Drain on paper towels and set aside.

Spice paste
Dry-roast the star anise, peppercorns and salt in a wok over medium heat until fragrant (1–2 minutes), stirring constantly to avoid burning. Pound to a fine powder using a mortar and pestle or spice grinder.

Using a mortar and pestle, pound the spice mix with the remaining ingredients until you achieve a smooth paste. Alternatively, pound to a coarse paste with a mortar and pestle and finish with a food processor.

Soup
Heat the peanut oil in a medium-sized pot and fry the Spice Paste until fragrant (around 5 minutes), stirring to make sure it doesn't catch. Add the fried pork, Fried Chili Peanuts, palm sugar, soy sauce, Shao Xing rice wine and Chicken Stock. Bring to a simmer, cover with a lid and cook until the meat is falling apart (around 45 minutes–1 hour).

To serve, stir through the coriander leaves and ladle the Soup into serving bowls. Serve the lime wedges on the side.

Lobster and tamarind soup with kaffir lime and betel leaves

Lobster
1 live lobster weighing around 4 lbs (2 kgs)
3 cups (750ml) vegetable oil, for frying
1¼ in (3 cm) peeled ginger, sliced into thin shreds
1 red finger-length chili, deseeded and finely sliced lengthwise
5 green onions (scallions), white ends only, finely sliced
½ cup (25 g) coriander leaves (cilantro)
2 kaffir lime leaves, finely sliced
10 betel leaves, torn

Spice paste
1¼ in (3 cm) peeled ginger, coarsely chopped
1¼ in (3 cm) peeled galangal root, coarsely chopped
¾ in (1½ cm) peeled fresh turmeric root, coarsely chopped
5 cloves garlic, coarsely chopped
1 stalk lemongrass, tender inner part of bottom third only, finely sliced
4 kaffir lime leaves, finely sliced
3 red bird's-eye chilies, deseeded and coarsely chopped
1 teaspoon Roasted Shrimp Paste (page 9)

Soup
1 tablespoon peanut oil
4 cups (1 liter) Asian Brown Chicken Stock (page 11)
¾ cup (250 g) Tamarind Paste (page 18)
3 tablespoons fish sauce
⅓ cup (80 ml) freshly-squeezed lime juice
2 tablespoons shaved palm sugar
1¾ oz (50 g) fresh egg noodles

Serves 6

You can substitute the lobster in this soup with crayfish, crab or even large mussels if you prefer. I like the sour taste of tamarind; however, if you find it too much add a little more palm sugar.

Make the Roasted Shrimp Paste and Asian Brown Chicken Stock by following the recipes on pages 9 and 11.

Spice paste
Use a mortar and pestle to pound the ingredients to a smooth paste (alternatively, pound to a coarse paste with a mortar and pestle and finish with a food processor).

Soup
Heat the peanut oil in a medium-sized pot and fry the Spice paste until fragrant (around 5 minutes), stirring to make sure it doesn't catch. Add the Chicken Stock and Tamarind Paste and bring to a boil. Simmer for 20 minutes or until reduced by a quarter, then set aside to cool.

Lobster
To kill the lobster, place it in a deep sink or pot of fresh water for 5 minutes or until the lobster drowns.

Hold the lobster with its head in one hand and tail in the other and gently twist and pull to separate them. Discard the head. Remove and crack the legs and claws. Use a cleaver or a large, sharp knife to cut the tail in half lengthwise. Cut each half into three large chunks with the shell attached so you are left with six pieces.

Heat the oil in a wok to 350°F (180°C) and add the lobster legs, claws and tail pieces. Fry, turning regularly, until the shells turn deep red (6–8 minutes). Drain on paper towels then extract the meat from the legs and claws. Keep the tail meat in the shells.

To serve
Reheat the Soup adding the fish sauce, lime juice and palm sugar. Taste for a balance of flavors, adjusting if required, then add the noodles and cook until al dente. Add the lobster pieces to the soup and reheat without boiling.

Divide the Soup among six serving bowls. Garnish with ginger, chili, green onions, coriander leaves, kaffir lime leaves and betel leaves and serve.

Omelet soup
with crab, bean sprouts and coriander

Despite how the recipe may look, this is quite a simple soup—the most time-consuming parts are extracting the crab meat and making the omelet.

Make the Asian Brown Chicken Stock by following the recipe on page 11.

Crab

1 live crab weighing at least 3 lbs (1½ kgs) (or several smaller crabs equalling the same weight)

Omelet

6 eggs
1 teaspoon oyster sauce
⅔ cup (150 ml) peanut oil
1 cup (50 g) bean sprouts
1 bunch (2½ oz/75 g) enoki mushrooms, bases trimmed
1 in (2½ cm) peeled ginger, sliced into thin shreds
5 green onions (scallions), finely sliced
1 cup (40 g) garlic chives, sliced into lengths
1 cup (50 g) coriander leaves (cilantro)

Broth

1⅔ cups (400 ml) Asian Brown Chicken Stock (page 11)
3 tablespoons sweet soy sauce
1 tablespoon fish sauce
¼ head iceberg lettuce, finely shredded
2 red finger-length chilies, deseeded and finely sliced lengthwise
½ cup (25 g) coriander leaves (cilantro)

Serves 6

Crab

Kill the crab quickly and humanely by turning it onto its back and inserting a large metal skewer in its middle where the flaps meet. Leave the skewer inside the crab for 3–4 minutes or until the crab has died. Alternatively, place the crab in a freezer for 1 hour, which will send it to sleep.

Bring a large pot of water to a boil. Calculate the cooking time—allow 7–8 minutes/lb of whole crab. (On this basis, a 3 lbs (1½ kgs) crab will need to be cooked for 20–22 minutes.) Add the crab to the pot and simmer for the correct time. The shell of the crab will turn a reddish brown when cooked. Remove the crab from the pot and plunge it in a basin of iced water to stop the cooking process. Leave the crab to cool in the basin for 10 minutes, then drain.

Use your fingers to pull the top shell away from the body. Discard the gills and rinse the crab. Twist off the legs and claws and use a mallet or the flat side of the cleaver to crack them. Use a crab pick or metal skewer to extract the meat from the legs, claws and body. Weigh 2 cups (250 g) of meat and refrigerate or freeze the rest for another use.

Omelet

Whisk the eggs with the oyster sauce. Heat the peanut oil in a wok until it begins to smoke then pour in the egg mixture. Gently move the wok over the heat in a circular motion to spread the egg out and ensure it cooks evenly. The omelet will bubble and float over the oil. When it has just set, drain any excess oil from the top and sprinkle on the crab meat, bean sprouts, enoki mushrooms, ginger, green onions, garlic chives and coriander leaves. When the Omelet begins to crisp around the edges and the topping has warmed through, carefully lift the Omelet out with two slotted spoons or other implements, drain off any excess oil, and place the Omelet into a warm serving bowl. Fold the Omelet over into a half-moon shape.

Broth

Place the stock, soy sauce and fish sauce in a saucepan and bring to a boil. Pour around the Omelet. Garnish the Omelet with the lettuce, chilies and coriander leaves. To serve, divide the Omelet into six pieces and spoon a little Omelet, Broth and garnish into each bowl.

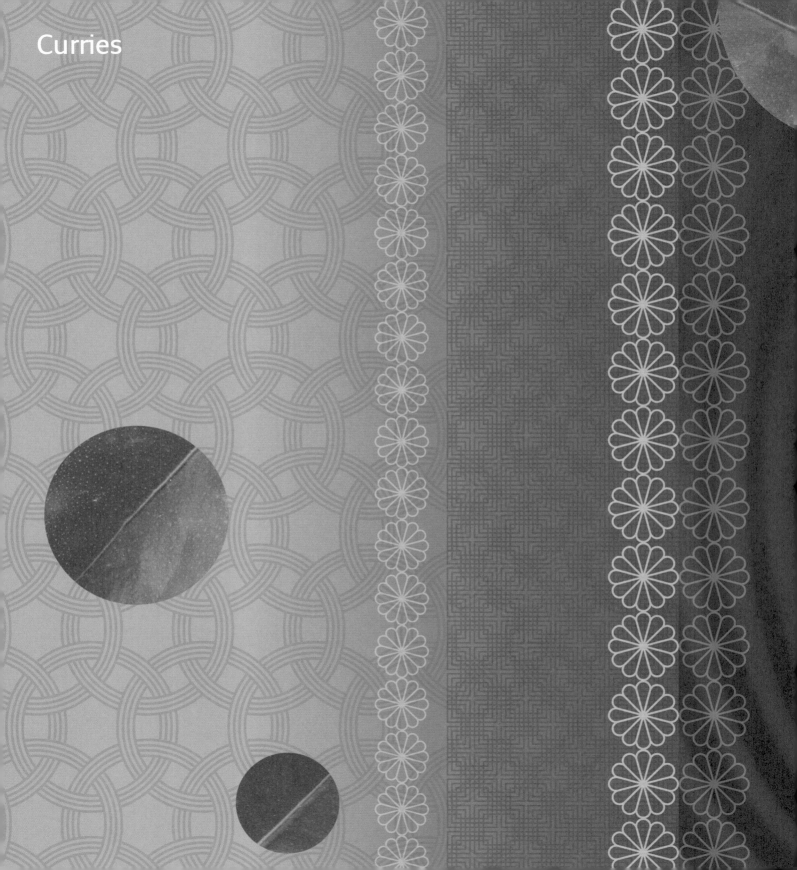

Curries

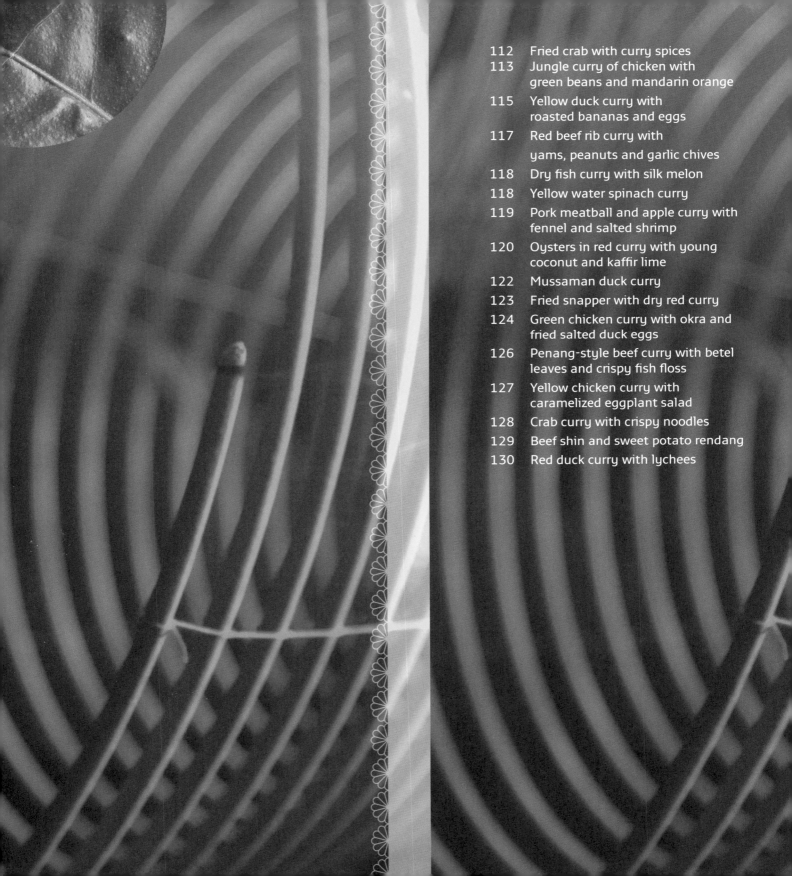

Fried crab with curry spices

This recipe uses dried curry spices instead of the traditional Southeast Asian aromatics, which makes for a spicier and more pungent curry to complement the sweetness of the crab. Deep-frying ensures the flavor of the crab is sealed inside.

1 live crab weighing around
   3 lbs (1½ kgs)
4 cups (1 liter) vegetable oil, for frying
1½ tablespoons peanut oil
1 small brown onion cut into 6 wedges
4 cloves garlic, finely chopped
3 dried red finger-length chilies, soaked in
   warm water for 30 minutes
¼ cup (50 g) shaved palm sugar
2 tablespoons fish sauce
1⅔ cups (400 ml) coconut milk
1 tablespoon soy sauce
2 tablespoons oyster sauce
1 tablespoon Curry Powder (page 10)
3 green onions (scallions), finely sliced
1 cup (50 g) coriander leaves (cilantro)
2 lemons, quartered

Serves 6

Make the Curry Powder by following the recipe on page 10.

Kill the crab quickly and humanely by turning it onto its back and inserting a large metal skewer in its middle where the flaps meet. Leave the skewer inside the crab for 3–4 minutes or until the crab has died.

Use your fingers to pull the top shell away from the body and discard. Discard the gills and rinse the crab. With a cleaver or a large, sharp knife, cut the crab into six pieces leaving the claws and legs attached. Crack the claws and legs with a mallet or the back of a cleaver (this helps them to cook evenly and allows the flavors to get in).

Heat the oil in a wok to 350°F (180°C) and add the crab pieces. Fry until the shells take on a deep red color (around 3 minutes). Drain on paper towels.

Remove the oil from the wok and wipe the wok clean. Heat the peanut oil in the wok and add the onion, garlic and chilies. Stir-fry until fragrant and beginning to brown. Add the palm sugar and fish sauce and cook until the mixture begins to caramelize.

Add the fried crab and stir-fry for 5 minutes, then add the coconut milk, soy sauce, oyster sauce and Curry Powder. Cover the wok with a lid or an upturned bowl and simmer the curry for a further 5 minutes.

Transfer to a serving dish and scatter with green onions and coriander leaves. Serve the lemon wedges on the side.

Jungle curry of chicken with green beans and mandarin orange

1 lb (500 g) chicken thighs

1 tablespoon peanut oil

3 cloves garlic, finely chopped

¾ in (1½ cm) peeled ginger, finely chopped

3 green bird's-eye chilies, finely chopped

3 kaffir limes leaves, torn

1 cup (150 g) green beans cut into lengths

2½ tablespoons oyster sauce

1⅔ cups (400 ml) Asian Brown Chicken Stock (page 11)

2 tablespoons sugar

1 green finger-length chili, finely sliced

2 mandarin oranges, peeled and segmented, seeds and pith removed

1 tablespoon fish sauce

1½ tablespoons freshly-squeezed lime juice

½ cup (20 g) Thai basil leaves

1 cup (50 g) coriander leaves (cilantro)

¼ cup (50 g) Fried Shallots (page 19)

Spice paste

6 green bird's-eye chilies, deseeded

3 green finger-length chilies, deseeded

5 Asian shallots

4 cloves garlic

1 in (2½ cm) peeled ginger

1 in (2½ cm) peeled galangal root

3 coriander (cilantro) roots, washed

1 stalk lemongrass, tender inner part of bottom third only

4 kaffir lime leaves

2 tablespoons fresh green peppercorns

½ tablespoon Roasted Shrimp Paste (page 9)

¼ cup (50 g) shaved palm sugar

1 teaspoon sea salt

Serves 6

Jungle curries originate from remote Thai villages where they were made mainly with wild boar. There are also many variations of vegetable jungle curries using ingredients such as pea eggplants, bamboo shoots and bean sprouts, as meat was sometimes scarce in northern Thailand. These curries are often very hot as they contain no coconut milk.

Make the Roasted Shrimp Paste, Asian Brown Chicken Stock and Fried Shallots by following the recipes on pages 9, 11 and 19.

Spice paste
Coarsely chop the chilies, shallots, garlic, ginger, galangal and coriander roots. Finely slice the lemongrass and shred the kaffir lime leaves. Using a mortar and pestle pound them all to a smooth paste with the remaining ingredients. Alternatively, pound to a coarse paste in a mortar and pestle and finish with a food processor.

Chicken curry
Finely chop the chicken thighs. Heat the peanut oil in a wok and add the chicken, garlic, ginger and bird's-eye chilies. Fry until the chicken begins to brown. Add the Spice Paste and stir-fry until fragrant (around 8 minutes), then add the kaffir lime leaves, green beans, oyster sauce, Chicken Stock and sugar. Simmer for 2 minutes then add the sliced chili and mandarin segments. Add the fish sauce and lime juice and taste for a balance of flavors, adjusting if required.

Remove from the heat and transfer to a serving dish. Garnish with the Thai basil, coriander leaves and Fried Shallots.

Yellow duck curry with roasted bananas and eggs

1 duck weighing around 4 lbs (2 kgs)

1 in (2½ cm) peeled ginger, bruised

2 cloves garlic, bruised

6 green onions (scallions), coarsely chopped

2 star anise pods

1 cinnamon stick, broken

½ cup (125 ml) Shao Xing rice wine

⅓ cup + 1 tablespoon (100 ml) sweet soy sauce

1 cup (40 g) Thai basil leaves

1 cup (50 g) coriander leaves (cilantro)

½ cup Fried Shallots (page 19)

Curry

1 tablespoon peanut oil

⅓ cup + 1 tablespoon (100 ml) coconut cream

¾ cup (150 g) Yellow Curry Paste (page 10)

2 cups (500 ml) coconut milk

1 cup (150 g) green beans cut into lengths

6 small sugar bananas

3 tablespoons freshly-squeezed lime juice

2 tablespoons fish sauce

3 tablespoons Palm Sugar Syrup (page 18)

Eggs

6 eggs

1 teaspoon sea salt

2 cups (500 ml) vegetable oil

Serves 6

This is quite an elaborate dish that you might make for a special occasion. The duck is steamed whole before it is carved up and simmered in the curry, which keeps it very tender and succulent. The bananas give a nice sweetness to the dish and the eggs, still runny in the middle, add a touch of luxury.

Make the Yellow Curry Paste, Palm Sugar Syrup and Fried Shallots by following the recipes on pages 10, 18 and 19

Rinse the duck inside and out. Stuff the cavity of the duck with the ginger, garlic, green onions, star anise and cinnamon. Carefully pour in the Shao Xing rice wine and seal the opening by threading a skewer through the flaps of skin.

Place the duck in a large bowl and add the soy sauce. Gently massage it into the skin with your fingers. Transfer the duck to the refrigerator to marinate for 3–4 hours (or overnight).

Remove the duck from the refrigerator and place it on a heatproof dish with a rim to catch any juices, and insert the dish into a large steamer. Steam for 1½ hours.

Remove the duck from the steamer and set aside to cool slightly. Reserve any juices that have pooled in the dish.

When the duck is cool enough to touch, remove the skewer and use a cleaver or a large, sharp knife to cut the duck in half lengthwise. Discard the stuffing. Cut the backbone away from the duck and discard. Slice off the wings where they meet the breasts and discard. Cut off the legs between the thigh and body and separate the thigh from the drumsticks by cutting through the joint. Cut the breasts from the rib cage (but leave them still attached to the breastplate). Cut the breasts and thighs through the bones into three pieces each. Leave the drumsticks whole.

Continued next page

Curry

Heat the peanut oil in a heavy-based pan or saucepan and add the coconut cream. Fry over medium heat until the coconut cream splits (when the oils and solids separate and it begins to smell nutty). Add the Yellow Curry Paste and fry until fragrant (around 5 minutes), stirring to make sure it doesn't catch.

Transfer the paste to a wok or medium-sized pot and add the coconut milk and reserved duck juices. Simmer for 5 minutes, then add the duck pieces and simmer for 20 minutes. Add the green beans and simmer for a further 5 minutes, then remove from the heat.

Heat a broiler grill or barbecue and cook the bananas in their skins until soft (around 4 minutes), turning them halfway through. Set aside to cool, then peel and cut them into large chunks and add them to the cooling curry.

Eggs

Place the eggs in a shallow bowl and cover with hot (but not boiling) water. Let them warm in the water for 3 minutes (this keeps them from cracking when boiled).

Bring a medium-sized pot of water to a boil and add the salt. When boiling, gently add the eggs and turn the heat down to a simmer. Cook the eggs until soft-boiled (3–4 minutes) then remove from the heat. Place the pot into the sink and run cold water into it to cool the eggs. (The water will run over the rim of the pot but the eggs should stay inside.) When the water is cold, turn off the tap and let the eggs cool completely in the water. Peel the eggs while still in the water and place them on paper towels to drain.

Heat the oil in a wok to 350°F (180°C) then add the eggs and fry until crisp and golden (around 4 minutes). Drain on paper towels.

To serve

Bring the curry back to a simmer and add the lime juice, fish sauce and Palm Sugar Syrup. Taste for a balance of flavors, adjusting if required. Transfer the curry to a serving dish. Slice the fried eggs in half (the yolks should still be runny) and scatter them over the curry. Garnish with Thai basil, coriander leaves and Fried Shallots.

Red beef rib curry with yams, peanuts and garlic chives

3 lbs (1½ kgs) beef ribs, cut into small pieces by your butcher

1 large or 2 small yams (5 oz/150 g), peeled and diced

½ cup (75 g) Fried Chili Peanuts (page 19) or roasted peanuts

1 tablespoon peanut oil

⅓ cup + 1 tablespoon (100 ml) coconut cream

½ cup (100 g) Red Curry Paste (page 10)

1½ tablespoons shaved palm sugar

1 tablespoon fish sauce

2 cups (500 ml) coconut milk

¾ cup (190 ml) Asian Brown Chicken Stock (page 11)

2 cassia sticks

2 star anise pods

1 bunch garlic chives, sliced into lengths (to make 2 cups/80 g)

2½ tablespoons freshly-squeezed lime juice

1 cup (50 g) coriander leaves (cilantro)

¼ cup (50 g) Fried Shallots (page 19)

1 tablespoon Chili Shrimp Oil (page 18), optional

Serves 6

Slowly cooked beef ribs are really tasty and tender. If yams are unavailable, substitute sweet potato or even taro.

Make the Red Curry Paste, Asian Brown Chicken Stock, Chili Shrimp Oil, Fried Chili Peanuts and Fried Shallots by following the recipes on pages 10, 11, 18 and 19.

Rinse the ribs and place them in a large pot. Cover them with cold water, adding a pinch of salt. Bring the pot to a boil then drain the ribs and refresh under cold running water. Transfer the ribs to a claypot or casserole dish. Add the yams and peanuts.

Preheat the oven to 325°F (160°C). Heat the peanut oil in a large heavy-based saucepan and add the coconut cream. Fry over medium heat until the coconut cream splits (when the oils and solids separate and it begins to smell nutty), then add the Red Curry Paste and fry until fragrant (around 5 minutes), stirring to make sure it doesn't catch.

Add the palm sugar and fish sauce and cook until the sugar caramelizes, turning a deep red color. Add the coconut milk, Chicken Stock, cassia and star anise and bring to a boil. Pour the liquid into the claypot, making sure everything is submerged, then cover with a lid and place in the oven. Cook for 2 hours or until the beef is tender.

To finish, remove the claypot from the oven and turn off the oven. Add the garlic chives to the pot and return the pot to the warm oven for 5–10 minutes. Remove from the oven and add the lime juice. Taste for seasoning then garnish with coriander leaves, Fried Shallots and Chili Shrimp Oil (if using), and serve.

Dry fish curry with silk melon

3 cups (750ml) vegetable oil

2 lbs (1 kg) hapuka fillets (substitute grouper fillets), skinned and cut into serving pieces

6 egg whites, lightly beaten

3 cups (375 g) rice flour

⅓ cup (80 ml) peanut oil

¾ cup (150 g) Green Curry Paste (page 9)

2 tablespoons shaved palm sugar

2 tablespoons fish sauce

1 silk melon or zucchini (weighing around 7 oz/200 g), peeled and sliced into bite-sized discs

3 tablespoons freshly-squeezed lime juice

3 tablespoons coconut cream

1 tablespoon cucumber oil (optional)

1 cup (40 g) Thai basil leaves

2 tablespoons Fried Shallots (page 19)

Serves 6

If you can't find hapuka, use another dense deep-sea fish such as grouper or snapper. Dry curries use little or no coconut milk or stock. Silk melon (a zucchini-shaped vegetable) is one of my favorite Asian swamp vegetables. It has a slightly earthy, muddy flavor.

Make the Green Curry Paste and Fried Shallots by following the recipes on pages 9 and 19.

Heat the oil in a wok to 350°F (180°C). Dip the fish fillets in the egg whites and then the rice flour, shaking off any excess. Fry the fish in batches until crisp and golden. Drain on paper towels.

Heat the peanut oil in a heavy-based pan or saucepan and fry the Green Curry Paste until fragrant (around 5 minutes), stirring to make sure it doesn't catch. Add the palm sugar and fish sauce and cook until it begins to caramelize.

Transfer the fried paste to a wok and add the silk melon. Stir-fry until tender (around 5 minutes). Gently toss the fried fish through the curry until heated through. Add the lime juice and taste for a good balance of flavors, adjusting if necessary.

Transfer the curry to a serving dish and drizzle with coconut cream and cucumber oil (if using). Sprinkle with Thai basil leaves and Fried Shallots and serve.

Yellow water spinach curry

1½ tablespoons peanut oil

⅓ cup (80 g) Yellow Curry Paste (page 10)

1⅔ cups (400 ml) coconut milk

2 tablespoons Tamarind Paste (page 18)

1 tablespoon Palm Sugar Syrup (page 18)

2 bunches water spinach, bases trimmed, cut into thirds

2 tablespoons freshly-squeezed lime juice

1 tablespoon fish sauce

½ cup (100 g) Fried Shallots (page 19)

Serves 6

This is a very simple dish I sometimes serve as an accompaniment to fish or poultry dishes. Yellow curries from Indonesia are the coolest of all curries, and the flavor of the fresh turmeric is unbeatable. You can substitute the water spinach with asparagus, silk melon, Chinese broccoli or a combination if you prefer. Sieving the curry before adding the spinach makes it smooth like a sauce.

Make the Yellow Curry Paste, Palm Sugar Syrup, Tamarind Paste and Fried Shallots by following the recipes on pages 10, 18 and 19.

Heat 1 tablespoon of the peanut oil in a heavy-based saucepan and add the Yellow Curry Paste. Fry until fragrant (around 5 minutes), stirring to make sure it doesn't catch. Add the coconut milk and bring to a simmer then remove from the heat. Set aside to cool and allow the flavors to infuse.

When the liquid is cool, puree it in a blender then push it through a sieve to extract as much flavor as possible. Discard the solids. Add the Tamarind Paste and Palm Sugar Syrup and set the sauce aside.

Heat the remaining peanut oil in a wok and add the water spinach. Stir-fry over high heat until tender (around a minute). Add the curry sauce and bring to a simmer. Add the lime juice and fish sauce and check for a balance of flavors, adjusting if necessary. Sprinkle with the Fried Shallots and serve.

Pork meatball and apple curry with fennel and salted shrimp

Pork and apple is a classic combination in Western cooking and works well in an Asian curry too. I like to use rose apples, which aren't true apples but a small, tropical, pear-shaped fruit with a faint rose aroma. While the result will be much sweeter, you can substitute Jonathans or other similar green apple varieties.

Make the Asian Brown Chicken Stock, Salted Shrimp and Sticky Rice by following the recipes on pages 11, 22 and 24.

Spicy paste
Using a mortar and pestle, pound the chilies, shallots, garlic, galangal and salt to a fine paste. Add the fermented fish paste and pound until well combined.

Pork meatballs
In a large mixing bowl, work the pork with your hands for several minutes until it becomes slightly elastic (this will help the meatballs to hold together). Add the remaining ingredients and combine thoroughly, then roll the mixture into 18 balls. Refrigerate for an hour to become firm.

Curry
Bring the Chicken Stock and sugar to a boil in a wok or medium-sized pot. Add the pork meatballs and simmer gently for 10 minutes, then add the Spice Paste and stir until it breaks up. Add the rose apples, cherry tomatoes and orange juice and cook until the apples are tender (around 3 minutes). Taste for seasoning then transfer the curry to a serving bowl. Garnish with the sliced fennel, betel leaves and Salted Shrimp.

Spice paste

- 6 dried red finger-length chilies, deseeded and soaked in warm water for 30 minutes, coarsely chopped
- 5 Asian shallots, coarsely chopped
- 4 cloves garlic, coarsely chopped
- 1 in (2½ cm) peeled galangal root, coarsely chopped
- 1 teaspoon sea salt
- 2 tablespoons fermented fish paste (or fish sauce)

Pork meatballs

- 1 lb (500 g) ground pork
- 1 cup (100 g) cooked Sticky Rice (page 24)
- 2 coriander (cilantro) roots, washed and finely chopped
- ½ tablespoon fish sauce
- Grated rind of 1 orange
- 1 teaspoon ground white pepper

Curry

- 2 cups (500 ml) Asian Brown Chicken Stock (page 11)
- 1 tablespoon sugar
- 6 rose apples or 3 green apples, cored and coarsely chopped (peel left on)
- 8 cherry tomatoes, halved
- Juice of 1 orange
- ½ large head fennel, finely sliced
- 1 cup betel leaves, torn
- 1 portion Salted Shrimp (page 22)

Serves 6

Oysters in red curry
with young coconut and kaffir lime

24 large unshucked oysters

1 young green coconut

1 cup (40 g) mint leaves

1 cup (50 g) coriander leaves (cilantro)

1 cup (40 g) Thai basil leaves, torn

1 red finger-length chili, deseeded and finely
  sliced lengthwise

½ cup (50 g) Fried Shallots (page 19)

1 tablespoon peanut oil

⅓ cup + 1 tablespoon (100 ml) coconut cream

3 tablespoons Red Curry Paste (page 10)

2 tablespoons shaved palm sugar

1 tablespoon fish sauce

1¼ cups (300 ml) coconut milk

4 kaffir lime leaves, finely sliced into thin
  shreds

1½ tablespoons freshly-squeezed lime juice

Serves 6

A great dish to serve as an appetizer, with very clean and refreshing flavors. The sweetness of the red curry complements the mild saltiness of the oysters. If you have a fishmonger who will shuck the oysters to order for you, and if you are going to use them right away, buy them shucked. Otherwise I recommend buying them closed and shucking them yourself (you will need an oyster knife for this).

Make the Red Curry Paste and Fried Shallots by following the recipes on pages 10 and 19.

Clean the oysters with a stiff brush under cold running water to remove any grit. To open, hold an oyster firmly in a glove or dish towel and insert an oyster knife between the shells near the hinge. Twist the knife to pry the shells apart and work the knife around the shells until they are completely loose. Open the shell and dislodge the oyster by gently sliding the knife between the oyster and the shell it is attached to. Discard the smaller shell, reserving the oyster in the larger one.

Pierce the coconut with a metal skewer and drain out the juice. Cut off the pointed top with a sharp knife or cleaver and scoop out the soft flesh inside with a large spoon, trying to keep it in large pieces. Refrigerate half the flesh for another use, and slice the other half into very fine strands.

Combine the mint and coriander leaves, Thai basil, chili and Fried Shallots and set aside.

Heat the peanut oil in a heavy-based saucepan and add the coconut cream. Fry over medium heat until the coconut cream splits (when the oils and solids separate and it begins to smell nutty). Add the Red Curry Paste and fry until fragrant (around 5 minutes), stirring to make sure it doesn't catch. Add the palm sugar and fish sauce and cook until the mixture begins to caramelize, turning a dark red color.

Add the coconut milk and simmer for 3–4 minutes. Add the kaffir lime leaves and sliced coconut and bring back to a simmer, then add the oysters and lime juice. Gently poach them for 20 seconds then turn off the heat. Scoop the oysters into a bowl with a slotted spoon to stop them cooking.

Arrange the oyster shells on a serving platter and return each oyster to a shell. Add a little coconut, kaffir lime leaf and sauce to each one, then scatter with the herb and shallot mixture. Serve immediately.

Mussaman duck curry

6 duck legs (marylands)

3 cups (750ml) vegetable oil

12 kipfler potatoes, peeled

8 Asian shallots

3 cups (750ml) coconut milk

4 cardamom pods, cracked

½ cup (75 g) Fried Chili Peanuts (page 19)
    or roasted peanuts

3 bay leaves

1 tablespoon peanut oil

⅓ cup + 1 tablespoon (100 ml) coconut cream

¼ cup (50 g) shaved palm sugar

2 tablespoons fish sauce

3 tablespoons Tamarind Juice (page 18)

2½ tablespoons guava juice

½ small seedless watermelon

1 green mango

½ cup (100 g) Fried Shallots (page 19)

1 cup (50 g) coriander leaves (cilantro)

Spice paste

2 tablespoons coriander seeds

1 tablespoon cumin seeds

4 whole cloves

2 whole nutmegs, cracked

2 cinnamon sticks, broken

4 cardamom pods, cracked

6 dried red finger-length chilies, deseeded
    and soaked in warm water for 30 minutes,
    coarsely chopped

6 Asian shallots, coarsely chopped

6 cloves garlic, coarsely chopped

1½ in (4 cm) peeled galangal root, coarsely
    chopped

1 stalk lemongrass, tender inner part of
    bottom third only, finely sliced

4 coriander (cilantro) roots, washed and
    coarsely chopped

¼ cup (40 g) Fried Chili Peanuts (page 19)
    or roasted peanuts

1 teaspoon sea salt

Serves 6

This Thai curry has an Indian influence, using dried spices such as cinnamon, cumin and coriander. It is usually made with beef. Cranberry juice is the best substitute for guava juice if you can't find it.

Make the Tamarind Juice, Fried Chili Peanuts and Fried Shallots by following the recipes on pages 18 and 19.

Spice paste

Dry-roast the coriander and cumin seeds, cloves, nutmeg, cinnamon and cardamom in a wok over medium heat until fragrant (around 1–2 minutes), stirring constantly to avoid burning. Remove from the heat and grind the spices to a fine powder with a mortar and pestle or spice grinder.

Using a mortar and pestle, pound the spice powder with the remaining ingredients until you achieve a smooth paste. Alternatively, pound to a coarse paste with a mortar and pestle and finish with a food processor.

Curry

Heat the vegetable oil in a wok to 350°F (180°C). With a cleaver or sharp knife, cut each duck leg (maryland) in half through the joint. Fry the pieces in batches until crisp and golden then drain on paper towels. Do the same with the whole potatoes and shallots.

Place the fried duck in a medium-sized pot and add the coconut milk, cardamom, peanuts and bay leaves and bring to a boil. Simmer for 1 hour, topping up with water occasionally as the liquid evaporates, then add the potatoes and shallots and cook for a further 45 minutes. By this time the duck should be tender and the potatoes and onions soft. Remove from the heat.

Heat the peanut oil in a heavy-based pan or saucepan and add the coconut cream. Fry over medium heat until the coconut cream splits (when the oils and solids separate and it begins to smell nutty). Add the Spice Paste and fry until fragrant (around 5 minutes). Add the palm sugar and cook until the mixture begins to caramelize, turning a dark red color. It should smell dense and earthy. Remove from the heat.

To serve

Cut the skin from the watermelon and dice the flesh into small cubes. Cut the skin from the mango and grate the flesh. Arrange the fruit in piles on a serving platter.

Add the fried Spice Paste to the pot containing the duck. Bring the pot back to a simmer for 5 minutes. Add the fish sauce, Tamarind Juice and guava juice and taste for a balance of flavors, adjusting if required.

Transfer the curry to a serving dish and sprinkle with Fried Shallots and coriander. Serve the fruit on the side.

Fried snapper with dry red curry

1 tablespoon peanut oil
⅓ cup + 1 tablespoon (100 ml) coconut cream
½ cup (100 g) Red Curry Paste (page 10)
3 tablespoons shaved palm sugar
1 tablespoon fish sauce
1¼ cups (300 ml) coconut milk
3 cups (750ml) vegetable oil, for frying
6 baby snapper fillets (skin on), weighing
    around 5 oz (150 g) each
2¾ cups (350 g) rice flour
1 cup (150 g) Fried Chili Peanuts (page 19)
    or roasted peanuts, coarsely chopped
18 fresh lychees, peeled and pitted,
    juices reserved
2 kaffir lime leaves, finely sliced
2 red finger-length chilies, finely sliced
2 tablespoons freshly-squeezed lime juice
1 cup (50 g) coriander leaves (cilantro)
8 Thai basil leaves, torn
½ cup (100 g) Fried Shallots (page 19)

Serves 6

This is a delicious curry and very simple. If you can get hold of them, try mangosteen segments instead of lychees.

Make the Red Curry Paste, Fried Chili Peanuts and Fried Shallots by following the recipes on pages 10 and 19.

Heat the peanut oil in a large heavy-based saucepan and add the coconut cream. Fry over medium heat until the coconut cream splits (when the oils and solids separate and it begins to smell nutty). Add the Red Curry Paste and fry until fragrant (around 5 minutes). Add the palm sugar and fish sauce and continue to cook until the sugar begins to caramelize, turning a deep red color. Add the coconut milk and bring to a simmer, then remove from the heat.

Heat the oil in a wok to 350°F (180°C). Dredge the snapper fillets in the rice flour, dusting off any excess, then fry the fish in batches until crisp and golden. Drain on paper towels.

Bring the curry back to a simmer and taste for seasoning. Stir through the peanuts, lychees (and juice), kaffir lime leaves, chilies and lime juice. Serve immediately with the curry spooned over the fried snapper. Garnish with coriander leaves, Thai basil and Fried Shallots.

Green chicken curry
with okra and fried salted duck eggs

6 large chicken thighs on the bone (skin on)

3 tablespoons fish sauce

3 cups (750ml) vegetable oil, for frying

1 tablespoon peanut oil

¾ cup (150 g) Green Curry Paste (page 9)

⅓ cup + 1 tablespoon (100 ml) coconut cream

2 cups (500 ml) coconut milk

10 okra, coarsely chopped

3 tablespoons freshly-squeezed lime juice

1½ tablespoons Palm Sugar Syrup (page 18)

1 cup (40 g) Thai basil leaves, torn

3 red finger-length chilies, deseeded and finely sliced lengthwise

½ cup (100 g) Fried Shallots (page 19)

Eggs

6 Salted Duck Eggs (page 22)

2 cups (500 ml) vegetable oil, for frying

Serves 6

Okra is a vegetable native to Africa but it is grown widely in tropical areas around the world and used frequently in Southeast Asian cooking. Okra has natural thickening properties when cooked for a long time, or if cooked for just a short time as in this dish, it adds a crunchy texture. Although this curry can be served without the salted duck eggs, they do add a nice richness.

Make the Green Curry Paste, Palm Sugar Syrup and Fried Shallots by following the recipes on pages 9, 18 and 19.

Make shallow incisions with a knife across the surface of the chicken thighs. Place them in a bowl and add 1½ tablespoons of the fish sauce, massaging it into the meat with your fingers. Transfer to the refrigerator to marinate for an hour.

Heat the oil in a wok to 350°F (180°C). Remove the chicken thighs from the marinade and pat dry with paper towels, then fry them in batches until crisp and golden (around 5 minutes). Drain on paper towels.

Heat the peanut oil in a heavy-based pan or saucepan and add the coconut cream. Fry over medium heat until the coconut cream splits (when the oils and solids separate and it begins to smell nutty) then add the Green Curry Paste. Fry until fragrant (around 5 minutes), stirring to make sure it doesn't catch.

Transfer the fried paste to a wok or medium-sized pot and add the coconut milk. Bring to a boil then add the chicken thighs and okra. Simmer for 10 minutes then remove from the heat while you prepare the Salted Duck Eggs by following the recipe on page 22.

Eggs

Heat the oil in a wok to 350°F (180°C). Blot any water from the Salted Duck Eggs with paper towels, then fry until crisp and golden. Drain on paper towels.

To serve

Bring the curry back to a simmer and add the remaining fish sauce, lime juice and Palm Sugar Syrup. Taste for a balance of flavors, adjusting if required.

Transfer the curry to a serving bowl and scatter with the fried Eggs. Sprinkle with the Thai basil, chilies and Fried Shallots.

Penang-style beef curry with betel leaves and crispy fish floss

2 lbs (1 kg) boneless beef shank, cubed

4 cups (1 liter) coconut milk

1 stalk lemongrass, tender inner part of bottom third only, bruised and cut in half

4 kaffir lime leaves, torn

Spice paste

1 whole nutmeg, grated

⅓ (50 g) cup roasted peanuts

6 Asian shallots, coarsely chopped

4 cloves garlic, coarsely chopped

1 in (2½ cm) peeled galangal root, coarsely chopped

8 dried red finger-length chilies, deseeded and soaked in warm water for 30 minutes, coarsely chopped

1 stalk lemongrass, tender inner part of bottom third only, finely sliced

4 coriander (cilantro) roots, washed and coarsely chopped

1 teaspoon sea salt

Curry

1 tablespoon peanut oil

⅓ cup + 1 tablespoon (100 ml) coconut cream

⅓ cup (60 g) shaved palm sugar

1¼ cups (300 ml) coconut milk

3 tablespoons freshly-squeezed lime juice

2 tablespoons fish sauce

1 cup betel leaves, torn

1 cup (300 g) Crispy Fish Floss (page 19)

Serves 6

Penang curry is a popular Thai curry that actually originated from Malaysia. It is traditionally based on chicken, but the slow-cooked beef shank provides a lovely gelatinous texture. A great substitute for the shank is oxtail.

Make the Crispy Fish Floss by following the recipe on page 19.

Bring a medium-sized pot of water to a boil and add the beef. Simmer for 10 minutes, then drain and refresh the beef under cold running water.

Rinse the pot and add the coconut milk, lemongrass and kaffir lime leaves. Bring to a boil and add the beef. Simmer gently for 3–4 hours or until tender, topping up with water occasionally as the liquid evaporates. Set aside.

Spice paste

Pound the ingredients to a fine paste using a mortar and pestle. Alternatively, pound to a coarse paste with a mortar and pestle and finish with a food processor.

Curry

Remove the beef from the stewing liquid with a slotted spoon. Reserve 1⅔ cups (400 ml) of the liquid.

Heat the peanut oil in a heavy-based pan or saucepan and add the coconut cream. Fry over medium heat until the coconut cream splits (when the oils and solids separate and it begins to smell nutty). Add the Spice Paste and fry until fragrant (around 5 minutes), stirring to make sure it doesn't catch. Add the palm sugar and cook until the mixture begins to caramelize, turning a dark red color.

Transfer the paste to a wok or medium-sized pot and add the reserved stewing liquid and coconut milk. Simmer for 20 minutes. Add the beef, and once heated through, add the lime juice and fish sauce. Taste for a balance of flavors, adjusting if necessary. Fold the betel leaves through the curry and transfer to a serving dish. Top with the Crispy Fish Floss and serve.

Yellow chicken curry with caramelized eggplant salad

6 large chicken thighs on the bone (skin on)

½ tablespoon Roasted Shrimp Paste (page 9)

3 tablespoons peanut oil

¾ cup (150 g) Yellow Curry Paste (page 10)

2½ cups (625 ml) coconut milk

3 tablespoons Tamarind Paste (page 18)

1 tablespoon fish sauce

2 tablespoons freshly-squeezed lime juice

1 tablespoon Palm Sugar Syrup (page 18)

Salad

2 medium Asian eggplants (long eggplants), peeled and cut into large chunks

⅓ cup + 1 tablespoon (100 ml) sweet soy sauce

⅓ cup + 1 tablespoon (100 ml) peanut oil

6 cloves garlic, unpeeled

5 Asian shallots, finely sliced

8 cherry tomatoes, halved

2 cups (300 g) green beans cut into lengths, blanched

2 tablespoons Fried Chili Peanuts (page 19) or roasted peanuts

1 stalk lemongrass, tender inner part of bottom third only, finely sliced

4 kaffir lime leaves, finely sliced

½ tablespoon dried shrimp

½ cup (25 g) coriander leaves (cilantro)

½ cup (20 g) mint leaves

8 Thai basil leaves, torn

2 tablespoons freshly-squeezed lime juice

1½ tablespoons fish sauce

1 tablespoon Palm Sugar Syrup (page 18)

Serves 6

This eggplant, tomato and green bean salad was inspired by a dish I had in Indonesia several years ago and is a great match for the curry. Eggplant is such an underrated vegetable in the West. The salad is made using the Thai technique of bruising the ingredients using a mortar and pestle.

Make the Roasted Shrimp Paste, Yellow Curry Paste, Palm Sugar Syrup, Tamarind Paste and Fried Chili Peanuts by following the recipes on pages 9, 10, 18 and 19.

Combine the chicken, Roasted Shrimp Paste and 2 tablespoons of the peanut oil in a bowl. Place in the refrigerator to marinate for 2–3 hours (or overnight), then place the chicken thighs in a steamer and steam for 25 minutes or until cooked through.

Heat the remaining peanut oil in a medium-sized pot and fry the Yellow Curry Paste over medium heat until fragrant (around 5 minutes), stirring to make sure it doesn't catch. Add the coconut milk and bring to a boil, then remove from the heat and set aside to cool while you make the Salad.

Salad

In a mixing bowl, coat the eggplant pieces in sweet soy sauce. Heat the peanut oil in a pan until smoking then add the eggplant. Pan-fry, turning regularly, until soft and caramelized (around 10 minutes).

Heat the oven to 350°F (180°C) and roast the garlic until tender (around 20 minutes). When cool enough to touch, slip the cloves out of their skins.

Using a large mortar and pestle, lightly pound the garlic, shallots, cherry tomatoes, green beans, peanuts, lemongrass, kaffir lime leaves, dried shrimp, coriander and mint leaves, and Thai basil until everything is slightly bruised. Add the caramelized eggplant, lime juice, fish sauce and Palm Sugar Syrup and combine.

To serve

Add the chicken thighs to the curry and simmer for 20 minutes. Add the Tamarind Paste, fish sauce, lime juice and Palm Sugar Syrup and taste for a good balance of flavors, adjusting if required. Transfer the curry to a serving bowl and accompany with the eggplant Salad.

Crab curry with crispy noodles

The idea behind the fried noodles is that by the time you are finished eating the crab, the noodles will have soaked up the curry juices and will be extremely flavorful. Begin this recipe the day before you plan to serve it.

Make the Roasted Shrimp Paste, Curry Powder and Asian Brown Chicken Stock by following the recipes on pages 9, 10 and 11.

Kill the crab quickly and humanely by turning it onto its back and inserting a large metal skewer in its middle where the flaps meet. Leave the skewer inside the crab for 3–4 minutes or until the crab has died.

Use your fingers to pull the top shell away from the body and discard. Discard the gills and rinse the crab. With a cleaver or a large, sharp knife, cut the crab into six pieces leaving the claws and legs attached. Crack the claws and legs with a mallet or the back of a cleaver (this helps them to cook evenly and allows the flavors to get in).

Combine the coconut milk, kaffir lime leaves, lemongrass and chilies in a deep bowl. Add the crab pieces. Coat the crab in the marinade and refrigerate overnight.

Spice paste
Pound the ingredients to a fine paste using a mortar and pestle. Alternatively, pound to a coarse paste with a mortar and pestle and finish with a food processor.

Crispy noodles
Heat the oil in a wok to 350°F (180°C) and fry the noodles until crisp (around 3 minutes). Drain on paper towels and let them cool to room temperature.

Curry
Remove the crab from the coconut marinade, reserving the marinade (there should be around 1⅔ cups (400 ml)—but if not, add extra coconut milk). Heat the peanut oil in a heavy-based pan or saucepan and add the coconut cream. Fry over medium heat until the coconut cream splits (when the oils and solids separate and it begins to smell nutty). Add the Spice Paste and fry until fragrant (around 5 minutes), stirring to make sure it doesn't catch.

Transfer the paste to a wok and add the crab pieces. Cook over medium heat until the shells begin to turn red (around 3 minutes). Add the reserved marinade, coconut milk and Chicken Stock and simmer for 5 minutes.

Add the palm sugar, fish sauce and lime juice and taste for a balance of flavors, adjusting if necessary. Transfer the curry to a large serving bowl and scatter with coriander leaves and the Crispy Noodles. Serve the lime wedges on the side.

---

1 live crab weighing around 3 lbs (1½ kgs)

2 cups (500 ml) coconut milk

4 kaffir lime leaves, torn

1 stalk lemongrass, tender inner part of bottom third only, bruised and cut in quarters

2 red bird's-eye chilies, split and deseeded

Spice paste

4 Asian shallots, coarsely chopped

6 cloves garlic, coarsely chopped

1 in (2½ cm) peeled ginger, coarsely chopped

1 in (2½ cm) peeled fresh turmeric root, coarsely chopped

3 dried red finger-length chilies, deseeded and soaked in warm water for 30 minutes, coarsely chopped

5 coriander (cilantro) roots, washed and coarsely chopped

1 teaspoon Roasted Shrimp Paste (page 9)

1 tablespoon Curry Powder (page 10)

Crispy noodles

2 cups (500 ml) vegetable oil, for frying

4 oz (100 g) fresh egg noodles

Curry

1 tablespoon peanut oil

¾ cup (190 ml) coconut cream

1¼ cups (300 ml) coconut milk

⅔ cup (150 ml) Asian Brown Chicken Stock (page 11)

1½ tablespoons shaved palm sugar

2½ tablespoons fish sauce

3½ tablespoons freshly-squeezed lime juice

2 cups (100 g) coriander leaves (cilantro)

2 limes, quartered

Serves 6

Beef shin and sweet potato rendang

3 lbs (1½ kgs) beef shin or beef brisket

¾ cup (200 ml) sweet soy sauce

6 cloves garlic, bruised

1 in (2½ cm) peeled ginger, bruised and
  chopped

1 tablespoon coriander seeds

3 cups (750ml) vegetable oil, for frying

Spice paste

2 tablespoons coriander seeds

1 tablespoon cumin seeds

12 Asian shallots, coarsely chopped

5 cloves garlic, coarsely chopped

¾ in (1½ cm) peeled ginger, coarsely
  chopped

1 in (2½ cm) peeled galangal root, chopped

¾ in (1½ cm) peeled fresh turmeric root,
  coarsely chopped

3 stalks lemongrass, tender inner part of
  bottom third only, finely sliced

4 dried red finger-length chilies, deseeded
  and soaked in warm water for 30 minutes,
  coarsely chopped

4 red bird's-eye chilies, deseeded and chopped

1 cup (100 g) grated fresh coconut, lightly
  dry-roasted

1 tablespoon Curry Powder (page 10)

Curry

1 tablespoon peanut oil

⅓ cup + 1 tablespoon (100 ml) coconut cream

2¾ cups (700 ml) coconut milk

2½ tablespoons fish sauce

6 curry leaves, torn (or 4 fresh bay leaves)

6 kaffir lime leaves, torn

1 sweet potato, peeled and cut into
  bite-size cubes

½ cup (20 g) mint leaves

¼ cup (50 g) Fried Shallots (page 19)

1 green finger-length chili, finely sliced

6 cherry tomatoes, halved

½ cup (25 g) bean sprouts

2 limes, quartered

Serves 6

Rendang curries originated in Indonesia but today they are made all over Asia. Beef and chicken are the most common ingredients. I like to use ox cheeks as they become very tender and are full of flavor.

Make the Curry Powder and Fried Shallots by following the recipes on pages 10 and 19.

Combine the ox cheeks in a large bowl with the sweet soy sauce, garlic, ginger and coriander seeds. Marinate in the refrigerator for 2–3 hours (or overnight).

Heat the oil in a wok to 350°F (180°C). Remove the ox cheeks from the marinade and pat dry with paper towels. Fry the meat in batches until crisp, dark and caramelized on the surface (around 10 minutes), then drain on paper towels. Set aside until needed.

Spice paste

Dry-roast the coriander and cumin seeds in a wok over medium heat until fragrant (1–2 minutes), stirring constantly to avoid burning. Remove from the heat and pound to a fine powder with a mortar and pestle. Add the remaining ingredients and pound to a fine paste. Alternatively, pound to a coarse paste with a mortar and pestle and finish with a food processor.

Curry

Heat the peanut oil in a medium-sized pot and fry the coconut cream over medium heat until the coconut cream splits (when the oils and solids separate and it begins to smell nutty). Add the Spice Paste and fry until fragrant (around 5 minutes), stirring to make sure it doesn't catch. Add the fried ox cheeks, coconut milk, fish sauce, curry leaves and kaffir lime leaves and bring to a simmer. Cook gently, covered with a lid, for 1½ hours, then add the sweet potato and simmer for a further 30 minutes or until the potato is tender. Taste for seasoning.

To serve, transfer the curry to a serving dish and garnish with the mint, Fried Shallots, chili, cherry tomatoes and bean sprouts. Serve the lime wedges on the side.

Red duck curry with lychees

2 tablespoons coriander seeds
1 tablespoon cumin seeds
4 star anise pods
1 whole nutmeg, cracked
1 teaspoon white peppercorns
1 duck weighing around 4 lbs (2 kgs)
3 cups (750ml) vegetable oil, for frying

Curry
1 tablespoon peanut oil
⅓ cup + 1 tablespoon (100 ml) coconut cream
¾ cup (150 g) Red Curry Paste (page 9)
2 cups (500 ml) coconut milk
18 fresh lychees, peeled and pitted
  (juices reserved)
3 tablespoons freshly-squeezed lime juice
2 tablespoons fish sauce
3 tablespoons Palm Sugar Syrup (page 18)
2 tablespoons coconut cream (optional)
1 cup (40 g) Thai basil leaves
½ cup (100 g) Fried Shallots (page 19)

Serves 6

Steaming and then frying poultry gives you the best of both worlds—moist flesh and crispy skin. By the time you're finished, the flavor of the spices rubbed into this duck will have gone right through the meat. Fresh lychees are a great marriage with this dish, adding a sweet, fragrant note.

Make the Red Curry Paste and Palm Sugar Syrup by following the recipe on pages 9 and 18.

Dry-roast the coriander, cumin, star anise, nutmeg and peppercorns in a wok over medium heat until fragrant (1–2 minutes), stirring constantly to avoid burning. Remove from the heat and grind to a fine powder using a mortar and pestle or spice grinder.

Use a cleaver or a large, sharp knife to cut the duck in half lengthwise. Cut the backbone away from the duck and discard. Slice off the wings where they meet the breasts and discard. Cut off the legs between the thigh and body and separate the thigh from the drumsticks by cutting through the joint. Cut the breasts from the rib cage (but leave them still attached to the breastplate). Cut the breasts and thighs through the bones into three pieces each. Leave the drumsticks whole.

Place the duck pieces in a mixing bowl and rub the spice powder into the flesh. Transfer the pieces to a heatproof dish and steam for 40 minutes or until cooked through. Set aside to cool, reserving any juices that have pooled in the dish. Chill the duck in the refrigerator (this helps the skin become crisp when deep-fried).

Heat the oil in a wok to 350°F (180°C) and fry the duck pieces in batches until crisp (around 5 minutes). Drain on paper towels.

Curry
Heat the peanut oil in a medium-sized pot and add the coconut cream. Fry over medium heat until the coconut cream splits (when the oils and solids separate and it begins to smell nutty). Add the Red Curry Paste and fry until fragrant (around 5 minutes), stirring to make sure it doesn't catch. Add the coconut milk, reserved steaming juices and lychee juices. Simmer for 5 minutes, then add the duck and simmer until just heated through. Add the lime juice, fish sauce and Palm Sugar Syrup and taste for a balance of flavors, adjusting if necessary.

Transfer the curry to a serving dish and drizzle with the coconut cream (if using). Scatter with the Thai basil, Fried Shallots and lychees.

Seafood

Salt and pepper oysters with roasted red bell pepper and black bean dressing

24 large unshucked oysters
3 cups (750 ml) vegetable oil
1 portion Tempura Batter (page 23)
1 tablespoon Salt and Pepper Mix
(page 11)

Dressing
2 red bell peppers
1 tablespoon olive oil
1 medium red onion, finely chopped
4 cloves garlic, finely chopped
1 in (2½ cm) peeled ginger, finely chopped
⅔ cup (150 ml) freshly-squeezed lime juice
3 tablespoons soy sauce
2 tablespoons dried salted black beans,
    gently rinsed

Serves 6

This dressing is one of my favorite—sweet from the bell peppers, salty from the black beans and soy sauce, and sour from the lime juice. It is great with most seafood.

Make the Salt and Pepper Mix and Tempura Batter by following the recipes on pages 11 and 23.

Dressing
Preheat the oven to 400°F (200°C). Brush the bell peppers with olive oil and roast until the skins start to blister (10–15 minutes). When cool enough to handle, peel the skins and scrape out the seeds. Finely dice the flesh.
    Combine the bell pepper in a bowl with the remaining ingredients and allow to rest for 10 minutes. Taste for a balance of flavors, adjusting if necessary.

Oysters
Clean the oysters with a stiff brush under cold running water to remove any grit. To open, hold an oyster firmly with a glove or dish towel and insert an oyster knife between the shells near the hinge end. Twist the knife to pry the shells apart, working the knife around the shells until they are completely loose. Open the shell and dislodge the oyster by gently sliding the knife between the oyster and the shell it is attached to. Discard the smaller shell, reserving the larger one.
    Heat the oil in a wok to 350°F (180°C). Dip the oysters in the Tempura Batter and fry them in batches until crisp (around 1 minute). Drain on paper towels.
    Gently toss the fried oysters in the Salt and Pepper Mix and place them back in their shells. Top each one with a tablespoon of the Dressing and serve immediately.

Fried shrimp with cucumber salad and lime chili syrup

18 fresh jumbo shrimp (about 1½ lbs/ 750 g)

3 cups (750 ml) vegetable oil, for frying

4 egg whites, lightly beaten

3 cups (375 g) rice flour

Lime chili syrup

⅔ cup (150 ml) water

1 cup (200 g) shaved palm sugar

1 red finger-length chili, deseeded and finely chopped

1 green finger-length chili, deseeded and finely chopped

Grated Rind and juice of 1 lime

Salad

2 limes

1 cucumber, peeled and diced

2 tablespoons Fried Chili Peanuts (page 19), coarsely chopped

8 cherry tomatoes, halved

1 medium red onion, finely sliced

2 red finger-length chilies, finely sliced

1 cup (40 g) mint leaves

1 cup (50 g) coriander leaves (cilantro)

Serves 6

Make the Fried Chili Peanuts by following the recipe on page 19.

Lime chili syrup

Place the water and palm sugar in a saucepan and bring to a boil. Simmer until the mixture begins to turn a light caramel color (around 10 minutes). You will need to brush or scrape the sides of the saucepan occasionally to stop crystals from forming. Remove from the heat and set aside to cool. Once cool, add the chilies, grated lime rind and juice.

Salad

Cut the peel from the limes and segment them by cutting as close to the membrane as possible on either side of each natural segment. Work your way around the limes until you have cut all the segments out. Combine with the remaining ingredients and place on a serving platter.

Shrimp

Shell the shrimp, leaving the heads and tail tips intact. With the tip of a sharp, small knife, make a small cut along the center of the tails and pull or scrape out the vein and discard.

Heat the oil in a wok to 350°F (180°C). Dip the shrimp in egg whites and then in the rice flour, dusting off any excess. Fry the shrimp in batches until crisp and golden (around 1 minute). Drain on paper towels.

Place the fried shrimp on top of the Salad and drizzle with the Lime Chili Syrup. Serve immediately.

Steamed scallops with pork and peanut caramel and thai herbs

18 large fresh scallops on the half-shell

Pork and peanut caramel
10 oz (300 g) lean pork belly
2 tablespoons fish sauce
2 cups (500 ml) vegetable oil, for frying
⅓ cup (60 g) shaved palm sugar
2½ tablespoons water
3 tablespoons Fried Chili Peanuts (page 19) or roasted peanuts
3 cloves garlic, coarsely chopped
¾ in (1½ cm) peeled ginger, coarsely chopped
1 red bird's-eye chili, deseeded and coarsely chopped
4 kaffir lime leaves, finely sliced into thin shreds
2 tablespoons freshly-squeezed lime juice

Garnishes
1 cup (50 g) coriander leaves (cilantro)
1 cup (40 g) mint leaves
1 cup (40 g) Thai basil leaves
½ teaspoon dried shrimp powder (made by processing several dried shrimp in a blender or food processor)
1 teaspoon Roasted Dried Shrimp (page 21)
2 red finger-length chilies, finely sliced
6 Asian shallots, finely sliced into rings
3 kaffir lime leaves, finely sliced into thin shreds

Serves 6

Make the Fried Chili Peanuts and Roasted Dried Shrimp by following the recipes on pages 19 and 21.

Pork and peanut caramel
Trim off the pork skin and discard. Place the pork in a bowl and add 1 tablespoon of the fish sauce. Coat thoroughly and marinate for 20 minutes.

Transfer the pork to a steamer and steam for 45 minutes until the pork is cooked through (test by inserting a skewer into the meat to see if the juices run clear). Set the pork aside to cool, then chill in the refrigerator for a few hours to firm.

Heat the vegetable oil in a wok to 350°F (180°C). Dice the pork into small cubes and fry until crisp. Remove from the oil with a slotted spoon and drain on paper towels.

Place the palm sugar and water in a saucepan and bring to a boil. Cook until the sugar begins to turn a light caramel color (around 10 minutes). You will need to brush or scrape the sides of the saucepan occasionally to stop crystals from forming. Remove from the heat.

Using a mortar and pestle pound the peanuts, garlic, ginger, chili and kaffir lime leaves to a fine paste.

Add the paste, pork, lime juice and remaining fish sauce to the caramel and combine. Check for a balance of flavors, adjusting with more lime juice or fish sauce if necessary.

To serve
Combine the Garnishes ingredients and set aside.

Remove the scallops from their shells. To clean the shells of any impurities, place them in a pot of water and bring to a boil. Refresh the shells under cold water then drain. Gently rinse the scallops and place them back in their shells.

Top each scallop with a tablespoon of the Pork and Peanut Caramel and place the scallop shells into a steamer (or several steamers). Steam for 3–5 minutes or until the scallops are firm to the touch. Remove from the steamer and top with the Garnishes. Serve immediately.

Tempura soft-shell crab with fried chilies

6 soft-shell crabs

3 cups (750 ml) vegetable oil, for frying

12 cloves garlic

4 tablespoons fresh green peppercorns

3 red finger-length chilies

3 green finger-length chilies

1⅓ cups (175 g) rice flour

1 portion Tempura Batter (page 23)

2 red bird's-eye chilies, deseeded and
   finely chopped

½ tablespoon sea salt

4 green onions (scallions), white ends only,
   finely sliced

Serves 6

Soft-shell crabs—crabs that have recently shed their shells and are protected by only a very thin skin—are eaten whole, shells and all. They are about the size of the palm of your hand and need to be handled very gently. They are generally sold frozen. I ate them in Thailand and was so impressed that I always go back to that same beach restaurant where they are served. In this dish the tempura becomes crisp, enclosing the beautiful sweet flavor of the crab within. Accompany this with some watercress, mint leaves and lemon wedges.

Make the Tempura Batter by following the recipe on page 23.

If the crabs are frozen, place them on a wire rack set above a large dish and leave them in the refrigerator to drain overnight. They need to be defrosted and dry when fried.

Heat the vegetable oil in a wok to 350°F (180°C). Pound the garlic and peppercorns to a fine paste using a mortar and pestle and fry the paste in the oil until crisp and fragrant. It will float on the surface and can be removed with a slotted spoon. Drain on paper towels.

Fry the whole red and green chilies until their skins begin to blister (3–4 minutes). Drain on paper towels.

Carefully dredge the crabs in the rice flour, shaking off any excess. Dip the crabs in the Tempura Batter and then fry them in batches until crisp (3–4 minutes). Drain on paper towels then cut them in half.

Combine the fried paste with the chopped chilies, salt and green onions. Add the whole fried chilies and crab halves and toss to combine. Serve immediately.

Steamed sea bass with mushrooms, soy mirin broth and XO sauce

2 lbs (1 kg) sea bass or cod fillet (skin on)
½ cup (125 ml) XO Sauce (page 17)

Broth
1⅔ cups (400 ml) Fish Stock (page 13)
⅔ cup (150 ml) soy sauce
⅓ cup (80 g) raw rock sugar crystals
⅓ cup (80 ml) mirin
½ cup (125 ml) rice wine vinegar
1 tablespoon sesame oil
¾ in (1½ cm) peeled ginger, sliced into thin shreds
4 dried black Chinese mushrooms
2 tablespoons instant dashi stock powder

Mushrooms
1 tablespoon peanut oil
8 oz (250 g) mixed fresh Asian mushrooms such as shiitake, oyster, enoki, straw, shimeji or wood ear, bases trimmed if necessary, sliced/torn
1 bunch (1 oz/40 g) garlic chives cut into lengths

Serves 6

This is a very delicate dish that we serve at **ezard** regularly. Asian sea bass is a great fish to steam. It is not quite as flavorsome as European sea bass, but the texture is similar. Substitute cod, whiting or perch if you can't find sea bass. The fish is served in just a small amount of broth and topped with XO sauce. Green vegetables such as peas, beans and asparagus can be used instead of mushrooms if preferred.

Make the Fish Stock and XO Sauce by following the recipes on pages 13 and 17.

Place the Broth ingredients in a saucepan and bring to a boil. Simmer for 3 minutes then remove from the heat. Set aside to allow the flavors to infuse while you prepare the fish and mushrooms.

Use a sharp knife to score the skin of the fish crosswise. Cut the fish into six pieces. Place the fish fillets onto a lightly oiled heatproof dish and insert into a steamer. Gently steam until cooked through (5–8 minutes).

Meanwhile, prepare the Mushrooms. Heat the peanut oil in a wok over high heat and add the mushrooms and chives. Stir-fry for a minute until lightly seared, then remove from the heat.

Strain and reheat the Broth. Divide the fish between serving bowls and follow with the Broth, Mushrooms and a tablespoon of the XO sauce.

Stir-fried squid with green beans, peanuts and Asian celery

3 fresh whole baby squid (combined weight of around 1½ lbs/750 g)

1 tablespoon peanut oil

1 cup (150 g) green beans sliced into pieces

2 red finger-length chilies, finely sliced

¼ cup (40 g) Fried Chili Peanuts (page 19), finely chopped

2½ tablespoons oyster sauce

⅓ cup + 1 tablespoon (100 ml) soy sauce

2 tablespoons Curry Powder (page 10)

8 cherry tomatoes, halved

4 coriander (cilantro) roots, washed and finely chopped

Leaves from 1 bunch Asian celery

¼ cup (50 g) Fried Shallots (page 19)

2 limes, quartered

Serves 6

Make the Curry Powder, Fried Chili Peanuts and Fried Shallots by following the recipes on pages 10 and 19.

To prepare the squid, twist and pull the tentacles away from the body—the internal organs and head will come away too. Cut the tentacles just below the head, discarding the head. Draw out the piece of transparent cartilage from the body and discard. Carefully peel off the wings then strip the wings and body of the dark membrane. Rinse the wings and tubes and pat dry.

Insert a knife into a tube and slit it open so it will open flat as a rectangle. On the outer surface score the tube in a criss-cross pattern with the tip of a knife, then slice the tube into bite-sized pieces. Repeat with the remaining tubes and do the same with the wings. Cut the tentacles into bite-sized pieces.

Heat the peanut oil in a wok over high heat then add the green beans, chilies and Fried Chili Peanuts and stir-fry for 1–2 minutes or until slightly charred. Add the squid and stir-fry for a further 30 seconds. Add the oyster sauce, soy sauce, Curry Powder and cherry tomatoes and bring to a simmer. Add the coriander roots, Asian celery and Fried Shallots and combine, then remove from the heat.

Transfer to a serving dish and serve the lime wedges on the side.

Tiger beer, chili jam and coconut mussels

4 lbs (2 kgs) large fresh mussels in the shell

2 tablespoons peanut oil

3 cloves garlic, finely chopped

10 garlic chives (or asparagus spears, bases trimmed) sliced into lengths

1 cup (250 ml) Tiger beer

½ cup (125 ml) Chili Jam (page 13)

¾ cup (200 ml) coconut cream

1 cup (40 g) Thai basil leaves

1 cup (50 g) coriander leaves (cilantro)

2 limes, quartered

Serves 6

Tiger beer has a fresh flavor and silky texture that goes well with Asian food, whether you're drinking it, cooking with it or both. Other crisp, refreshing beers also work well in this dish.

Make the Chili Jam by following the recipe on page 13.

Scrub the mussels thoroughly under cold water. De-beard them by giving the beard a firm pull down towards the tip of the mussel.

Heat the peanut oil in a wok and add the garlic and garlic chives or asparagus. Stir-fry until fragrant (1–2 minutes). Turn up the heat, add the beer and Chili Jam and bring to a simmer. Add the mussels. Place a lid or an upturned bowl over the wok and steam until the mussels open (around 1–2 minutes). Discard any mussels that don't open.

Transfer to a serving dish and drizzle with the coconut cream. Scatter with Thai basil and coriander leaves and serve the lime wedges on the side.

Lime cured scallop salad
with sour cream and cucumber oil

24 large sea scallops (roe removed)

1 teaspoon sea salt

Juice of 2 limes

2 kaffir lime leaves, finely sliced into thin
shreds

1 stalk lemongrass, tender inner part of
bottom third only, finely sliced

2 large red chilies, finely sliced

1 cup (50 g) coriander leaves (cilantro)

1 cup (40 g) mint leaves, torn

⅓ cup (80 ml) Hot and Sour Dressing
(page 17)

⅓ cup + 1 tablespoon (100 ml) sour cream

⅓ cup (50 g) Fried Chili Peanuts (page 19),
coarsely chopped

2 tablespoons salmon roe

1 tablespoon cucumber oil (page 233)

Sea scallops, sometimes called Pacific scallops, are larger, milder and firmer than other scallops, which makes them ideal for a dish like this. They are generally sold without the shell and frozen. Sour cream and salmon roe add a wonderful creaminess to the lime and chili in this salad.

Make the Hot and Sour Dressing and Fried Chili Peanuts by following the recipes on pages 17 and 19.

If the scallops are frozen, place them on a wire rack set above a large dish and cover with a damp cloth. Leave them in the refrigerator to drain and defrost for 2 hours.

Slice each scallop in half lengthwise. Place the scallops in a wide bowl and sprinkle with the salt. Add the lime juice and gently rub the salt and lime into the scallops with your fingertips. Once all the scallops have been briefly massaged, let them stand for 30 seconds and then drain (without rinsing).

Combine the kaffir lime leaves, lemongrass, chilies, coriander leaves and mint in a mixing bowl. Toss through the scallops. Divide the salad between six small serving bowls and pour a little of the Hot and Sour Dressing over each one. Place a heaped teaspoon of sour cream on top and garnish with peanuts and salmon roe. Drizzle with the cucumber oil and serve.

Serves 6

Tempura fish with spiced chili salt and cucumber mint pickle salad

Salad

1 cup (40 g) mint leaves

1½ tablespoons rice wine vinegar

Juice of half a lemon

2 tablespoons sugar

1 tablespoon water

2 cucumbers, diced

6 Asian shallots, finely sliced

3 red finger-length chilies, finely sliced

Tempura Fish

2 lbs (1 kg) catfish fillets or flathead tails

1 portion Tempura Batter (page 23)

3 cups (750 ml) vegetable oil, for frying

2 tablespoons Spiced Chili Salt (page 11)

Serves 6

This is a quick dish with refreshing summer flavors. Make the mint pickle dressing as close to serving as possible, for maximum flavor. If you cannot find flathead fish, catfish is a good substitute.

Make the Spiced Chili Salt and Tempura Batter by following the recipes on pages 11 and 23.

Salad

To make the mint pickle dressing, place the mint, vinegar, lemon juice, sugar and water in a blender and puree. Taste for a good balance of sweet and sour flavors, adjusting if necessary. Combine the dressing in a bowl with the cucumber, shallots and chilies and set aside.

Tempura fish

Heat the oil in a wok to 350°F (180°C). Dip the fish pieces in the Tempua Batter and fry in batches until crisp and golden (2–3 minutes). Toss the fried fish in the Spiced Chili Salt and serve accompanied with the Salad.

Shrimp with roasted tomato sambal and toasted coconut

18 fresh jumbo shrimp (about 1½ lbs/ 750 g)

⅓ cup (80 ml) peanut oil

8 cherry tomatoes, halved

¾ cup (185 ml) Roasted Tomato Sambal (page 16)

2 kaffir lime leaves, sliced into thin shreds

1 stalk lemongrass, tender inner part of bottom third only, finely sliced

½ cup Toasted Coconut (page 21)

1 tablespoon Palm Sugar Syrup (page 18)

1 tablespoon fish sauce

2 tablespoons freshly-squeezed lime juice

½ cup (25 g) coriander leaves (cilantro)

Serves 6

Make the Roasted Tomato Sambal, Palm Sugar Syrup and Toasted Coconut by following the recipes on pages 16, 18 and 21.

Shell the shrimp, leaving the heads and tail tips intact. With the tip of a sharp, small knife, make a small cut along the center of the tails and pull or scrape out the veins. Combine the shrimp and peanut oil in a bowl.

Heat a wok over high heat and add half the shrimp. Stir-fry until the bodies turn white and the heads turn red. Remove and repeat with the remaining shrimp.

Return all the shrimp to the wok along with the cherry tomatoes, Roasted Tomato Sambal, kaffir lime leaves, lemongrass and Toasted Coconut. Bring to a simmer and add the Palm Sugar Syrup, fish sauce and lime juice. Taste for a balance of flavors, adjusting if necessary.

Transfer to a serving dish and garnish with the coriander leaves.

Crispy garlic calamari with green papaya and bean sprouts salad

3 fresh whole baby squid (combined weight of around 1½ lbs/750 g)

3 tablespoons fresh green peppercorns

5 cloves garlic, finely chopped

1 tablespoon shaved palm sugar

1½ tablespoons sea salt

3 cups (750 ml) vegetable oil, for frying

1¼ cups (150 g) rice flour

¾ cup (100 g) cornstarch

Salad

½ small green papaya, peeled and grated

½ cup (75 g) Fried Chili Peanuts (page 19)

½ cup (25 g) fresh bean sprouts

8 cherry tomatoes, halved

2 kaffir lime leaves, finely sliced into thin shreds

1 stalk lemongrass, tender inner part of bottom third only, finely sliced

½ cup (25 g) coriander leaves (cilantro)

½ cup (20 g) mint leaves

½ cup (20 g) Thai basil leaves

Dressing

2½ tablespoons freshly-squeezed lime juice

2½ tablespoons lemon juice

¼ cup (50 g) shaved palm sugar

½ tablespoon fish sauce

1 red bird's-eye chili, deseeded and finely chopped

Serves 6

Make the Fried Chili Peanuts by following the recipe on page 19.

Combine the Salad ingredients in a bowl. Combine the Dressing ingredients in another bowl and taste for a balance of flavors, adjusting if required—it should taste a little like lemonade.

To prepare the squid, twist and pull the tentacles away from the body—the internal organs and head will come away too. Cut the tentacles just below the head, discarding the head. Draw out the piece of transparent cartilage from the body and discard. Carefully peel off the wings and strip the wings and body of the dark membrane. Rinse the wings and tubes and pat dry. Slice the tubes into very thin rings, the wings into thin strips, and the tentacles into bite-sized pieces.

Heat the oil in a wok to 350°F (180°C). Pound the peppercorns, garlic, palm sugar and salt to a fine paste using a mortar and pestle, then fry the paste in the oil until crisp and fragrant. It will float on the surface and can be removed with a slotted spoon. Drain on paper towels.

Combine the rice flour and cornstarch in a bowl and thoroughly dredge the squid pieces. Try to get the flour inside the rings as well—a good coating of flour will make the squid crisp instead of chewy. Shake off any excess flour and fry the squid in batches until crisp and golden (40–50 seconds). Drain on paper towels.

Toss the squid in the fried paste. Combine the Salad and Dressing and place on a serving platter. Top with the squid and serve.

Steamed oysters in soy dressing with green onions and toasted sesame oil

24 large unshucked oysters
⅓ cup (80 ml) mirin
1 teaspoon sugar
1 cup (50 g) coriander leaves (cilantro)
6 green onions (scallions), finely sliced
1½ tablespoons sesame oil

Dressing
1 clove garlic, finely chopped
2 red bird's-eye chilies, deseeded and finely
  chopped
1 in (2½ cm) peeled ginger, finely chopped
1 teaspoon sugar
⅔ cup (150 ml) soy sauce
1½ tablespoons mirin
1 tablespoon rice wine vinegar

Serves 6

I like the simple Cantonese style of this dish. Heating the sesame oil before drizzling it over the oysters brings out its fragrance and flavor.

Combine the Dressing ingredients, stirring until the sugar dissolves, and set aside.

Clean the oysters with a stiff brush under cold running water to remove any grit. To open, hold an oyster firmly with a glove or dish towel and insert an oyster knife between the shells near the hinge end. Twist the knife to pry the shells apart, working the knife around the shells until they are completely loose. Open the shell and dislodge the oyster by gently sliding the knife between the oyster and the shell it is attached to. Discard the smaller shell, reserving the oyster in the larger one.

Combine the mirin and sugar, stirring until the sugar dissolves. Moisten each oyster with a small amount of the mirin and place the oysters into a steaming basket (or several steaming baskets). Steam for 1–2 minutes then transfer to a serving platter. Drizzle the Dressing over the oysters and garnish with the coriander leaves and green onions. Heat the sesame oil in a saucepan until smoking and drizzle it over the oysters and herbs. Serve immediately.

Salmon with Asian gazpacho and avocado fennel salad

2 lbs (1 kg) fresh salmon fillets (skin on)
2 tablespoons olive oil
½ tablespoon sea salt
3 tablespoons sour cream
3 tablespoons salmon roe

Gazpacho

2 cucumbers, peeled, deseeded and coarsely chopped
2 large ripe tomatoes, coarsely chopped
1 small red onion, coarsely chopped
2 green finger-length chilies, deseeded and finely chopped
4 cloves garlic, finely chopped
1 in (2½ cm) peeled ginger, finely chopped
½ cup (120 ml) rice wine vinegar
⅓ cup (80 ml) lemon juice
½ cup (120 ml) soy sauce
1 tablespoon Worcestershire sauce
¾ cup (200 ml) olive oil
10 Thai basil leaves
½ cup (25 g) coriander leaves (cilantro)
½ cup (20 g) mint leaves

Salad

2 limes
4 large ripe tomatoes, diced
2 ripe avocados, peeled and pitted, diced
1 small bulb fennel, diced
¼ cup dried black olives (or 10 fresh pitted olives)

Serves 6

A great dish to make during summer. The gazpacho is used as a sauce and is fantastic with most fish and seafood, or it can be served alone as an appetizer. The salad uses dried olives rather than olives in oil or brine as they have a stronger flavor and crunchy texture. You can find them at gourmet food stores.

Gazpacho

Combine the cucumbers, tomatoes, onion, chilies, garlic and ginger in a food processor and puree. (You can do this in batches if necessary.) Add the vinegar, lemon juice, soy sauce, Worcestershire and olive oil and pulse until blended. Taste for seasoning then add the Thai basil, coriander leaves and mint leaves and pulse until they are finely chopped but not pureed. Refrigerate the Gazpacho for 1 hour before using.

Salad

Cut the peel from the limes and segment them by cutting as close to the membrane as possible on either side of each natural segment. Work your way around the limes until you have cut all the segments out.

Combine the lime with the remaining ingredients and set aside.

To serve

With a pair of kitchen pliers or tweezers carefully remove the pin bones from the salmon, then cut the fillets into six portions.

Preheat the oven to 340°F (170°C). Heat the olive oil over high heat in a large skillet or pan. Season the skin of the salmon pieces with salt and place them into the skillet skin-side down. Fry until the skin is crisp (1–2 minutes). Place the skillet in the oven (or transfer the salmon to a hot oven tray) and cook for 4–5 minutes, or until cooked on the outside but still slightly pink in the middle.

Place the Gazpacho in wide serving bowls followed by the salmon and Salad. Garnish with sour cream and salmon roe.

Peppered crab with lemon

1 live crab weighing around 3 lbs/1½ kgs (or several smaller crabs equalling the same weight)

2½ tablespoons peanut oil

6 cloves garlic, finely chopped

2½ tablespoons oyster sauce

1¼ cups (300 ml) Asian Brown Chicken Stock (page 11)

4 green bird's-eye chilies, bruised

6 green onions (scallions) cut into lengths

1 tablespoon black peppercorns, lightly roasted and ground

1 lemon, quartered, plus the juice of 1 lemon

1 cup (50 g) coriander leaves (cilantro)

2 lemons, quartered, extra

Serves 6

This simple, flavorsome dish is wonderful in summer with cold beer.

Make the Asian Brown Chicken Stock by following the recipe on page 11.

Kill the crab quickly and humanely by turning it over on its back and inserting a large metal skewer in its middle where the flaps meet. Leave the spike inside the crab for 3–4 minutes or until the crab has died. Alternatively, place the crab in a freezer for 1 hour, which will send it to sleep.

Pull the top shell of the crab away from the body and discard. Discard the gills and rinse the crab. With a large sharp knife or cleaver, cut the crab into six pieces with the legs and claws attached. Crack the claws and legs with a mallet or the back of a cleaver (this helps them to cook evenly and allows the flavors to get in).

Heat the peanut oil in a wok and fry the garlic until fragrant and beginning to brown. Turn up the heat and add the crab pieces, oyster sauce, Chicken Stock, chilies, green onions, pepper, lemon wedges and lemon juice. Cover with a lid or an upturned bowl and steam the crab for around 8 minutes or until the shells turn deep red. Add a little extra Chicken Stock or water if the liquid evaporates too quickly, but allow the liquid to reduce at the end so that there is just enough sauce to coat the crab.

Transfer the crab and sauce to a serving dish and garnish with the coriander leaves. Serve the extra lemon wedges on the side.

Fried crabs with roasted bell pepper and yellow bean dressing

6 large fresh crabs (around 10 oz/300 g each)
⅓ cup + 1 tablespoon (100 ml) fish sauce
3 cups (750 ml) vegetable oil, for frying
3 cups (375 g) tapioca or rice flour
1 cup (50 g) coriander leaves (cilantro)
2 lemons, quartered

Dressing
1 red bell pepper
½ tablespoon olive oil
1 cup (250 ml) coconut cream
⅓ cup (80 ml) yellow bean paste
3 cloves garlic, finely chopped
4 Asian shallots, finely chopped
2 red bird's-eye chilies, deseeded and finely chopped
2 tablespoons shaved palm sugar
1 tablespoon fish sauce
2 tablespoons freshly-squeezed lime juice

Serves 6

This dish is one to eat with your hands, and with plenty of napkins. The sweet and sour flavors of the dressing go well with all kinds of seafood.

Dressing
Preheat the oven to 400°F (200°C). Brush the bell pepper with olive oil and roast until the skin starts to blister (10–15 minutes). When cool enough to handle, peel the skin and scrape out the seeds. Finely dice the flesh.

Heat the coconut cream in a saucepan until the coconut cream splits (when the oils and solids separate and it begins to smell nutty). Add the bell pepper, yellow bean paste, garlic, shallots and chili and simmer for 2 minutes. Add the palm sugar, fish sauce and lime juice and remove from the heat.

Crab
Use your fingers to pull the top shells of the crabs away from their bodies. Discard the gills and innards and rinse the crabs under cold running water. Use a cleaver or sharp knife to cut each crab into quarters (legs and claws attached). Crack the claws with a mallet or the back of a cleaver to help them cook evenly and let the flavors get in.

In a large bowl coat the crab pieces in fish sauce and marinate for 10 minutes. Drain.

Heat the vegetable oil in a wok to 350°F (180°C). Toss the marinated crab pieces in the tapioca or rice flour, dusting off any excess, and fry them in batches until the shells turn red (around 5 minutes). For garnish, fry a few of the top shells if you desire. Drain on paper towels.

Transfer the crabs to a serving platter and garnish with the coriander leaves and lemon wedges. Serve the Dressing on the side.

Stir-fried lobster with chili, black beans and Asian celery

2 live lobsters each weighing 1¼ to 1¾ lbs (600g to 800 g)

⅓ cup + 1 tablespoon (100 ml) peanut oil

3 green onions (scallions) sliced into lengths, plus 5 extra green onions, finely sliced

6 cloves garlic, finely chopped

1 in (2½ cm) peeled ginger, finely chopped

4 dried red finger-length chilies, deseeded and soaked in warm water for 30 minutes, coarsely chopped

¼ cup (15 g) dried salted black beans, gently rinsed

2 cups (500 ml) Asian Brown Chicken Stock (page 11)

3 tablespoons oyster sauce

2 tablespoons soy sauce

⅓ cup + 1 tablespoon (100 ml) Shao Xing rice wine

½ tablespoon sesame oil

1½ tablespoons black Chinese vinegar

1 tablespoon sugar

1 cup (50 g) coriander leaves (cilantro)

Leaves from 1 bunch Asian celery

Serves 6

Chicken stock is used here instead of fish stock as its body and meatiness goes well with lobster. This stir-fry has some broth, so serve it with soup spoons.

Make the Asian Brown Chicken Stock by following the recipe on page 11.

To kill the lobster, place it in a deep sink or pot of fresh water for 5 minutes or until the lobster drowns.

Hold the lobster with its head in one hand and tail in the other and gently twist and pull to separate them. Discard the head and rinse the tail. Twist off the legs and claws and crack them with a mallet or the back of a cleaver (this will help them to cook evenly and allow the flavors to get in), then chop them in half. Use a cleaver or a large, sharp knife to cut the tail in half lengthwise. Cut each half into three chunks with the shell attached so you have six pieces per lobster.

Heat the peanut oil in a wok and fry the green onion (sliced into lengths), garlic, ginger, chilies and black beans until fragrant and beginning to brown. Turn up the heat and add the lobster pieces and legs. Cook, stirring, until the shells start to turn red (around 5 minutes). Strain off as much oil as you can then add the Chicken Stock, oyster sauce, soy sauce, Shao Xing rice wine, sesame oil, black Chinese vinegar and sugar. Bring to a simmer then reduce the heat. Cover with a lid or an upturned bowl and cook for a further 5 minutes. Remove from the heat and toss through the finely sliced green onions, coriander leaves and Asian celery, and serve.

Swordfish with caramelized eggplant and roasted tomato sambal

2 lbs (1 kg) swordfish or snapper fillets (skin on)

2 tablespoons olive oil

½ tablespoon sea salt

Sambal

2 medium Asian eggplants (long eggplants), peeled and coarsely diced

⅓ cup + 1 tablespoon (100 ml) sweet soy sauce

⅓ cup + 1 tablespoon (100 ml) peanut oil

8 cloves garlic, unpeeled

1 cup (250 ml) Roasted Tomato Sambal (page 16)

6 coriander (cilantro) roots, washed and finely chopped

1½ tablespoons Pat Chun sweetened vinegar

Herb garnish

1 cup (50 g) coriander leaves (cilantro)

1 cup (40 g) mint leaves

3 green onions (scallions), finely sliced

6 Asian shallots, finely sliced

1 red finger-length chili, finely sliced

3 tablespoons Hot and Sour Dressing (page 17)

Serves 6

Cooking with sambals is one of my favorite things; this one has great tomato and lime flavors.

Make the Roasted Tomato Sambal and Hot and Sour Dressing by following the recipes on pages 16 and 17.

Sambal

In a mixing bowl coat the eggplant pieces in the sweet soy sauce. Heat the peanut oil in a pan until smoking then add the eggplant. Pan-fry, turning regularly, until soft and caramelized (around 10 minutes). Leave to cool in the pan.

Heat the oven to 350°F (180°C) and roast the garlic until tender (around 20 minutes). When cool enough to touch, slip the cloves out of their skins.

Add the roasted garlic, Roasted Tomato Sambal, coriander roots and Pat Chun vinegar to the pan containing the eggplant. Bring to a gentle simmer then remove from the heat.

To serve

Combine the ingredients for the Herb Garnish.

Preheat the oven to 340°F (170°C). Cut the fish fillets into six portions. Heat the olive oil over high heat in a large skillet or pan. Season the skin of the fish pieces with salt and place them in the skillet skin-side down. Fry until the skin is crisp (1–2 minutes). Place the skillet in the oven (or transfer the fish to a hot oven tray) and cook for 7–8 minutes, or until cooked through.

To serve, warm the Sambal if necessary and place onto serving plates. Top with the fish and Herb Garnish.

Fried whole snapper
with chili jam and coconut cream

2 cups (500 ml) coconut cream

3 cups (750 ml) vegetable oil, for frying

1 whole snapper weighing 3–4 lbs (1½–2 kgs), scaled and cleaned

3 tablespoons fish sauce

½ cup (125 ml) Chili Jam (page 13)

½ cup (25 g) coriander leaves (cilantro)

½ cup (20 g) mint leaves

½ cup (20 g) Vietnamese mint leaves

½ cup (20 g) Thai basil leaves

Serves 6

Whole fish, as opposed to fish fillets, are more commonly served throughout Asia. Whether fried or steamed, this has to be one of the most impressive dishes to serve at a shared meal among family and friends.

Make the Chili Jam by following the recipe on page 13.

Place the coconut cream in a saucepan and bring to a boil. Simmer until it has reduced by a half to two-thirds and is thick like semi-whipped cream. Remove from the heat and set aside.

Heat the oil in the wok to 350°F (180°C). Cut four to six diagonal slits along either side of the snapper (this will help it to cook evenly). Place the fish in a large bowl or dish and rub it with the fish sauce. Let it stand for a few minutes. Then, holding onto the head and tail, carefully submerge the snapper in the oil. Fry the fish until crisp (8–10 minutes)—there should be enough oil to cover the fish so it won't need to be turned. Drain on paper towels.

Place the fried snapper on a serving plate and top with the Chili Jam, reduced coconut cream and herbs.

Crispy fried fish with silk melon, garlic chives and peanuts

3 cups (750 ml) vegetable oil

2 lbs (1 kg) wild barramundi fillets (substitute perch or asian seabass), skinned and cut into bite-sized pieces

9 egg whites, lightly beaten

3 cups (375 g) rice flour

2 tablespoons Spiced Chili Salt (page 11)

2 tablespoons peanut oil

1 in (2½ cm) peeled ginger, finely chopped

3 cloves garlic, finely chopped

2 red finger-length chilies, finely sliced

½ silk melon or zucchini (around 4 oz/100 g), peeled and sliced into bite-sized discs

1 bunch (1 oz/40 g) garlic chives sliced into lengths

½ cup (75 g) Fried Chili Peanuts (page 19) or roasted peanuts

⅓ cup + 1 tablespoon (100 ml) Shao Xing rice wine

⅓ cup + 1 tablespoon (100 ml) oyster sauce

⅓ cup + 1 tablespoon (100 ml) Asian Brown Chicken Stock (page 11)

3 green onions (scallions), finely sliced

1 cup (50 g) coriander leaves (cilantro)

Serves 6

If you can't find wild barramundi then use another firm-fleshed fish such as perch or asian seabass. Asparagus or zucchini can easily be substituted for silk melon.

Make the Asian Brown Chicken Stock, Spiced Chili Salt and Fried Chili Peanuts by following the recipes on pages 11 and 19.

Heat the vegetable oil in a wok to 350°F (180°C). Dip the fish pieces in egg whites and then in the rice flour, shaking off any excess. Fry the fish in batches until crisp and golden (2–3 minutes). Drain on paper towels. Toss the fried fish in the Spiced Chili Salt and keep warm in a low oven.

Heat the peanut oil in a wok and add the ginger, garlic and chilies. Stir-fry until fragrant (1–2 minutes). Add the silk melon, garlic chives and peanuts and cook until everything is slightly charred. Add the Shao Xing rice wine, oyster sauce and Chicken Stock and simmer until reduced and thickened.

At the last minute, toss through the fried fish, green onions and coriander leaves and serve.

Steamed scallops with red-bean paste and roasted bell pepper dressing

18 large fresh scallops on the half-shell
3 red bell peppers
1½ tablespoons olive oil
1 tablespoon peanut oil
1 large red onion, finely chopped
3 cloves garlic, finely chopped
1 in (2½ cm) peeled ginger, finely chopped
3 tablespoons dried salted black beans,
   gently rinsed
2 red bird's-eye chilies, finely sliced
¾ cup (150 g) unsweetened red bean paste
⅓ cup (80 ml) sake
2½ tablespoons mirin
2½ tablespoons rice wine vinegar
1 tablespoon shaved palm sugar
1 cup (50 g) coriander leaves (cilantro)
6 green onions (scallions), finely sliced

Serves 6

The dense texture and savory flavor of unsweetened red bean paste (adzuki bean paste) make it a great base for sauces and dressings—the red bell pepper adds a sweet note.

Remove the scallops from their shells. To clean the shells of any impurities, place them in a pot of water and bring to a boil. Refresh the shells in cold water then drain. Gently rinse the scallops and place them back in their shells.

Preheat the oven to 400°F (200°C). Brush the bell peppers with olive oil and roast until the skins start to blister (10–15 minutes). When cool enough to handle, peel the skins and scrape out the seeds. Finely dice the flesh.

Heat the peanut oil in a wok and fry the onion, garlic and ginger until fragrant and beginning to brown. Add the bell pepper. When the oil has started to turn red, add the black beans, chilies and red bean paste. Cook, stirring, until the paste begins to caramelize and stick a little on the bottom of the wok. Add the sake, mirin, vinegar and palm sugar and simmer until the liquid has reduced by a quarter. Remove from the heat.

Top each scallop with a tablespoon of red bean and bell pepper mixture and place the shells in a steamer (or several steamers). Steam for 3–5 minutes or until the scallops are firm to the touch. Remove from the steamer and top with the coriander leaves and green onions, and serve.

Steamed crab and silken tofu with chili, green onions and coriander

1 live crab weighing at least 3 lbs/1½ kgs (or several smaller crabs equalling the same weight)
¾ cup (200 ml) Fish Stock (page 13)
⅓ cup (80 ml) soy sauce
2½ tablespoons mirin
2 tablespoons rice wine vinegar
2½ tablespoons (40 g) raw rock sugar crystals
¾ in (1½ cm) peeled ginger, bruised
6 dried black Chinese mushrooms
1 tablespoon instant dashi stock powder
1 lb (500 g) silken (soft) tofu
2 red finger-length chilies, finely sliced
5 green onions (scallions), finely sliced
1 cup (50 g) coriander leaves (cilantro)
1 tablespoon sesame oil
½ cup (100 g) Fried Shallots (page 19)

Serves 6

Silken tofu is fantastic to combine with crab. I make this dish with plenty of tofu and crab and just a touch of broth, but you could make it into a soup by adding more broth if you prefer.

Make the Fish Stock and Fried Shallots by following the recipes on pages 13 and 19.

Kill the crab quickly and humanely by turning it onto its back and inserting a large metal skewer in its middle where the flaps meet. Leave the skewer inside the crab for 3–4 minutes or until the crab has died. Alternatively, place the crab in a freezer for 1 hour, which will send it to sleep.

Bring a large pot of water to a boil. Calculate the cooking time—allow 7–8 minutes/lb of whole crab. (On this basis, a 3 lbs (1½ kgs) crab will need to be cooked for 20–22 minutes.) Add the crab to the pot and simmer for the correct time. The shell of the crab will turn a reddish brown when cooked. Remove the crab from the pot and plunge it in a basin of iced water to stop the cooking process. Leave the crab to cool in the basin for 10 minutes, then drain.

Use your fingers to pull the top shell away from the body. Discard the gills and rinse the crab. Twist off the legs and claws and use a mallet or the flat side of the cleaver to crack them. Use a crab pick or metal skewer to extract the meat from the legs, claws and body. Measure 2 cups (250 g) of meat and refrigerate or freeze the rest for another use.

Combine the Fish Stock, soy sauce, mirin, vinegar, rock sugar, ginger, mushrooms and dashi powder in a saucepan and bring to a boil. Simmer for 3 minutes then remove from the heat. Allow the flavors to infuse for at least 20 minutes.

Slice the tofu into bite-sized pieces and place on a heatproof serving dish. Scatter with the crab meat. Strain the broth over the tofu and crab and place the dish in a steamer. Steam until the ingredients are heated through (2–3 minutes) then remove from the heat and garnish with the chili, green onions and coriander leaves.

Place the sesame oil in a saucepan and heat until smoking. Drizzle the hot oil over the garnish. Top with the Fried Shallots and serve immediately.

Steamed mussel salad with toasted coconut and tamarind dressing

4 lbs (2 kgs) large fresh mussels in their shells

¾ cup (200 ml) white wine

⅔ cup (150 ml) Hot and Sour Dressing (page 17)

⅓ cup (80 ml) Tamarind Juice (page 18)

1 stalk lemongrass, tender inner part of bottom third only, finely sliced

3 kaffir lime leaves, finely sliced into thin shreds

¾ in (1½ cm) peeled ginger, sliced into thin shreds

5 Asian shallots, finely sliced

½ cup (50 g) grated fresh coconut, lightly roasted

2 red finger-length chilies, finely sliced

1 cup (50 g) coriander leaves (cilantro)

1 cup (40 g) mint leaves

¼ cup (40 g) Fried Chili Peanuts (page 19), coarsely chopped

2 tablespoons salmon roe

1 banana leaf (optional)

½ cup (100 g) Fried Shallots (page 19)

Serves 6

Make the Hot and Sour Dressing, Tamarind Juice, Fried Chili Peanuts and Fried Shallots by following the recipes on pages 17, 18 and 19.

Scrub the mussels thoroughly under cold water. De-beard them by giving the beard a firm pull down towards the tip of the mussel.

Find a pot that has a lid and will accommodate all of the mussels. Heat the empty pot for a minute then add the mussels followed by the wine. Cover with the lid and steam until the mussels open (around 1–2 minutes). Discard any that do not open. Remove from the heat and strain, discarding the cooking liquid. Remove the mussels from their shells, discarding the shells.

Combine the Hot and Sour Dressing and Tamarind Juice in a bowl. Add the mussels and marinate them for 5 minutes. Add the lemongrass, kaffir lime leaves, ginger, shallots, coconut, chilies, coriander leaves, mint, Fried Chili Peanuts and salmon roe and gently combine.

Line a large serving bowl (or six individual serving bowls) with a square of banana leaf (if using) and place the salad on top. Garnish with the Fried Shallots and serve.

Grilled stingray with chili jam and pomelo and coconut sambal

4 lbs (2 kgs) fresh stingray or skate wing

¾ cup (200 ml) sweet soy sauce

1 in (2½ cm) peeled ginger, bruised and coarsely chopped

5 cloves garlic, bruised

1 cup (250 ml) Chili Jam (page 13)

1 banana leaf cut into 6 plate-sized squares (optional)

2 limes, quartered

Sambal

1 young green coconut

1 pomelo (or 2 large grapefruits)

10 cherry tomatoes, halved

⅓ cup (80 ml) Pat Chun sweetened vinegar

1 tablespoon fish sauce

1½ tablespoons freshly-squeezed lime juice

½ cup (50 g) grated fresh coconut, lightly roasted

4 red bird's-eye chilies, finely sliced

2 stalks lemongrass, tender inner part of bottom third only, finely sliced

4 kaffir lime leaves, finely sliced into thin shreds

½ cup (25 g) coriander leaves (cilantro)

8 Thai basil leaves, torn

Serves 6

Stingray (or skate) wings are filleted in the same way as other fish—the process is quite straightforward. It has a firm texture and very mild flavor, making it a great fish to marinate. Serve this dish with Coconut Rice (page 24).

Make the Chili Jam by following the recipe on page 13

Begin filleting the stingray wing at the thick, open end. Use a large sharp knife and try to cut as close as possible between the flesh and the bone that runs through the center, making your way to the tip of the wing. The idea is to cut the fillet off in one piece, but as your knife is probably smaller than the width of the wing, you may need to do the right and left sides separately. Flip the wing over and do the same on the other side so that you are left with two large fillets (one side is usually thicker than the other). Cut the fillets into three pieces each so you have six pieces in total (or, if you end up with several awkward pieces, cut them into smaller pieces and serve more than one piece per person).

Place the stingray pieces in a bowl and add the sweet soy sauce, ginger and garlic and combine thoroughly. Marinate in the refrigerator for at least 4–5 hours (or overnight).

Sambal

Pierce the coconut with a metal skewer and drain out the juice. Cut off the pointed top with a sharp knife or cleaver and scoop out the soft flesh with a spoon, trying to keep it in large pieces. Cut the pieces into very fine strands.

Cut the skin away from the pomelo and segment it by cutting as close to the membrane as possible on either side of each natural segment. Work your way around the pomelo until you have cut all the segments out.

Place the cherry tomatoes and Pat Chun in a non-reactive saucepan and bring to a boil. Simmer for a few minutes until the tomatoes are soft. Allow to cool then add the fish sauce and lime juice. Combine in a bowl with the pomelo, young coconut, roasted coconut, chilies, lemongrass, kaffir lime leaves, coriander leaves and Thai basil.

To serve

Heat a broiler grill or barbecue and add the stingray pieces. Cook each piece for 3–4 minutes on one side (or a little less for the thinner pieces) and 2–3 minutes on the other. Before they've finished cooking, spread the tops with the Chili Jam.

Place the stingray pieces jam-side up onto plates or banana leaves and top with the Sambal. Serve the lime wedges on the side.

Poultry

Mu shu chicken
in lettuce cups

18 Lettuce Cups (page 21)

3 tablespoons peanut oil

6 eggs, lightly beaten

1 lb (500 g) skinless chicken breasts,
  finely chopped

⅓ cup + 1 tablespoon (100 ml) oyster sauce

5 cloves garlic, finely chopped

1 in (2½ cm) peeled ginger, finely chopped

2 red finger-length chilies, finely sliced

4 garlic chives cut into lengths

1 cup (150 g) green beans cut into lengths

⅓ cup (80 g) sugar

⅔ cup (150 ml) Shao Xing rice wine

⅓ cup (75 ml) soy sauce

2½ tablespoons black Chinese vinegar

¾ cup (200 ml) Asian Brown Chicken Stock
  (page 11)

1 teaspoon sesame oil

1 small bunch (1 oz/30 g) enoki mush–
  rooms, bases trimmed

3 green onions (scallions), finely sliced

1 cup (50 g) coriander leaves (cilantro)

1 tablespoon sesame seeds, lightly roasted

½ tablespoon Sichuan Pepper-Salt Powder
  (page 11)

Serves 6

Mu shu is a traditional dish from northern China made with pork and served with Mandarin pancakes and plum or hoisin sauce. Common ingredients are lily buds, mushrooms and bamboo shoots. This version uses chicken instead of pork, and lettuce cups instead of pancakes. It's a great dish for parties—for people to share.

Make the Asian Brown Chicken Stock, Sichuan Pepper-Salt Powder and Lettuce Cups by following the recipes on pages 11 and 21.

Heat half of the peanut oil in a wok until it begins to smoke. Add the eggs and stir-fry until they are firmly scrambled. Remove from the wok.

Toss the chicken in half of the oyster sauce and set aside. Heat the remaining peanut oil in the wok and add the garlic, ginger, chilies and garlic chives. Stir-fry for a few minutes then add the chicken and fry until beginning to brown. Add the green beans and sugar and cook until the mixture begins to caramelize. Add the remaining oyster sauce, Shao Xing rice wine, soy sauce, black Chinese vinegar, Chicken Stock and sesame oil and cook until the liquid reduces by a third.

Add the scrambled eggs, enoki mushrooms, green onions and coriander leaves and combine. Transfer the mixture to a serving dish and sprinkle with the sesame seeds and Sichuan Pepper-Salt Powder. Serve accompanied with the Lettuce Cups.

Spiced chicken in a claypot with green onion buns

2 cinnamon sticks

1 teaspoon fennel seeds

4 pieces dried mandarin peel

1 dried red finger-length chili

1 teaspoon Sichuan peppercorns

1 teaspoon cardamom pods

5 star anise pods

2 pieces liquorice root

2 tablespoons peanut oil

6 chicken thighs on the bone, skin on

2 tablespoons (25 g) raw rock sugar crystals

1 in (2½ cm) peeled ginger, finely chopped

5 cloves garlic, finely chopped

6 dried black Chinese mushrooms

1 cup (250 ml) Shao Xing rice wine

½ cup (120 ml) soy sauce

⅓ cup (80 ml) sweet soy sauce

⅓ cup (80 ml) oyster sauce

2 cups (500 ml) water

6 dried Chinese sausages (*lup cheong*), sliced

1 cup (150 g) green beans sliced into pieces

3 baby bok choy, halved

8 oyster mushrooms, torn

3 green onions (scallions), white ends only, finely sliced

1 cup (50 g) coriander leaves (cilantro)

Green onion buns

1 portion Yeast Bun Dough (page 23)

1 teaspoon peanut oil

8 green onions (scallions), green ends only, coarsely chopped

1 in (2½ cm) peeled ginger, finely chopped

3 tablespoons hoisin sauce

Serves 6

The steamed green onion buns are a good accompaniment to this dish—an Asian version of dinner rolls.

Roughly pound the cinnamon sticks, fennel seeds, mandarin peel, chili, Sichuan peppercorns, cardamom, star anise and liquorice roots with a mortar and pestle. Tie the spices in a square of muslin cloth.

Preheat the oven to 325°F (160°C). Heat the oil in a pan and fry the chicken thighs until browned all over.

Combine the rock sugar, ginger, garlic, shiitake mushrooms, Shao Xing rice wine, soy sauce, oyster sauce and water in a large saucepan and bring to a simmer, stirring until the sugar dissolves. Transfer the liquid to a claypot or a casserole dish with a lid and add the spice bag, fried chicken and dried Chinese sausages. Cover with the lid and cook in the oven for 1–1½ hours or until the chicken is falling off the bone and the dried Chinese sausages are tender.

Green onion buns

Make the Yeast Bun Dough by following the recipe on page 23.

Heat the oil in a wok or pan and fry the green onions and ginger until fragrant and softened. Drain on paper towels.

Portion the Yeast Bun Dough into 12 balls. On a floured surface, roll each ball into a circle and place a teaspoon of hoisin and a teaspoon of green onions in the center. Bring the edges up around the filling and pinch them together at the top to seal.

To serve

Place the buns into a steamer, allowing space for rising. Steam for 10–12 minutes, or until the tops have cracked open.

Meanwhile, remove the claypot from the oven and turn off the oven. Add the green beans and bok choy to the pot and return to the warm oven for 5–10 minutes. Remove from the oven and stir through the oyster mushrooms.

Garnish with green onions and coriander leaves and serve accompanied with the Green Onion Buns.

Stir-fried egg noodles with crispy chicken and shrimp

1 lb (500 g) skinless chicken breasts,
 coarsely chopped

14 oz (400 g) fresh shrimp, peeled and
 deveined (to make 7 oz/200 g),
 coarsely chopped

2½ tablespoons fish sauce

1½ tablespoons Shao Xing rice wine

3 tablespoons peanut oil

1 large brown onion, finely sliced

3 cloves garlic, finely chopped

3 dried red finger-length chilies, deseeded
 and softened in warm water for 30
 minutes, then coarsely chopped

4 green onions (scallions), cut into lengths

1 teaspoon sugar

½ tablespoon Curry Powder (page 10)

½ bunch Chinese broccoli leaves

8 oyster mushrooms, torn

12 oz (350 g) fresh egg noodles

1 tablespoon soy sauce

2 red finger-length chilies, finely sliced

1 cup coriander leaves (cilantro)

2 limes, quartered

Serves 6

Make the Curry Powder by following the recipe on page 10.

Place the chicken and shrimp meat in separate bowls. Add 1 tablespoon of fish sauce and Shao Xing rice wine to the chicken and ½ tablespoon of fish sauce and the remaining wine to the shrimp. Toss to combine and leave to marinate for a few minutes.

Heat the peanut oil in a wok and fry the chicken over high heat until lightly browned. Add the shrimp and stir-fry for a further minute, or until both the chicken and shrimp are browned and crisp. Remove the meat from the wok, leaving some of the oil.

Return the wok to the heat and add the onion, garlic, dried chilies and green onions. Stir-fry until fragrant and beginning to brown, then add the sugar, Curry Powder, Chinese broccoli, oyster mushrooms and noodles and stir-fry for another minute. Add the fried chicken and shrimp, remaining fish sauce and soy sauce and combine. Transfer to a serving dish and garnish with the fresh chilies and coriander leaves. Serve the lime wedges on the side.

Peking duck with mandarin pancakes

1 large pekin duck weighing around
    4 lbs (2 kgs), head attached

1 in (2½ cm) peeled ginger, bruised

2 cloves garlic, bruised

6 green onions (scallions), coarsely chopped

2 star anise pods

1 cinnamon stick

½ cup (125 ml) Shao Xing rice wine

1 cup (250 ml) Maltose Liquid (page 18)

Accompaniments

18 Mandarin Pancakes (page 23)

1 teaspoon Sichuan Pepper-Salt Powder
    (page 11)

1 tablespoon Toasted Sesame Oil
    (page 17)

½ cup (125 ml) plum or hoisin sauce

9 green onions (scallions), white ends only,
    halved lengthwise

1 cucumber, peeled and sliced into thin
    sticks

2½ in (6 cm) peeled ginger, finely sliced into
    thin shreds

Serves 6

The pekin duck is a Chinese breed known for its juicy and tender meat. It is sold with the head attached, which is suited to the preparation of Peking duck, one of Beijing's most famous dishes. The method of preparing the duck for this dish is quite involved—pumping air underneath the skin and then hardening it with hot maltose syrup—but the result you get is unbeatably crisp.

Make the Maltose Liquid by following the recipe on page 18.

Rinse the duck inside and out. Bring a large pot of water to a rapid boil and add the duck. Blanch for 20 seconds then drain (this helps to tighten the skin).

Stuff the cavity of the duck with the ginger, garlic, green onions, star anise and cinnamon. Carefully pour in the Shao Xing rice wine and seal the opening by threading a skewer through the flaps of skin.

Loosely wrap a piece of twine around the base of the neck of the duck. Make a small nick in the skin in the neck area above the level of the twine and carefully insert the nozzle of a bicycle pump (see Note on opposite page). Pump air underneath the skin until it lifts from the flesh. Carefully move the nozzle deeper beneath the skin and repeat. Keep doing so until you have separated as much of the skin as possible without tearing it. Remove the pump and tie the twine tightly around the neck, trying to keep some air trapped under the skin.

Bring the Maltose Liquid to a boil. When it boils, brush the duck (breasts and legs mainly) with the syrup in one even layer. Bring the syrup back to a boil and repeat. Continue this process until the duck is well coated. To dry the duck, hang it by its neck (but not by the twine, or the skin may rip) or elevate it on a wire rack set above a dish and place it in front of a fan for at least 2 hours, or until the skin is hard like parchment. Alternatively, refrigerate the duck on a rack uncovered overnight.

Preheat the oven to 400°F (200°C). Fill a small dish or tray with water and place it in the bottom of the oven (this will create steam and keeps the skin from burning). Cut off the head and neck of the duck just above the twine. Place the duck on a tray and roast for 15 minutes, then lower the temperature to 340°F (170°C) and roast for a further 40 minutes or until the juices run clear when a skewer is inserted into a thigh (there is no need to turn the duck during cooking). Remove the duck from the oven, cut away the twine and remove the skewer. Allow the duck to rest for 20 minutes before removing the meat.

To remove the meat, cut off the legs between the thigh and body. Remove the leg meat by making slits to the bone and using your fingers to pull the meat away (in one piece ideally). To remove the breasts, locate the breastbone and run a knife down either side of it, slicing as close to the bone as possible. Continue to trace around each breast then use a small, sharp knife to cut each one away from the breastplate. Discard the wings and carcass. You can refrigerate the duck meat skin-side up and uncovered if not planning to serve it right away.

To serve

Make the Sichuan Pepper-Salt Powder, Toasted Sesame Oil and Mandarin Pancakes by following the recipes on pages 11, 17 and 23.

Arrange the duck meat on a tray skin-side up and gently reheat it under a broiler grill. Once hot, place on paper towels to drain off any excess fat.

Gently heat the Mandarin Pancakes in a steamer for 1–2 minutes then transfer to a warm serving plate. Carve the duck meat into long, thin strips and place on another warm serving plate. Sprinkle the duck with the Sichuan Pepper-Salt Powder. Place the Toasted Sesame Oil, plum or hoisin sauce, green onions, cucumber and ginger in separate bowls or dishes and bring them to the table.

To serve, brush each warm pancake with a little of the Toasted Sesame Oil. Smear with half a teaspoon of plum or hoisin sauce and top with a few strips of duck, a piece of green onion, and some cucumber and ginger. Roll up the pancakes and eat immediately.

Note A bike pump with a ball valve is the best thing to use to separate the skin and flesh for Peking duck. But if you don't have one on hand you can leave this procedure out—the skin won't be quite as crisp.

Crispy fried quail or chicken with chili and green peppercorns

2 dried red finger-length chilies, deseeded and softened in warm water for 30 minutes, then coarsely chopped

3 cloves garlic

2 tablespoons fresh green peppercorns

3 tablespoons sea salt

1 tablespoon shaved palm sugar

½ tablespoon fish sauce

1 tablespoon freshly-squeezed lime juice

6 large quail (about 2 lbs/1 kg in total) or 2½ lbs (1¼ kgs) chicken fillets, sliced

3 cups (750 ml) vegetable oil, for frying

1 portion Tempura Batter (page 23)

⅓ cup + 1 tablespoon (100 ml) soy sauce

2 limes, quartered

1 cup (50 g) coriander leaves (cilantro)

1 cup (40 g) mint leaves

Serves 6

Make the Tempura Batter by following the recipe on page 23.

Using a mortar and pestle pound the chilies, garlic, peppercorns, salt and palm sugar to a fine paste. Add the fish sauce and lime juice and combine.

Remove the wing tips from the quail by cutting through the first wing joint with a pair of kitchen snips. Hold a quail in the palm of your hand and insert the snips into the cavity of the bird and cut along either side of the backbone. Remove the backbone. Open the quail up, flatten it with the palm of your hand and gently pull out the breastplate.

Detach the ribs with the tip of a small paring knife and gently pull them out. Cut out the connecting bone between the thigh and backbone. Check the quail for any remaining bones—it should be left with leg and upper wing bones only. Repeat with the remaining quail.

Lay the quail or chicken fillets out flat in a steamer (or several steamers) and steam for 6–7 minutes. Set aside to cool a little.

Heat the oil in a wok to 350°F (180°C) and fry the green peppercorn paste until crisp and fragrant. It will float on the surface and can be removed with a slotted spoon. Drain on paper towels.

Dip the quail or chicken fillets in the Tempura Batter, shaking off any excess, then fry them in batches until crisp and golden (around 5 minutes). Drain on paper towels.

Cut the quail (if using) in half then toss them in the paste. Arrange on a serving plate and accompany with the soy sauce, lime wedges, coriander and mint leaves.

Roast duck with orange caramel sauce and green peppercorns

1 duck weighing around 4 lbs (2 kgs)
1 in (2½ cm) peeled ginger, bruised
2 cloves garlic, bruised
6 green onions (scallions), coarsely chopped
2 star anise pods
1 cinnamon stick
½ cup (125 ml) Shao Xing rice wine
1 cup (250 ml) Maltose Liquid (page 18)

Orange caramel sauce
1½ cups (300 g) shaved palm sugar
¾ cup (200 ml) water
4 pieces dried mandarin orange peel
1 red finger-length chili, finely sliced
1 green finger-length chili, finely sliced
Grated rind of 1 orange
2 tablespoons fish sauce
3 tablespoons freshly-squeezed lime juice
2 small mandarin oranges, peeled and
   segmented, seeds and pith removed
2 tablespoons fresh green peppercorns

Serves 6

Make this dish when you can find fresh green peppercorns—they are sold on the stem and are available in summer/autumn, and are a common Southeast Asian ingredient. Green peppercorns in brine can be used as a substitute but they don't have the same pungency. Serve this dish with Pickled Cucumber (page 22).

Make the Maltose Liquid by following the recipe on page 18.

Rinse the duck inside and out. Bring a large pot of water to a rapid boil and add the duck. Blanch for 20 seconds then drain (this helps to tighten the skin). Pat the duck dry with paper towels.

Stuff the cavity of the duck with the ginger, garlic, green onions, star anise and cinnamon. Carefully pour in the Shao Xing rice wine and seal the opening by threading a skewer through the flaps of skin.

Bring the Maltose Liquid to a boil. When it boils, brush the duck (breasts and legs mainly) with the syrup in one even layer. Bring the syrup back to a boil and repeat. Continue this process until the duck is well coated. To dry the duck, elevate it on a wire rack set above a dish and place it in front of a fan for at least 2 hours, or until the skin is hard like parchment. Alternatively, refrigerate the duck on a rack uncovered overnight.

Preheat the oven to 400°F (200°C). Fill a small dish or tray with water and place it in the bottom of the oven (this will create steam and keeps the skin from burning). Place the duck on a tray and roast for 15 minutes, then lower the temperature to 340°F (170°C) and roast for a further 40 minutes or until the juices run clear when a skewer is inserted into a thigh (there is no need to turn the duck during cooking). Remove the duck from the oven and remove the skewer. Rest the duck for 20 minutes.

Continued next page

To carve the duck, use a cleaver or a large, sharp knife to cut it in half lengthwise. Discard the stuffing. Cut the backbone away and discard. Cut off the legs between the thigh and body and separate the thighs from the drumsticks by cutting through the joint. Cut the breasts away from the rib cage (but leave them still attached to the breastplate). Cut the breasts and thighs through the bones into three pieces each so you have 12 pieces of breast and thigh. Leave the drumsticks whole. Discard the carcass and wings.

Orange Caramel Sauce
Place the palm sugar, water and mandarin orange peel in a heavy-based saucepan and bring to a boil. Simmer until the mixture begins to turn a light caramel color (around 10 minutes), then watch it closely and take it off the heat just before it becomes dark brown. (You will need to brush or scrape the sides of the saucepan occasionally to stop crystals from forming.) Remove from the heat and stir in the remaining ingredients. Check for a balance of flavors, adding a little more fish sauce or lime juice if necessary. Set aside to cool.

To serve
Arrange the duck meat on a tray skin-side up and gently reheat under a broiler grill.
Transfer the hot duck to a serving platter and spoon over the Orange Caramel Sauce.

Barbecued quail with mandarin pancakes and cucumber herb salad

6 large quail (about 2 lbs/1 kg in total)

1 teaspoon sea salt

Juice of half a lemon

1/3 cup (75 ml) hoisin sauce

1/3 cup (75 ml) tomato ketchup

1/2 tablespoon sesame oil

3 tablespoons honey

18 Mandarin Pancakes (page 23)

2 tablespoons Roasted Rice Powder (page 21)

Salad

1 tablespoon olive oil

2 tablespoons lemon juice

1½ tablespoons soy sauce

1 red bird's-eye chili, deseeded and finely chopped

2 limes

1¾ oz (50 g) dried rice vermicelli

1 cucumber, deseeded and sliced into thin sticks

5 Asian shallots, finely sliced

4 green onions (scallions), finely sliced

1 red finger-length chili, deseeded and finely sliced lengthwise

1 cup (40 g) mint leaves

1 cup (50 g) coriander leaves (cilantro)

Serves 6

Char siu is traditionally a dish using pork, although it works well with quail too. It's a simple and fast way of marinating meat and giving it flavor. If you don't have the patience to debone quail, ask your butcher to do it.

Make the Roasted Rice Powder and Mandarin Pancakes by following the recipes on pages 21 and 23.

Cut off the wings of the quail and discard. Holding the quail in the palm of your hand, insert a pair of kitchen snips into the cavity and cut along either side of the backbone. Remove the backbone. Open the bird up, flatten it with the palm of your hand and gently pull out the breastplate.

Detach the ribs with the tip of a small paring knife and gently pull them out. To debone the legs, make a slit to the bone making sure you don't go all the way through. Carefully open the leg up and cut around the bone to detach it from the meat. Ease it out. Check the quail for any remaining bones, then debone the rest of the quail.

Place the quail in a bowl and rub with the salt and lemon juice. Marinate for 10 minutes. Add the hoisin, tomato sauce, sesame oil and 2 tablespoons of honey and coat the quail thoroughly. Place in the refrigerator to marinate for 2 hours.

Salad

Combine the olive oil, lemon juice, soy sauce and bird's-eye chili and set aside.

Cut the peel from the limes and segment them by cutting as close to the membrane as possible on either side of each natural segment. Work your way around the limes until you have cut all the segments out.

Cover the dried noodles with boiling water and leave until tender (around 1 minute). Drain and refresh under cold water.

Combine all the ingredients and place in a serving bowl.

To serve

Heat a broiler grill or barbecue and cook the quail for 5 minutes, turning halfway through. When they are almost cooked, glaze the quail with the remaining 1 tablespoon of honey.

Gently reheat the Mandarin Pancakes in a steamer for 1–2 minutes.

Slice each quail in three then place on a serving plate and sprinkle with the Roasted Rice Powder. Each person gets three Pancakes—top each Pancake with a piece of quail and some Salad, then roll it up and eat.

Cripsy red braised chicken with black vinegar dressing

1 large organic free-range chicken (weighing around 3 lbs/1½ kgs)

1¼ in (3 cm) peeled ginger, bruised

6 green onions (scallions), coarsely chopped

8 cups (2 liters) Master Stock (page 12)

4 cups (1 liter) vegetable oil, for frying

Black vinegar dressing

4 green bird's-eye chilies, finely sliced

6 Asian shallots, finely sliced

6 cloves garlic, finely chopped

1 in (2½ cm) peeled ginger, finely chopped

4 coriander (cilantro) roots, washed and finely chopped

3 green onions (scallions), finely sliced

½ teaspoon dried shrimp powder (made by processing several dried shrimp in a blender or food processor)

3 tablespoons oyster sauce

3 tablespoons Shao Xing rice wine

⅓ cup + 1 tablespoon (100 ml) soy sauce

⅔ cup (150 ml) black Chinese vinegar

2½ tablespoons Palm Sugar Syrup (page 18)

Serves 6

Red-cooking involves the slow braising of meats in Master Stock before deep-frying or roasting them. Master stock is one of the secrets of great Chinese cooking—it imparts a beautiful rich red color and an incredible flavor and aroma from the Shao Xing rice wine and aromatics. If you take the Chinese approach and purify and refresh the stock after each use so that it can be used again, master stock simply gets richer and richer. Our Master Stock at **ezard** is entering its fifth year—when we cook with it the smell goes right through the restaurant. Accompany this dish with Jasmine or Coconut Rice and greens. Instead of the Black Vinegar Dressing, I sometimes like to serve this with Shrimp, Tomato and Peanut Relish (page 203).

Make the Master Stock and Palm Sugar Syrup by following the recipes on pages 12 and 18.

Rinse the chicken inside and out. Stuff the cavity with ginger and green onions and seal the opening by threading a skewer through the flaps of skin.

Bring the Master Stock to a boil in a large pot. Add the chicken, cover the pot with a lid and gently poach for 45 minutes. Remove the pot from the heat and allow the chicken to completely cool in the stock.

Once cool, remove the chicken from the Stock and elevate it on a wire rack set above a dish. Refrigerate the chicken uncovered overnight. In the morning, the skin should be hard like parchment.

Black vinegar dressing
Combine all the ingredients in a bowl and set aside to allow the flavors to develop while you fry the chicken.

To serve
Heat the vegetable oil in a wok to 350°F (180°C). Remove the skewer from the chicken and use a large knife or cleaver to cut it in half lengthwise. Remove the ginger and green onions and pat the inside of the chicken dry. Gently lower one chicken half into the hot oil and fry until crisp and golden (7–8 minutes). Remove from the oil, drain on paper towels and repeat with the other half.

To carve the chicken, cut away the backbone and discard. Cut off the legs between the thigh and body and separate the thighs from the drumsticks by cutting through the joint. Cut the breasts away from the rib cage (but leave them still attached to the breastplate). Cut the breasts and thighs through the bones into three pieces each so you have 12 pieces of breast and thigh. Leave the drumsticks whole. Discard the carcass and wings.

Drizzle the chicken with the Black Vinegar Dressing and serve.

Chinese chicken salad with sweet and sour peanut dressing

6 chicken legs (marylands)
⅓ cup (80 g) raw rock sugar crystals
2 in (5 cm) peeled ginger, bruised

Peanut dressing
½ cup (75 g) Fried Chili Peanuts (page 19)
    or roasted peanuts
½ cup (120 ml) Shao Xing rice wine
⅓ cup + 1 tablespoon (100 ml) soy sauce
2 tablespoons black Chinese vinegar
1 tablespoon Toasted Sesame Oil
    (page 17)
2½ tablespoons water
2 tablespoons sugar
2 tablespoons honey
3 tablespoons freshly-squeezed lime juice
1½ in (4 cm) peeled ginger, finely chopped
3 green onions (scallions), finely sliced
½ cup (20 g) garlic chives, finely sliced

Salad
1¾ oz (50 g) dried glass noodles
1 cucumber, deseeded and sliced
    into sticks
½ teaspoon dried red chili flakes
1 in (2½ cm) peeled ginger, finely sliced in
    thin shreds
4 green onions (scallions), finely sliced
8 wood ear mushrooms, torn
½ cup (75 g) Fried Chili Peanuts (page 19)
    or roasted peanuts
¼ cup (30 g) sesame seeds, lightly roasted
½ cup (25 g) coriander leaves (cilantro)
½ cup (20 g) mint leaves
½ cup (20 g) watercress sprigs

Serves 6

This dish originates from the Sichuan province, where it goes by the name of "Bang Bang Chicken." "Bang bang" refers to the traditional technique of hammering the chicken to loosen the meat fibers before shredding it. There are several versions of this dish; this one has a traditional peanut dressing. The salad is served cold, which highlights the sweet and sour flavors.

Make the Toasted Sesame Oil and Fried Chili Peanuts by following the recipes on pages 17 and 19.

Bring a large pot of water to a rapid boil. Rinse the chicken legs then place them in the pot to boil for 10 seconds. Refresh them under cold running water.

Rinse out the pot and refill it with fresh water. Add the rock sugar and ginger and heat, stirring, until the sugar dissolves. Add the chicken legs and gently poach them for 40 minutes. Remove from the heat and allow the chicken to cool in the cooking liquid. Once cool, remove from the liquid. Peel the skin off the chicken and finely slice it. Remove the meat from the bones with your fingers and shred it into fine strands.

Peanut dressing
Pound the peanuts to a coarse paste with a mortar and pestle. Add the remaining ingredients and stir until the sugar dissolves. Taste for a balance of flavors, adjusting if necessary.

To serve
For the Salad, cover the noodles with boiling water and leave until tender (around 1 minute). Drain and refresh under cold water. Combine the noodles in a bowl with the remaining Salad ingredients. Add the chicken and Peanut Dressing and toss to combine. Serve lime wedges on the side if you wish.

Roast duck with seared scallops and green ginger wine sauce

1 Roast Duck (page 177–78)

1 teaspoon peanut oil

12 large sea scallops (roe removed)

1 bunch asparagus spears, bases trimmed, cut into lengths

⅓ cup (50 g) green beans, ends trimmed, cut into lengths

½ cup (50 g) snow peas, ends trimmed and strings removed

Green ginger wine sauce

½ tablespoon sesame oil

1 in (2½ cm) peeled ginger, finely chopped

3 cloves garlic, finely chopped

1½ cups (350 ml) Stones green ginger wine (purchased)

3 cups (700 ml) Veal Stock (page 12)

Serves 6

Roast duck and sea scallops are a great combination. The crisp duck contrasts with the smoothness of the scallops, and the sauce adds a light tang. If the scallops are frozen (sea scallops generally come this way—for more on these scallops, see page 144), then defrost them on a wire rack in the refrigerator for a few hours. Produced in England since 1740, Stone's Original Green Ginger Wine has been made in Australia to the same ancient formula since the early 1960's. Ginger is one of the oldest herbs known to man, and is popular in oriental cooking and confectionery. Ginger has also been linked with many therapeutic values.

Prepare the Roast Duck by following the recipe on pages 177–78.

Green ginger wine sauce
Make the Veal Stock by following the recipe on page 12.

Heat the sesame oil in a large saucepan and fry the ginger and garlic until fragrant and beginning to brown. Add the green ginger wine, bring it to a boil and ignite it with a match to burn off the alcohol. When the flame goes out, remove the saucepan from the heat and strain the liquid. Place it back in the saucepan and add the Veal Stock. Simmer until the sauce has reduced by half and is thick enough to coat the back of a spoon. Season to taste.

To serve
Arrange the duck meat on a tray skin-side up and gently reheat under a broiler grill.

Meanwhile, heat the peanut oil in a pan over high heat and sear the scallops for 5–10 seconds on each side (they should be lightly browned). Keep them warm while you stir-fry the asparagus, beans and snow peas until just tender.

To serve, transfer the duck pieces to a serving plate and top with the scallops and vegetables. Drizzle with the Green Ginger Wine Sauce.

Grilled coconut chicken with green mango salad

6 boneless chicken breasts, skin on

1½ tablespoons fish sauce

5 cloves garlic

1¼ in (3 cm) peeled ginger

¾ in (1½ cm) peeled galangal root

1 in (2½ cm) peeled fresh turmeric root

2 red bird's-eye chilies, deseeded

1 green finger-length chili, deseeded

5 coriander (cilantro) roots, washed

1 stalk lemongrass, tender inner part of bottom third only

5 kaffir lime leaves

1 teaspoon Roasted Shrimp Paste (page 9)

1 teaspoon coriander seeds, lightly roasted

2 tablespoons shaved palm sugar

1¼ cups (300 ml) coconut cream

½ cup (125 ml) Chili Jam (page 13)

Green mango salad

2 tablespoons cashew nuts, lightly roasted

1 teaspoon Roasted Dried Shrimp (page 21)

1 stalk lemongrass, tender inner part of bottom third only, finely sliced

3 kaffir lime leaves, finely sliced into thin shreds

1 red bird's-eye chili, finely sliced

10 cherry tomatoes, halved

1 cup (150 g) green beans cut into lengths, blanched

2 cups grated green mango

½ cup (20 g) mint leaves

½ cup (25 g) coriander leaves (cilantro)

½ cup (20 g) Thai basil leaves

1 tablespoon Tamarind Juice (page 18)

1 tablespoon fish sauce

1½ tablespoons freshly-squeezed lime juice

Serves 6

Make the Roasted Shrimp Paste, Chili Jam, Tamarind Juice and Roasted Dried Shrimp by following the recipes on pages 9, 13, 18 and 21.

Place the chicken breasts in a bowl, add the fish sauce and rub the fish sauce into the meat. Leave to marinate for 1 hour.

Coarsely chop the garlic, ginger, galangal, turmeric, chilies and coriander roots. Finely slice the lemongrass and kaffir lime leaves. Using a mortar and pestle, pound them all to a fine paste with the Roasted Shrimp Paste and coriander seeds. Add the palm sugar and coconut cream then add the mixture to the chicken breasts. Marinate in the refrigerator overnight.

Green mango salad

Using a mortar and pestle pound the cashews, Roasted Dried Shrimp, lemongrass, kaffir lime leaves, chili, cherry tomatoes and beans to a coarse paste. Add the mango, herbs, Tamarind Juice, fish sauce and lime juice and gently pound to combine. Taste for a balance of flavors, adjusting if necessary.

To serve

Heat a broiler grill or barbecue to medium heat. Remove the chicken from the marinade and place on the grill skin-side down. Cook for 5 minutes, or until the skin is crisp and caramelized, then turn and cook for another 5 minutes or until cooked through. Baste the chicken with the remaining marinade as it cooks.

Serve the chicken with the Green Mango Salad and Chili Jam.

Drunken chicken
with lemon sesame dressing

1 large organic free-range chicken (weighing
  around 3 lbs/1½ kgs)
4 cups (1 liter) sake
4 cups (1 liter) water
⅓ cup (80 g) raw rock sugar crystals
1 pandanus leaf
½ head iceberg lettuce, finely sliced into
  thin shreds
1 cup (40 g) mint leaves

Lemon sesame dressing
3 tablespoons sesame seeds, lightly roasted
⅓ cup + 1 tablespoon (100 ml) lemon juice
⅓ cup + 1 tablespoon (100 ml) freshly-
  squeezed lime juice
2 tablespoons shaved palm sugar
⅓ cup + 1 tablespoon (100 ml) olive oil

Serves 6

Sometimes I like to serve this with a chili mayonnaise (such as the one on page 72) as a second sauce.

Bring a large pot of water to a boil and blanch the chicken for 10 seconds. Remove and shock in a large bowl or sink of iced water. Repeat the process three times, taking care not to tear the skin. This will help tighten the skin and keep it intact, and bring out any excess fat.

Rinse the pot and add the sake, water, rock sugar and pandanus leaf and bring to a boil, stirring until the sugar dissolves. When the liquid is boiling, add the chicken. Cover the pot with a lid and gently poach the chicken for 45 minutes.

Remove the pot from the heat and allow the chicken to cool in the liquid. Refrigerate the chicken in the liquid overnight.

Lemon sesame dressing
Pound the sesame seeds to a powder in a mortar and pestle. Combine the lemon juice, lime juice and palm sugar in a mixing bowl, stirring until the sugar dissolves. Add the olive oil and ground sesame seeds. Taste for a good balance of sweet and sour flavors, adjusting if required.

To serve
Remove the chicken from the poaching liquid, being careful not to tear the skin. Use a cleaver or a large, sharp knife to cut the chicken in half lengthwise. Cut out the backbone and discard. Slice off the wings and trim the knuckles from the base of the wings to expose the two small bones on either side. Pull out the bones. Cut off the legs between the thigh and body and separate the thighs from the drumsticks by cutting through the joint. Cut the breasts away from the rib cage (but leave them still attached to the breastplate). Cut the breasts and thighs through the bones into three pieces each so you have 12 pieces of breast and thigh. Leave the drumsticks whole.

Place the shredded lettuce and mint on a serving plate and arrange the chicken pieces on top. Pour over the Lemon Sesame Dressing and serve.

Red-cooked crispy quail

6 large quail (about 2 lbs/1 kg in total)

6 star anise pods

3 cinnamon sticks

1 in (2½ cm) peeled ginger, bruised and cut into 6 pieces

1 head garlic, peeled and bruised

2 green onions (scallions), coarsely chopped

4 cups (1 liter) Master Stock (page 12)

3 cups (750 ml) vegetable oil, for frying

1 tablespoon Sichuan Pepper-Salt Powder (page 11)

2 limes, quartered

Serves 6

In this recipe the quail are stuffed without being deboned—the Chinese love to cook poultry with the bones in, even quail, because sucking the flavorsome meat from the bones is half the fun.

Make the Sichuan Pepper-Salt Powder and Master Stock by following the recipes on pages 11 and 12.

Rinse the quail inside and out. Coarsely pound the star anise and cinnamon with a mortar and pestle. Place an equal amount of ginger, garlic, green onions, star anise and cinnamon in the cavity of each quail. Seal the openings by threading toothpicks through the skin.

Place the Master Stock and quail in a large pot and gently bring to a boil. When it boils, remove from the heat. Leave the quail in the stock for 10 minutes.

Remove the quail from the stock and elevate them on a wire rack set above a dish. Refrigerate the quail uncovered for a few hours, or until the skin of the quail is hard like parchment.

Heat the oil in a wok to 350°F (180°C). Fry the quail in batches until crisp. Drain on paper towels.

To serve, remove the toothpicks and split the quail in half. Discard the stuffing. Arrange the quail on a serving platter and sprinkle with the Sichuan Pepper-Salt Powder. Serve the lime wedges on the side.

Fried chicken with lemon and honey

1 lb (500 g) skinless chicken breasts, coarsely diced

2½ tablespoons fish sauce

1 tablespoon shaved palm sugar

½ teaspoon ground white pepper

1 tablespoon peanut oil

1 in (2½ cm) peeled ginger, finely chopped

2 cloves garlic, finely chopped

2 green finger-length chilies, finely sliced

3 green onions (scallions) cut into lengths

1 cup (150 g) green beans, cut into lengths

¼ cup (40 g) Fried Chili Peanuts (page 19) or roasted peanuts

⅓ cup (80 ml) Shao Xing rice wine

⅔ cup (150 ml) lemon juice

2 tablespoons honey

8 Thai basil leaves, torn

¼ cup (50 g) Fried Shallots (page 19)

Serves 6

Make the Fried Chili Peanuts and Fried Shallots by following the recipes on page 19.

Combine the chicken, fish sauce, palm sugar and pepper in a bowl. Leave to marinate for 10 minutes.

Heat the peanut oil in a wok and add the chicken. Stir-fry until the mixture begins to caramelize then add the ginger, garlic, chilies, green onions, green juice and honey and cook until the liquid has reduced and thickened to a sauce.

Transfer to a serving dish and garnish with the Thai basil and Fried Shallots.

Beef and pork

Barbecued pork omelet
with Chinese greens and XO sauce

4 eggs

1 teaspoon sesame oil

2 tablespoons oyster sauce

½ cup (120 ml) peanut oil

5 oz (150 g) Char Siu Pork (page 24, or bought from a restaurant), finely chopped

1 dried Chinese sausage (*lup cheong*), finely sliced

1 cup (50 g) fresh bean sprouts

¼ bunch Chinese broccoli leaves, finely chopped

3 green onions (scallions), finely sliced

1 in (2½ cm) peeled ginger, sliced into thin shreds

½ cup (20 g) garlic chives cut into lengths

½ cup (25 g) coriander leaves (cilantro)

1 teaspoon Sichuan Pepper-Salt Powder (page 11)

¼ cup (65 ml) XO Sauce (page 17)

2 lemons, quartered

Serves 6

Cooking omelets in a wok is just as easy as cooking them in a pan, and I like the crisp, crunchy texture of wok omelets (because you use a little more oil). Double the quantities to make two omelets or one large omelet if you want to serve this dish as a main meal. Roast duck can be used instead of the char siu pork if you prefer.

Make the Sichuan Pepper-Salt Powder, XO Sauce and Char Siu Pork by following the recipes on pages 11, 17 and 24.

Whisk the eggs with the sesame oil and 1 tablespoon of the oyster sauce. Heat the peanut oil in a wok until it begins to smoke then pour in the egg mixture. Gently move the wok over the heat in a circular motion to spread the egg out and make sure it cooks evenly. The omelet will bubble and float over the oil. When it is just set, drain away any excess oil from the top if necessary and spoon on the remaining oyster sauce. Top with the Char Siu Pork, dried Chinese sausage, bean sprouts, Chinese broccoli leaves, green onions, ginger, garlic chives and coriander leaves. When the omelet begins to crisp around the edges and the topping has warmed through, carefully lift the omelet out with two slotted spoons or other implements, drain off any excess oil, and place the omelet onto a serving plate. Fold the omelet over and sprinkle with the Sichuan Pepper-Salt Powder. Slice into portions and serve with the XO sauce and lemon wedges on the side.

Grilled coconut beef
with pickled bean sprout salad

4 cloves garlic, coarsely chopped

1 in (2½ cm) peeled ginger, coarsely chopped

¾ in (1½ cm) peeled galangal root, coarsely chopped

1 stalk lemongrass, tender inner part of bottom third only, finely sliced

2 kaffir lime leaves, finely sliced into thin shreds

2 red bird's-eye chilies, deseeded and coarsely chopped

4 coriander (cilantro) roots, washed and coarsely chopped

1 tablespoon Roasted Shrimp Paste (page 9)

3 tablespoons shaved palm sugar

1 cup (250 ml) coconut cream

2 lbs (1 kg) beef tenderloin, trimmed

Salad

2 cups (100 g) Pickled Bean Sprouts (page 22)

1 cucumber, sliced into thin sticks

1 stalk lemongrass, tender inner part of bottom third only, finely sliced

3 kaffir lime leaves, finely sliced into thin shreds

1 red onion, finely sliced

1 in (2½ cm) peeled ginger, finely sliced into thin shreds

2 red finger-length chilies, finely sliced

½ cup (20 g) mint leaves

1 tablespoon fish sauce

2 tablespoons freshly-squeezed lime juice

1 tablespoon shaved palm sugar

Serves 6

This salad is a favorite of mine—the pickled bean sprouts are slightly sweet and go well with the coconut beef.

Make the Roasted Shrimp Paste and Pickled Bean Sprouts by following the recipes on pages 9 and 22.

Using a mortar and pestle pound the garlic, ginger, galangal, lemongrass, kaffir lime leaves, chilies, coriander roots and Roasted Shrimp Paste to a fine paste. Alternatively, pound to a coarse paste with a mortar and pestle and finish off in a food processor. Add the palm sugar and coconut cream and combine.

Place the beef in a bowl or dish and cover with the coconut mixture. Marinate in the refrigerator overnight.

To serve

Combine the Salad ingredients and taste for a balance of flavors, adjusting if necessary.

Heat a broiler grill or barbecue to medium heat. Remove the beef from the marinade and cook, turning frequently, for around 10 minutes for medium-rare. Baste the beef with the leftover marinade as it cooks.

To serve, slice the beef against the grain and arrange the pieces on a serving plate. Serve the Salad on the side.

Crispy five spice pork cubes with chili jam and lime

2 lbs (1 kg) lean pork belly

2½ tablespoons Shao Xing rice wine

1 tablespoon soy sauce

4 cloves garlic, bruised

6 cardamom pods, cracked

5 star anise pods

2 cinnamon sticks, broken

2 nutmegs, cracked

3 tablespoons Sichuan peppercorns

3 tablespoons sea salt

3 cups (750 ml) vegetable oil, for frying

½ cup (125 ml) Chili Jam (page 13)

⅓ cup + 1 tablespoon (100 ml) coconut cream

2 limes, quartered

Serves 6

To get great aroma and flavor it is best to make your own five spice powder from fresh spices.

Make the Chili Jam by following the recipe on page 13.

Cut off the pork skin and discard. Cut the pork into three pieces and place in a bowl or dish. Cover with the Shao Xing rice wine, soy sauce and garlic and marinate in the refrigerator for 2–3 hours (or overnight).

Remove the pork pieces from the marinade and place in a steamer. Steam gently for 1 hour or until the pork is cooked through (test by inserting a skewer into the meat to see if the juices run clear). Remove from the steamer and set aside to cool, then chill in the refrigerator for a few hours to firm.

Dry roast the cardamom, star anise, cinnamon, nutmeg, Sichuan pepper and salt in a wok over medium heat until fragrant (2–3 minutes), stirring constantly to avoid burning. Remove from the heat and grind the mixture to a fine powder using a mortar and pestle or spice grinder. Sift the powder.

Heat the oil in a wok to 350°F (180°C). Dice the pork into bite-sized cubes and toss them in the spice powder, shaking off any excess. Fry the pork in batches until crisp. Drain on paper towels. Transfer the pork to a serving plate and serve with the Chili Jam, coconut cream and lime.

Meatball and ox tongue casserole

6 fresh shiitake mushrooms

6 oyster mushrooms, torn

3 baby bok choy, halved

Ox tongue

1 pickled ox tongue (about 3 lbs/1½ kgs)

1 medium brown onion, coarsely chopped

2 large carrots, coarsely chopped

1 leek, coarsely chopped

3 stalks celery, coarsely chopped

1 tablespoon black peppercorns

1 tablespoon sea salt

2 tablespoons olive oil

Meatballs

8 oz (250 g) ground beef

5 oz (150 g) ground pork

1 cup (100 g) cooked Jasmine Rice (page 24)

6 cloves garlic, finely chopped

1 in (2½ cm) peeled ginger, finely chopped

Grated rind of 1 orange

Grated rind of 1 lemon

2 red bird's-eye chilies, deseeded

3 green onions (scallions), finely sliced

3 coriander (cilantro) roots, washed

½ tablespoon soy sauce

1 teaspoon sesame oil

Claypot

6 cups (1½ liters) Asian Brown Chicken
    Stock (page 11)

1¼ cups (300 ml) Shao Xing rice wine

2 tablespoons soy sauce

3 tablespoons oyster sauce

4 pieces dried mandarin orange peel

4 dried black Chinese mushrooms

5 cloves garlic, finely chopped

1 in (2½ cm) peeled ginger, finely chopped

2 cinnamon sticks

6 star anise pods

5 green onions (scallions), finely sliced

1 cup (50 g) coriander leaves (cilantro)

2 tablespoons Chili Shrimp Oil (page 18), optional

Pickled ox tongues are available from most continental butchers. "Pickled" really means brined, which keeps the tongue pink and makes it more flavorful. If you prefer, you can also make this dish with just the meatballs.

Make the Asian Brown Chicken Stock, Chili Shrimp Oil and Jasmine Rice by following the recipes on pages 11, 18 and 24.

Ox tongue

Place the ox tongue, onion, carrots, leek, celery, pepper and salt in a large pot and cover with water. Bring to a gentle simmer and poach for 2–3 hours, or until the tongue is tender (test by squeezing the center of the tongue between your fingers—it should give easily). You may need to top up the liquid from time to time to ensure that the tongue and vegetables stay covered.

Leave the tongue in the liquid until it is cool enough to handle, then remove it from the liquid and peel away the skin, starting from the back of the tongue and ending at the tip. Place the tongue back in the liquid and allow to cool completely, then refrigerate in the liquid overnight.

Remove the tongue from the liquid. Cut it in half and set one half aside for another use. Slice the remaining half crosswise into ½ in (1 cm) thick slices.

Heat the olive oil in a pan or skillet and add the slices of tongue. Season with extra salt and pepper and brown the slices on both sides. For a smokier flavor, you could do this on a barbecue.

Meatballs

Finely chopped the bird's-eye chilies and coriander roots. Combine all the ingredients thoroughly in a mixing bowl and roll into bite-sized balls. Refrigerate for 1–2 hours to become firm.

Claypot

Place the chicken stock in a large pot and bring to a boil. Reduce it by a third to a half then add the Shao Xing rice wine, soy sauce, oyster sauce, mandarin orange peel, dried black Chinese mushrooms, garlic, ginger, cinnamon and star anise. Simmer for 5 minutes then remove from the heat.

Preheat the oven to 325°F (160°C). Place the tongue and meatballs in a claypot (or use a casserole dish with a lid) and pour in the contents of the pot. Cover with the lid and cook for 45 minutes, then turn off the oven and leave the claypot in the oven for 10 minutes (to avoid it cracking).

Garnish the claypot with green onions and coriander leaves and drizzle with Chili Shrimp Oil (if using). Trim the stems of the shiitake mushrooms and quarter them. Lightly stir-fry the shiitake mushrooms, oyster mushrooms and bok choy and serve on the side.

Serves 6

Grilled lemongrass beef with glass noodle salad

3 Asian shallots, coarsely chopped

4 cloves garlic, coarsely chopped

1 in (2½ cm) peeled ginger, coarsely chopped

2 stalks lemongrass, tender inner part of bottom third only, finely sliced

2 kaffir lime leaves, finely sliced into thin shreds

1 red bird's-eye chili, deseeded and coarsely chopped

1 tablespoon Fried Chili Peanuts (page 19) or roasted peanuts

1 tablespoon shaved palm sugar

1 tablespoon fish sauce

2 tablespoons freshly-squeezed lime juice

1½ lb (750 g) beef tenderloin, trimmed

¼ cup (50 g) Fried Shallots (page 19)

Salad

3½ oz (100 g) dried glass noodles

⅔ cup (100 g) green beans, sliced in half diagonally and blanched

3 tablespoons Candied Chilies (page 16)

¼ cup (50 g) Peanut Brittle (page 21), finely chopped

½ cup (20 g) mint leaves

½ cup (20 g) Thai basil leaves

2 tablespoons fish sauce

2 tablespoons freshly-squeezed lime juice

Serves 6

Make the Candied Chilies, Fried Chili Peanuts, Fried Shallots and Peanut Brittle by following the recipes on pages 16, 19 and 21.

Using a mortar and pestle pound the shallots, garlic, ginger, lemongrass, kaffir lime leaves, chili and peanuts to a fine paste. Alternatively, pound to a coarse paste with a mortar and pestle and finish off in a food processor. Add the palm sugar, fish sauce and lime juice and combine. Place the beef in a bowl, cover with the marinade and refrigerate for 1 hour.

Salad

Cover the noodles with boiling water and leave until tender (around 1 minute). Drain and refresh under cold water. Combine with the remaining Salad ingredients and taste for a balance of flavors, adjusting if required.

To serve

Place the ox tongue, onionHeat a broiler grill or barbecue to medium heat. Remove the beef from the marinade and cook, turning frequently, for around 10 minutes for medium-rare. Thinly slice the beef against the grain and toss the slices through the Salad. Garnish with the Fried Shallots and serve.

Roast pork with chili caramel sauce and green apple salad

1⅔ cups (400 ml) Shao Xing rice wine

⅓ cup + 1 tablespoon (100 ml) soy sauce

⅓ cup (60 g) sugar

1 head garlic, peeled and bruised

1 in (2½ cm) peeled ginger, bruised and coarsely chopped

2 cinnamon sticks, broken

6 star anise pods

5 cardamom pods, cracked

2 lbs (1 kg) pork belly, with skin on

2 cups (500 ml) vegetable oil, for frying

4 tablespoons sea salt

1 cup (250 ml) Chili Caramel Sauce (page 13)

Green apple salad

1½ tablespoons Stones green ginger wine

1 tablespoon lemon juice

1 tablespoon shaved palm sugar

2 green apples, peeled and cored and finely sliced into thin shreds

1 large red onion, finely sliced into rings

2 red finger-length chilies, deseeded and finely sliced lengthwise

1 in (2½ cm) peeled ginger, sliced into thin shreds

½ cup (25 g) coriander leaves (cilantro)

Serves 6

The longer you marinate the pork, the more the flavor of the spices intensifies. Marinate overnight at least, although several days is even better.

Make the Chili Caramel Sauce by following the recipe on page 13.

In a large bowl combine the Shao Xing rice wine, soy sauce and sugar and whisk until the sugar dissolves. Add the garlic, ginger, cinnamon, star anise and cardamom. Dip each side of the pork in the marinade to make sure it is thoroughly coated, then leave it in the bowl skin-side up and refrigerate for at least one night. Leave the pork uncovered to allow the skin to dry out.

Heat the oil in a wok to 350°F (180°C). Remove the pork from the marinade (reserving the marinade) and pat it dry with paper towels. Lower the pork into the oil skin-side down and fry without turning until the skin is covered in air bubbles (3–5 minutes). Remove from the oil and drain on paper towels.

Preheat the oven to 275°F (140°C). Transfer the pork skin-side up to an ovenproof dish. Strain the marinade, discarding the solids, and pour it around the pork. Season the skin of the pork with the salt and roast for 1½ hours.

Green apple salad

Combine the ginger wine, lemon juice and palm sugar in a mixing bowl, stirring until the sugar dissolves. Add the shredded apple and toss it immediately to stop the apple going brown, then add the remaining ingredients and combine.

To serve

Use a sharp knife to cut the crackling off the roast pork. Slice the pork, arrange the meat on a serving plate and drizzle it with the Chili Caramel Sauce. Serve the crackling and Green Apple Salad on the side.

Wagyu beef with black beans, mushrooms and garlic chives

1½ lbs (750 g) boneless wagyu beef rib eye
   (or other aged beef rib eye)
2 tablespoons sweet soy sauce
2 tablespoons Sichuan Pepper-Salt Powder
   (page 11)
2 tablespoons peanut oil
1 small red onion, finely sliced
3 cloves garlic, finely chopped
2 tablespoons dried salted black beans,
   gently rinsed
3 dried red finger-length chilies, softened in
   warm water for 30 minutes
1 tablespoon sugar
2½ tablespoons Shao Xing rice wine
1 teaspoon sesame oil
1 tablespoon oyster sauce
1½ tablespoons soy sauce
1 tablespoon black Chinese vinegar
2 cups (80 g) garlic chives cut into lengths
   (or substitute asparagus)
10 oyster mushrooms, torn
1 cup (50 g) coriander leaves (cilantro)
½ cup (20 g) Thai basil leaves

Serves 6

Wagyu beef is the best choice for quick-cooked dishes as its dense marbling makes it very tender and full-flavored. The saltiness and spiciness of the other ingredients are a great complement to the natural flavor of the beef.

Make the Sichuan Pepper-Salt Powder by following the recipe on page 11.

Place the beef in a bowl and rub with the sweet soy sauce and Sichuan Pepper-Salt Powder. Heat 1 tablespoon of the peanut oil in a pan over medium heat and fry the meat, turning frequently, for around 10 minutes for medium-rare. If you would like to cook the beef more, place in a 400°F (200°C) oven and cook for a further 5 or 10 minutes. Leave the beef to rest in a warm place.

Heat the remaining peanut oil in a wok and fry the onion, garlic, black beans and chilies until fragrant and beginning to brown. Add the sugar, Shao Xing rice wine, sesame oil, oyster sauce, soy sauce and black Chinese vinegar. When the liquid begins to reduce, add the garlic chives and oyster mushrooms and stir-fry for a minute. Remove from the heat and transfer the stir-fry to a serving dish.

Thinly slice the beef against the grain and place on top of the vegetables. Garnish with the coriander leaves and Thai basil.

Red-cooked pork hocks with red dates and black mushrooms

2 deboned pork hocks weighing around
   1 lb (500 g) each
8 cups (2 liters) Master Stock (page 12)
10 dried red dates
8 dried black Chinese mushrooms
6 cloves garlic, bruised
5 cardamom pods, cracked
5 star anise pods
2 cinnamon sticks
4 pieces dried mandarin orange peel
2 pieces dried liquorice root
1 tablespoon peanut oil
1 bunch *choy sum* (or substitute other
   Chinese greens), coarsely chopped
2 green onions (scallions), finely sliced
½ cup (50 g) coriander leaves (cilantro)

Serves 6

This is a simple Chinese dish of pork hocks braised in Master Stock. I love the gelatinous texture of pork hocks cooked this way, and the extra spices added to the stock make it wonderfully aromatic. Serve this with Jasmine or Coconut Rice (page 24) or with Fried Sticky Rice Balls (page 68).

Make the Master Stock by following the recipe on page 12.

Cut the pork hocks into four or six pieces each. Transfer them to a claypot or casserole dish with a lid.

Preheat the oven to 325°F (160°C). Bring the Master Stock to a boil in a large pot and pour it over the hocks. Add the dried red dates, black Chinese mushrooms, garlic, cardamom, star anise, cinnamon, mandarin orange peel and liquorice root. Cover with the lid and cook for 2–3 hours or until the meat is tender.

Heat the peanut oil in a wok and lightly stir-fry the *choy sum*. Serve the pork hocks moistened with a little stock and with the dried red dates, shiitake mushrooms and spices spooned on top. Garnish with green onions and coriander leaves and serve the *choy sum* on the side.

Grilled turmeric spareribs

1½ in (4 cm) peeled fresh turmeric root,
   coarsely chopped
¾ in (1½ cm) peeled ginger, minced
5 cloves garlic, coarsely chopped
1 stalk lemongrass, tender inner part of
   bottom third only, finely sliced
3 kaffir lime leaves, sliced into thin shreds
1 red bird's-eye chili, deseeded and minced
1 tablespoon coriander seeds, lightly roasted
1 tablespoon shaved palm sugar
1 cup (250 ml) coconut cream
2 lbs (1 kg) boneless pork spareribs
¼ cup (40 g) Fried Chili Peanuts (page 19)
1 cup (40 g) mint leaves

Serves 6

Serve these ribs on their own or tossed through a green mango salad (page 185) or a green papaya salad (page 68).

Make the Fried Chili Peanuts by following the recipe on page 19.

Using a mortar and pestle pound the turmeric, ginger, garlic, lemongrass, kaffir lime leaves, chili and coriander seeds to a fine paste. Alternatively, pound to a coarse paste in a mortar and pestle and finish off in a food processor. Add the palm sugar and coconut cream and combine.

Place the pork spareribs in a large mixing bowl and add the coconut mixture. Toss the spareribs to coat and refrigerate them for 2–3 hours (or overnight).

Heat a broiler grill or barbecue to medium heat and cook the spareribs, turning and basting with leftover marinade, for 10 minutes. The surface of the spareribs will caramelize. Transfer to a serving plate and garnish with the Fried Chili Peanuts and mint leaves.

Braised beef shin with sweet soy, peanuts, chili and lemon

3 lbs (1½ kgs) ox beef shin or beef brisket

⅔ cup (150 ml) sweet soy sauce

1½ in (4 cm) peeled ginger, bruised

8 cloves garlic, bruised

3 cups (750 ml) vegetable oil, for frying

1 medium red onion

2 red bird's-eye chilies

4 coriander (cilantro) roots, washed

1 tablespoon peanut oil

¾ cup (200 ml) Shao Xing rice wine

4 cups (1 liter) Asian Brown Chicken Stock (page 11)

¼ cup (50 g) raw rock sugar crystals

3 tablespoons oyster sauce

2 tablespoons black Chinese vinegar

2 heaped tablespoons (50 g) Tamarind Paste (page 18)

1 pandanus leaf, knotted

2 red finger-length chilies, finely sliced

2 lemons, quartered

Peanut paste

3 cloves garlic

1 in (2½ cm) peeled ginger

2 red bird's-eye chilies, deseeded

4 coriander (cilantro) roots, washed

3 kaffir lime leaves

½ cup (75 g) Fried Chili Peanuts (page 19) or roasted peanuts

1 teaspoon sea salt

1 tablespoon peanut oil

¼ cup (50 g) shaved palm sugar

2 tablespoons fish sauce

3 tablespoons freshly-squeezed lime juice

Serves 6

Serve this dish with fresh cucumber or crunchy greens.

Make the Asian Brown Chicken Stock, Tamarind Paste and Fried Chili Peanuts by following the recipes on pages 11, 18 and 19.

Trim the ox cheeks of any fat or sinew. Combine them in a bowl with the sweet soy sauce and half of the ginger and garlic. Marinate in the refrigerator overnight.

Heat the vegetable oil in a wok to 350°F (180°C). Remove the ox cheeks from the marinade and pat dry with paper towels. Fry the ox cheeks one at a time until crisp and dark. Drain on paper towels then transfer to a casserole dish.

Preheat the oven to 325°F (160°C). Coarsely chop the onion, chilies and coriander roots. Heat the peanut oil in a medium-sized pot and fry them with the remaining garlic and ginger until fragrant and beginning to brown. Add the remaining ingredients and bring to a boil. Pour the hot stock into the dish containing the ox cheeks and cover with a tight-fitting lid or foil. Cook for 2 hours, or until the cheeks are tender. Keep the ox cheeks in the hot liquid while you prepare the Peanut Paste.

Peanut paste

Coarsely chop the garlic, ginger, chilies and coriander roots and finely shred the kaffir lime leaves. Using a mortar and pestle pound them to a fine paste with the peanuts and salt. Alternatively, pound to a coarse paste with a mortar and pestle and finish with a food processor.

Heat the peanut oil in a wok over medium heat and fry the paste and palm sugar until fragrant and caramelized (around 10 minutes), stirring to make sure it doesn't catch. Add the fish sauce and the ox cheeks. Toss to combine and reheat if necessary, then add the lime juice. Taste for a balance of flavors, adjusting if necessary.

To serve

Transfer the ox cheeks to a serving dish and garnish with the chilies. Sprinkle with extra finely chopped peanuts and shredded kaffir lime leaves if you desire. Serve the lemon wedges on the side.

Thai pork and oxtail sausages

2 tablespoons peanut oil

2 lbs (1 kg) oxtail pieces (to yield around 1 lb/500 g cooked meat)

6 cups (1½ liters) Veal Stock (page 12)

10 oz (300 g) ground pork

3 Asian shallots, finely chopped

5 cloves garlic, finely chopped

1 in (2½ cm) peeled ginger, finely chopped

1 stalk lemongrass, tender inner part of bottom third only, finely sliced

2 kaffir lime leaves, finely sliced

1 green bird's-eye chili, deseeded, finely chopped

1 red bird's-eye chili, deseeded, finely chopped

4 coriander (cilantro) roots, washed, chopped

1 tablespoon Fried Chili Peanuts (page 19) or roasted peanuts, finely chopped

3 tablespoons Green Curry Paste (page 9)

1 teaspoon dried shrimp powder (made by processing several dried shrimp in a blender or food processor)

1 tablespoon fish sauce

2 tablespoons freshly-squeezed lime juice

Juice of half a lemon

1 teaspoon sea salt

3-ft (1-meter) sausage casing (see note)

⅓ cup + 1 tablespoon (100 ml) coconut cream

18 betel leaves

¼ cup (50 g) Fried Shallots (page 19)

Salad

½ cup (25 g) coriander leaves (cilantro)

½ cup (20 g) mint leaves

½ cup (20 g) Thai basil leaves

1 in (2½ cm) peeled ginger, finely sliced

6 Asian shallots, finely sliced

1 teaspoon dried shrimp powder (made by processing several dried shrimp in a blender or food processor)

3 tablespoons Hot and Sour Dressing (page 17)

These sausages, made with oxtail and pork, have a beautiful richness. Lettuce cups or Chinese cabbage can be used instead of betel leaves if you cannot find them.

Make the Green Curry Paste, Paste Veal Stock, Hot and Sour Dressing, Fried Chili Peanuts and Fried Shallots by following the recipes on pages 9, 12, 17 and 19.

Preheat the oven to 325°F (160°C). Heat the peanut oil in a large pan or skillet and brown the oxtail pieces. Transfer to a casserole dish. Bring the Veal Stock to a boil and pour it over the oxtail. Cover the dish with a tight-fitting lid or foil and place in the oven for 2–3 hours, or until the meat is falling off the bone.

When cool enough to handle, remove the oxtail from the stock and pick off the meat, breaking it into small pieces. Discard the bones and refrigerate or freeze the cooking stock for another use. Proceed with the next part of the recipe right away so the oxtail meat remains warm.

Combine the ground pork in a bowl with the shallots, garlic, ginger, lemongrass, kaffir lime leaves, chilies, coriander roots, peanuts, Green Curry Paste, dried shrimp powder, fish sauce and lime juice. Gently fold in the oxtail meat.

Fill a large bowl with water and add the lemon and salt. Wash the sausage casing thoroughly to remove any grit, then drain. Tie a knot in one end.

Fit a piping bag with a nozzle smaller than the width of the sausage casing. Fill the bag with the sausage mixture, pressing down to remove any air bubbles. Insert the nozzle into the open end of the casing. Carefully gather the casing over the nozzle until it reaches the knot and begin piping. Once all the mixture has been piped in, tie off the casing at the end of the mixture, discarding any excess casing. Curl the sausage into a spiral and refrigerate for at least 2 hours to allow the meat to set.

To serve

Combine the Salad ingredients in a bowl.

Heat a broiler grill or barbecue on medium heat and add the sausage spiral. Cook, turning and basting with coconut cream, for 10–12 minutes.

Arrange the betel leaves on a serving plate. Slice the sausage diagonally into 18 pieces and place each piece on a leaf. Top with the Salad and garnish with the Fried Shallots.

Note Sausage casings are available from most good continental-style butchers. Some butchers may be willing to fill the casing for you.

Serves 6

Sweet braised pork with shrimp

2 lbs (1 kg) pork belly

1 tablespoon peanut oil

1 small red onion, coarsely chopped

6 cloves garlic, bruised

1 in (2½ cm) peeled ginger, bruised and coarsely chopped

2 red bird's-eye chilies, coarsely chopped

4 coriander (cilantro) roots, washed and coarsely chopped

2 heaped tablespoons (50 g) Tamarind Paste (page 18)

½ cup (100 g) raw rock sugar crystals

2½ tablespoons oyster sauce

3 tablespoons black Chinese vinegar

1⅓ cups (350 ml) Shao Xing rice wine

4 cups (1 liter) Asian Brown Chicken Stock (page 11)

3 cups (750 ml) vegetable oil, for frying

Relish

½ tablespoon peanut oil

5 oz (160 g) fresh shrimp, peeled and deveined (to make 2½ oz/80 g), halved lengthwise

2 green finger-length chilies, deseeded and coarsely chopped

2 red finger-length chilies, deseeded and coarsely chopped

1 red bird's-eye chili, deseeded and chopped

3 cloves garlic, coarsely chopped

¾ in (1½ cm) peeled ginger, chopped

1 teaspoon Roasted Dried Shrimp (page 21)

6 cherry tomatoes, halved

2 kaffir lime leaves, finely sliced

1 cup (40 g) mint leaves, coarsely chopped

1 cup (50 g) coriander leaves (cilantro), coarsely chopped

3½ oz (100 g) Peanut Brittle (page 21), finely chopped

3 tablespoons shaved palm sugar

3 tablespoons freshly-squeezed lime juice

2 tablespoons fish sauce

Pork with shrimp is one of my favorite combinations. The flavors of this relish go well also with other meats as well, such as chicken or fish.

Make the Asian Brown Chicken Stock, Tamarind Paste and Roasted Dried Shrimp by following the recipes on pages 11, 18 and 21.

Preheat the oven to 325°F (160°C). Cut the pork belly in half and place the halves in a casserole dish skin-side up—the dish should be small enough so that when the liquid is added it will cover the pork. Heat the peanut oil in a medium-sized pot and fry the onion, garlic, ginger, chilies and coriander roots until fragrant and beginning to brown. Add the remaining ingredients except the vegetable oil and bring to a boil. Pour the hot liquid over the pork. Cover the dish with a tight-fitting lid or foil and place in the oven for 2–3 hours, or until the pork is tender.

Allow the pork to cool completely in the cooking liquid, then remove the pork from the liquid and pat it dry with paper towels. Refrigerate the pork uncovered for a few hours (or overnight) to become firm.

Relish

Heat the peanut oil in a pan or wok and fry the shrimp halves until slightly charred. Set them aside to cool and then finely chop them.

Using a mortar and pestle pound the chilies, garlic and ginger to a fine paste. Add the Roasted Dried Shrimp, tomatoes, kaffir lime leaves, mint and coriander leaves and pound until smooth (alternatively, you could do this in a food processor). Stir through the shrimp, Peanut Brittle, palm sugar, lime juice and fish sauce and taste for a balance of flavors, adjusting if necessary.

To serve

Heat the vegetable oil in a wok to 350°F (180°C) and fry the pork halves separately until crisp and the skin is covered in bubbles (around 10 minutes). If the oil doesn't completely cover the pork, you will need to turn the pieces halfway through. Drain on paper towels.

Use a sharp knife to cut the crackling off the pork. Slice the pork and arrange the slices on a serving plate. Spoon over the Relish and serve the crackling on the side.

Serves 6

Wagyu beef with young coconut salad and red curry sauce

1 tablespoon peanut oil
2 lbs (1 kg) boneless wagyu beef rib eye (or other aged beef rib eye)

Curry sauce
1 tablespoon peanut oil
⅓ cup + 1 tablespoon (100 ml) coconut cream
½ cup (100 g) Red Curry Paste (page 10)
¼ cup (50 g) shaved palm sugar
1⅔ cups (400 ml) coconut milk
1 cup torn betel leaves
½ cup (75 g) Fried Chili Peanuts (page 19)
2 tablespoons fish sauce
3 tablespoons freshly-squeezed lime juice

Caramelized pumpkin and green beans
12 oz (350 g) butternut pumpkin, peeled and chopped into ¾ in (1½ cm) cubes to yield 3 cups
6 cloves garlic, unpeeled
⅓ cup (80 ml) sweet soy sauce
1 tablespoon shaved palm sugar
3 cups (450 g) green beans cut into lengths, blanched

Young coconut salad
1 young coconut
1 medium red onion, finely sliced into rings
2 red finger-length chilies, finely sliced
½ cup (25 g) coriander leaves (cilantro)
½ cup (20 g) mint leaves
½ cup (20 g) Thai basil leaves
2½ tablespoons Hot and Sour Dressing (page 17)

Serves 6

This is a popular dish at our restaurant. The rich wagyu, pungent curry sauce and fresh coconut salad are simply fantastic together. You can serve the caramelized pumpkin and green beans as an accompaniment to other dishes as well.

Make the Red Curry Paste, Hot and Sour Dressing, and Fried Chili Peanuts by following the recipes on pages 10, 17 and 19.

Curry sauce
Heat the peanut oil in a heavy-based saucepan and add the coconut cream. Fry over medium heat until the coconut cream splits. Add the Red Curry Paste and fry until fragrant (around 5 minutes), stirring to make sure it doesn't catch. Add the palm sugar and cook until the mixture begins to caramelize, turning a dark red color. Add the coconut milk and bring to a boil, then remove from the heat. Set aside.

Caramelized pumpkin and green beans
Boil the pumpkin in a pot of boiling water until still slightly firm in the center. Drain and set aside.
   Heat the oven to 350°F (180°C) and roast the garlic until tender (around 20 minutes). When cool enough to touch, slip the cloves out of their skins.
   Place the garlic, sweet soy sauce and palm sugar in a deep pan and simmer until reduced by half. Add the pumpkin and cook until the surface begins to caramelize and it is cooked through without being too soft. Stir through the green beans then remove from the heat.

Young coconut salad
Pierce the coconut with a metal skewer and drain out the juice. Cut off the pointed top with a sharp knife or cleaver and scoop out the soft flesh with a spoon, trying to keep it in large pieces. Cut the pieces into very fine strands. Combine the coconut with the remaining ingredients apart from the Hot and Sour Dressing and set aside.

To serve
Heat the peanut oil in a large pan or skillet over medium heat. Add the beef and cook, turning frequently, for around 10 minutes for medium-rare. If you would like to cook the beef more, place in a 400°F (200°C) oven and cook for a further 5 or 10 minutes. Rest the beef in a warm place while you prepare the other ingredients.
   Reheat the curry without boiling, adding the betel leaves, peanuts, fish sauce and lime juice. Taste for a balance of flavors, adjusting if necessary.
   Dress the Salad and gently reheat the pumpkin and green beans in the pan.
   Slice the beef into six slices. Divide the Caramelized Pumpkin and Green Beans between serving plates and place a slice of beef on top. Spoon over some curry sauce and top with the Young Coconut Salad.

Roast pork with plum relish and vinegar ginger rice

1 portion Roast Pork (page 196)
1 cup (50 g) coriander leaves (cilantro)

Relish
10 blood plums, pitted and coarsely
  chopped
1 medium red onion, finely chopped
3 cloves garlic, finely chopped
3 red bird's-eye chilies, deseeded and finely
  chopped
2 coriander (cilantro) roots, washed and
  finely chopped
1 cinnamon stick
2 whole cloves
⅔ cup (150 ml) sweet soy sauce
⅓ cup (60 g) shaved palm sugar
⅔ cup (150 ml) water
1 tablespoon fish sauce
2 tablespoons freshly-squeezed lime juice

Vinegar rice
3 cups (300 g) cooked Sticky Rice (page 24)
3 cups (300 g) cooked Jasmine Rice (page 24)
1½ in (4 cm) peeled ginger, finely chopped
3 coriander (cilantro) roots, washed and
  finely chopped
5 green onions (scallions), finely sliced
⅓ cup + 1 tablespoon (100 ml) rice wine
  vinegar

Serves 6

Make this dish in summer or autumn, when sweet, juicy blood plums are in season. Vinegar rice is a robust accompaniment to sweet dishes and also to pork, as it cuts through any fattiness. Mixing Jasmine and Sticky Rice together gives you the best of both worlds—fragrance and taste, and texture—but you can make this with just Jasmine Rice if you prefer.

Make the Jasmine Rice and Sticky Rice by following the recipes on page 24. To make the Roast Pork, follow the recipe on page 196.

Relish
Place the plums, onion, garlic, chilies, coriander roots, cinnamon stick, cloves, sweet soy sauce, palm sugar and water in a saucepan. Bring to a boil then simmer for 20 minutes until soft and reduced. Remove from the heat and add the fish sauce and lime juice. Taste for a balance of flavors, adjusting if necessary.

Vinegar rice
Combine the ingredients for the Vinegar Rice in a mixing bowl, then transfer to a smaller heatproof bowl that will fit inside a steamer. Alternatively, you can divide the rice between six individual heatproof serving bowls. Steam for 5–10 minutes, or until the rice has heated through.

To serve
Take the pork from the oven and use a sharp knife to cut the crackling off. Slice the pork and arrange the meat on a serving plate. Spoon over the Relish and garnish with the coriander leaves. Serve the crackling and Vinegar Rice on the side, either in the bowl it was steamed in or inverted onto a warm plate.

Osso buco with wasabi potato dumplings and Sichuan pepper sauce

2½ tablespoons olive oil

6 thick slices veal osso buco

6 cups (1½ liters) Veal Stock (page 12)

1 teaspoon Sichuan Pepper-Salt Powder (page 11)

1 cup (50 g) coriander leaves (cilantro)

Sichuan pepper sauce

1 fresh cob corn, kernels removed for another use, cob coarsely chopped

5 cloves garlic, bruised

2 coriander (cilantro) roots, washed and coarsely chopped

1½ tablespoons Sichuan peppercorns, lightly roasted and ground

3 tablespoons black Chinese vinegar

1 tablespoon Dijon mustard

Wasabi potato dumplings

14 oz (400 g) waxy potatoes such as Desiree or Nicola, peeled and diced

4 tablespoons (80 g) unsalted butter, diced

2½ tablespoons heavy cream

1 teaspoon wasabi paste

12 wonton skins

Stir-fried lettuce

1½ tablespoons peanut oil

4 cloves garlic, finely sliced

8 green onions (scallions), cut into lengths

½ head iceberg lettuce, shredded

Serves 6

These unusual flavors work beautifully together—the dish has appeared on the menu at ezard on many occasions in winter.

Make the Sichuan Pepper-Salt Powder Veal Stock by following the recipes on pages 11 and 12.

Preheat the oven to 325°F (160°C). Heat the olive oil in a large pan or skillet and brown the osso buco slices. Transfer to a casserole dish. Bring the Veal Stock to a boil and pour it over the osso buco. Cover the dish with a tight-fitting lid or foil and place it in the oven for 2–3 hours, or until the meat is falling off the bone.

Allow the meat to cool completely in the stock then remove the meat and refrigerate until needed. Reserve the stock for the Sichuan Pepper Sauce.

Sichuan pepper sauce

Strain the osso buco stock into a large pot. Bring it to a boil, skimming the surface of any impurities, and reduce the stock by half. Add the corn cob and reduce the stock by another third, then remove the cob. (The corn helps the sauce to thicken naturally.) Add the remaining ingredients and simmer for a further 5 minutes then remove from the heat. The sauce should lightly coat the back of a spoon.

Wasabi potato dumplings

Boil the potatoes in salted water until tender. Drain and then mash them, preferably with a potato ricer. Add the butter, cream and wasabi paste and mix thoroughly. Season to taste.

Lay six of the wonton skins out on a clean work surface and place a heaped tablespoon of the potato mixture in the center of each one. Lightly brush around the edges with water. Top with the remaining six wonton skins and press the edges together to seal. Make sure you push out any air. Cut the Dumplings into circles with a knife or a cookie cutter and refrigerate them, covered in plastic wrap, until needed.

To serve

Place the osso buco pieces in a large pan or skillet and strain the Sichuan Pepper Sauce into the pan. Gently reheat the meat and Sauce.

Meanwhile, place the Dumplings in a steamer and steam for 5 minutes.

For the Stir-fried Lettuce, heat the peanut oil in a wok and fry the garlic and green onions until fragrant and beginning to soften. Add the lettuce and stir-fry over high heat until slightly charred and wilted. Remove from the heat before the lettuce begins to stew. For the best result, do this in two or three batches.

To serve, divide the Stir-fried Lettuce between serving plates. Add a piece of osso buco to each one and place a Dumpling on top. Drizzle the Sauce around the sides and sprinkle with the Sichuan Pepper-Salt Powder. Garnish with coriander leaves.

Desserts

Caramelized pineapple with tamarind granita

Granita
2 cups (500 ml) water
⅓ cup (100 g) Tamarind Paste (page 18)
¾ cup (150 g) sugar

Pineapple
1 medium pineapple
⅓ cup (80 g) brown sugar
2 tablespoons (40 g) unsalted butter

Serves 6

Tamarind is quite a sour and unusual flavor to use in dessert, but it teams well with the sweetness of pineapple.

Make the Tamarind Paste by following the recipe on page 18.

Granita
Combine all the ingredients in a saucepan and heat, stirring, until the sugar dissolves. Set aside to cool.

Pour into a shallow dish or container and place in the freezer. Use a fork to scrape and mix the ice every 45 minutes until it becomes a frozen ice slush—you will need to do this four or five times in total. It is best to serve the granita the day it is made.

Pineapple
Cut the peel from the pineapple. Remove the eyes by cutting channels in the pineapple all the way around. Slice the pineapple into quarters. Trim off the portions of core and slice the quarters crosswise into three pieces each. Place the pieces in a bowl and toss in brown sugar.

Heat the butter in a pan until it melts, then add the pineapple and any sugar left in the bowl. Cook, turning, until the pineapple is sticky and caramelized. Leave to cool to room temperature.

To serve
Give the Granita another scrape to refresh it. Place the caramelized Pineapple in serving bowls and top with the Granita.

Sweet taro dumplings with chocolate, coconut and candied chilies

¾ cup (150 g) dark chocolate, coarsely chopped

2½ tablespoons coconut cream

½ cup (90 g) unsweetened desiccated coconut, lightly roasted

1 tablespoon Candied Chilies (page 16), coarsely chopped

1 lb (500 g) taro, peeled and diced

1 tablespoon (20 g) clarified butter or ghee

½ cup (50 g) cornstarch

1 teaspoon superfine (caster) sugar

1 teaspoon baking soda

3 cups (750 ml) vegetable oil, for frying

Chocolate sugar

2 tablespoons confectioner (icing) sugar

1 tablespoon cocoa

Serves 6

These dumplings are a twist on the savory taro dumplings regularly served at dim sum (page 56). Eat them warm, with the filling still melted inside.

Make the Candied Chilies by following the recipe on page 16.

Place the chocolate and coconut cream in a bowl set over a pot of simmering water and heat, stirring occasionally, until the mixture is melted and smooth.

Add the toasted coconut and Candied Chilies and combine. Pour the mixture onto a small tray lined with greaseproof paper to cool, then portion the mixture into 12 small balls (it should be firm but pliable). Refrigerate the balls.

Place the taro on a heatproof dish and insert into a steamer. Steam for 30 minutes or until tender. Transfer to a mixing bowl and mash with the clarified butter or ghee until there are no lumps. Leave the mash to cool a little, then stir in the cornstarch, sugar and baking soda. The dough should have the consistency of soft mashed potato (add a little water if it seems too thick). Lift the dough onto a floured surface and knead briefly. Roll into a sausage shape and portion into 12 pieces. Shape each piece into a ball.

Hold a ball of dough in one hand and flatten it with your other hand. Place a ball of chocolate mixture in the center and mold the dough around the chocolate to form a torpedo shape. Repeat with the rest of the dough. Refrigerate the Dumplings for at least 20 minutes before cooking.

For the Chocolate Sugar, combine the confectioner (icing) sugar and cocoa, ensuring there are no lumps. Set aside.

Heat the oil in a wok to 350°F (180°C) and fry the Dumplings in batches until fluffy and golden (around 3 minutes). Drain on paper towels. Dust with the Chocolate Sugar and serve.

Pandanus dumplings
with palm sugar syrup

Palm Sugar Syrup

1½ cups (300 g) shaved dark palm sugar

4 pieces dried mandarin orange peel

2 pandanus leaves, knotted

2 star anise pods

2 cinnamon sticks

1⅔ cups (400 ml) water

Pandanus dumplings

2⅓ cups (350 g) self-raising flour

4 tablespoons (80 g) unsalted butter, diced

2 tablespoons shaved palm sugar

2 eggs

½ tablespoon pandanus essence

⅓ cup + 1 tablespoon (100 ml) milk

Serves 6

The long, spear-shaped pandanus leaf is from the screwpine tree, a tropical plant found across Asia. The leaves and essence have a vanilla-like character.

Palm Sugar Syrup

Combine the ingredients in a saucepan and bring to a boil, stirring until the sugar dissolves. Simmer until reduced by a third and lightly syrupy—it will thicken a little more as it cools.

Pandanus dumplings

Sift the flour into a mixing bowl and add the butter and palm sugar. Rub the mixture with your fingertips until it resembles fine breadcrumbs. Add the eggs, pandanus essence and milk and combine. Don't over work the dough or it may toughen.

Using wet hands, form the dough into six Dumplings. Cut a pattern such as a crisscross on the top of each one if you desire. Place the Dumplings into a steamer lined with greaseproof paper and steam for 15–20 minutes—they will have risen slightly.

To serve, strain and reheat the Palm Sugar Syrup and pour a generous amount into the bottom of each bowl. Place a hot Dumpling on top. Serve with cream or ice cream if you desire.

Caramelized bananas
with cardamom custard

5 cardamom pods
2½ tablespoons (50 g) unsalted butter
1⅓ cups (170 g) superfine (caster) sugar
2 ripe sugar bananas, peeled and
    halved lengthwise
8 egg yolks
2⅔ cups (600 ml) heavy cream
½ cup (100 g) brown sugar

Serves 6

Crack the cardamom pods, remove the seeds and grind the seeds to a powder using a mortar and pestle. Place the butter and ¼ cup (50 g) of the caster sugar in a pan or saucepan and heat until the butter melts. Add the bananas and cardamom powder and cook, turning, until the bananas are soft and caramelized. Puree the bananas and any juices from the pan in a blender.

In a mixing bowl whisk together the egg yolks and remaining caster sugar until the sugar dissolves.

Place the cream in a saucepan and heat until almost boiling. Slowly whisk the hot cream into the egg and sugar mixture. Add the banana puree and combine.

Preheat the oven to 300°F (150°C). Pour the custard into six small ramekins or heatproof dishes and place them in a deep baking tray lined with a dish towel (this keeps the dishes from moving around). Pour boiling water into the tray to come between half and two-thirds of the way up the sides of the dishes. Cover the tray loosely with a sheet of foil and place in the oven to bake for 20 minutes or until the custard are just set. Cool and refrigerate the custard until you are ready to serve.

To serve, preheat your broiler grill to its highest temperature. Remove the custard from the refrigerator and sprinkle them evenly with the brown sugar. Place them under the grill until the sugar caramelizes, then leave them to cool for a few minutes until the sugar sets hard. Alternatively, you can caramelize the tops with a gas blowtorch.

Fried peanut brittle ice cream with cardamom sugar

3 vanilla pods
2 cups (500 ml) milk
2 cups (500 ml) heavy cream
12 egg yolks
2 cups (250 g) superfine (caster) sugar
½ cup (100 g) Peanut Brittle (page 21), finely chopped
3 cups (750 ml) vegetable oil, for frying
3 cups (375 g) rice flour
1 portion Beer Batter (page 23)
⅓ cup + 1 tablespoon (100 ml) Palm Sugar Syrup (page 18)
⅓ cup + 1 tablespoon (100 ml) coconut cream (optional)

Cardamom sugar
10 cardamom pods
2 tablespoons superfine (caster) sugar

Serves 6

As a shortcut you can make this with good-quality bought vanilla ice cream—simply fold through the peanut brittle and refreeze.

Make the Palm Sugar Syrup, Peanut Brittle and Beer Batter by following the recipes on pages 18, 21 and 23.

Split the vanilla pods and scrape the seeds into a saucepan, adding the pods too. Add the milk and cream and bring to a simmer then remove from the heat and leave to infuse for 20 minutes.

In a mixing bowl whisk together the eggs and sugar until they become thick and pale. Remove the vanilla pods from the warm milk mixture and slowly pour it over the eggs, whisking to combine. Set the bowl over a pot of simmering water and heat gently for 5–10 minutes, stirring constantly, until the custard thickens enough to coat the back of a spoon.

Place the bowl in a sink of iced water to cool. Pour the custard into an ice cream machine and churn according to the manufacturer's instructions. Fold through the Peanut Brittle then transfer to a container and place in the freezer. Alternatively, pour the custard into a shallow dish or container and place in the freezer until frozen at the edges. Scrape back into the bowl and beat with electric beaters, then return to the dish and place back in the freezer. Repeat this process 2–3 times, folding through the Peanut Brittle the last time.

When the ice cream is thoroughly frozen, scoop out 12 golf ball-sized balls. Place the balls on a tray and freeze overnight.

To serve
For the Cardamom Sugar, crack the cardamom pods, remove the seeds and grind the seeds to a powder using a mortar and pestle. Combine with the sugar.

Heat the oil in a wok to 350°F (180°C). Remove the ice cream balls from the freezer and, working quickly, dredge the balls in rice flour, dusting off any excess, then dip them in the Beer Batter. Fry the balls in batches until crisp and golden. Drain on paper towels. Sprinkle the balls with the Cardamom Sugar and serve drizzled with the Palm Sugar Syrup and coconut cream (if using).

Red bean pancakes with vanilla ice cream

1¼ cups (300 ml) boiling water
1⅓ oz (40 g) unsalted butter
2 cups (300 g) all-purpose (plain) flour
1 cup (200 g) sweetened red bean paste
2 tablespoons peanut oil
½ cup (125 ml) sugar treacle syrup
Vanilla ice cream

Serves 6

Red bean pancakes are popular throughout China, but are perhaps more similar to flat bread than to the Western idea of pancakes. The red bean paste filling is quite sweet and dry, so treacle and vanilla ice cream are a great match. Use good quality bought vanilla ice cream or follow the ice cream recipe (page 216) but omit the Peanut Brittle.

Pour the boiling water into a large mixing bowl and add the butter. Sift in the flour and stir the mixture until it comes together as a dough. Turn out onto a lightly floured surface and gently knead until smooth—add more water if the dough seems too firm or more flour if too soft. Roll the dough into a sausage shape and portion into 12 pieces. Shape each piece into a ball.

Divide the red bean paste into 12 smaller pieces by cutting it with a knife or pinching it off with your fingers.

Flatten a ball of dough in your hand and place a piece of red bean paste in the center. Fold the edges of dough into the middle to encase the paste then gently flatten the dough into a pancake. Carefully roll it out with a rolling pin so it is around ⅛ in (3 mm) thick and the size of a large pikelet. Repeat with the remaining dough and paste.

Fry the pancakes in batches until golden brown on each side, adding a small amount of the peanut oil to the pan with each new batch. Divide the pancakes between serving plates and drizzle with treacle. Top with a scoop of vanilla ice cream and serve immediately.

Fried bananas with palm sugar syrup and coconut ice cream

Coconut ice cream
1½ cups (140 g) grated fresh coconut,
   lightly roasted
2 cups (500 ml) milk
1⅓ cups (350 ml) heavy cream
9 egg yolks
1⅓ cups (170 g) superfine (caster) sugar
⅔ cup (150 ml) Palm Sugar Syrup (page 18)
⅓ cup + 1 tablespoon (100 ml) coconut
   cream

Cinnamon sugar
2 tablespoons superfine (caster) sugar
1 teaspoon ground cinnamon

Fried bananas
3 cups (750 ml) vegetable oil, for frying
6 ripe sugar bananas
1 portion Beer Batter (page 23)

Serves 6

Make the Palm Sugar Syrup and Beer Batter by following the recipes on pages 18 and 23.

Coconut ice cream

Place the grated coconut, milk and cream in a saucepan and bring to a boil, then remove from the heat. Leave for 20 minutes to allow the coconut flavor to infuse.

In a mixing bowl whisk together the eggs and sugar until they become thick and pale. Gently strain in the warm infused milk and whisk to combine.

Set the bowl over a pot of simmering water and heat gently for 5–10 minutes, stirring constantly, until the custard thickens enough to coat the back of a spoon. Place the bowl in a sink of iced water to cool.

Pour the custard into an ice cream machine and churn according to the manufacturer's instructions, then transfer the ice cream to a container and place in the freezer until ready to serve. Alternatively, pour the custard into a shallow dish or container and place in the freezer until frozen at the edges. Scrape back into the bowl and beat with electric beaters, then return to the dish and place back in the freezer. Repeat this process 2–3 times.

To serve

For the Cinnamon Sugar, combine the sugar and cinnamon and set aside.

Heat the oil in a wok to 350°F (180°C). Peel the bananas and dip them in the batter, shaking off any excess. Fry them in batches until crisp and golden (around 3 minutes). Drain on paper towels.

Place the Fried Bananas in serving bowls and sprinkle with the Cinnamon Sugar. Drizzle with Palm Sugar Syrup and coconut cream and top with a scoop of Coconut Ice Cream.

Mango and pineapple with tapioca salad and coconut caramel sauce

1⅓ cups (200 g) dried tapioca pearls
1¼ cups (250 g) shaved palm sugar
⅓ cup + 1 tablespoon (100 ml) water
⅓ cup + 1 tablespoon (100 ml) coconut
  cream
2 limes
1 ripe mango, peeled, flesh finely diced
½ small ripe pineapple, peeled, cored and
  finely diced

Serves 6

Fill a pot with water and bring to a boil. Add the dried tapioca pearls, stirring at first to make sure they don't stick. Simmer until they are almost completely transparent with just a small speck of white left in the middle (around 10 minutes). Drain and refresh under cold water and set aside to cool.

For the coconut caramel, combine the palm sugar and water in a saucepan and bring to a boil. Simmer until it begins to turn into a light brown caramel (around 10 minutes), then watch it closely and take it off the heat just before it becomes dark brown. (You will need to brush or scrape the sides of the saucepan occasionally to keep crystals from forming.) Add the coconut cream, shaking the saucepan to combine. Set aside to cool.

Cut the peel from the limes and segment them by cutting as close to the membrane as possible on either side of each natural segment. Work your way around the limes until you have cut all the segments out. Coarsely dice the segments.

Combine the lime, mango, pineapple, tapioca and coconut caramel in a mixing bowl. Spoon into individual bowls and serve.

Egg and coconut custard

1¼ cups (300 ml) heavy cream
3 tablespoons grated fresh coconut,
  lightly roasted
8 duck egg yolks
1¼ cups (150 g) superfine (caster) sugar
1¼ cups (300 ml) coconut cream
1 tablespoon Malibu liquer

Serves 6

Duck eggs lend a wonderful richness to these custard (although use chicken eggs if you prefer—you'll need ten egg yolks instead of eight). For a rustic look I sometimes cook these in halved coconuts.

Place the cream and grated fresh coconut in a saucepan and bring to a simmer, then remove from the heat. Leave for 20 minutes to allow the coconut flavor to infuse.

Whisk the egg yolks and sugar until thick and pale, then slowly strain in the warm infused cream and combine. Whisk in the coconut cream and Malibu liquer.

Preheat the oven to 300°F (150°C). Pour the custard into six small ramekins or heatproof dishes and place them in a deep baking tray lined with a dish towel (this keeps the dishes from moving around). Pour boiling water into the tray to come between half and two-thirds of the way up the sides of the dishes. Cover the tray loosely with a sheet of foil and place in the oven to bake for 20 minutes, or until the custard are just set.

Serve the custard warm.

Sweet black rice pudding with mango cheeks and coconut cream

2¼ cups (430 g) uncooked black glutinous rice, soaked for 4 hours (or overnight)

1 cup (275 ml) coconut cream

¾ cup (170 g) sugar

1 teaspoon sea salt

1 pandanus leaf, knotted

1½ tablespoons rice flour

3 ripe mangoes, peeled, cheeks sliced off and scored

6 mint sprigs

¼ cup (50 g) Fried Shallots (page 19)

Serves 6

Try to find black glutinous rice from Thailand or Bali—these countries produce the best black rice, with a reddish brown color when cooked and a beautiful nuttiness. I prefer to steam rather than boil rice puddings as the texture remains light and the flavor of the rice is retained.

Make the Fried Shallots by following the recipe on page 19.

Rinse the soaked glutinous rice thoroughly under cold running water to remove any excess starch. Drain. Place the rice into a deep dish that will fit into a steamer. Add enough water to cover the rice by 1 in (2½ cm) and cover the dish with foil. Steam until the rice is tender (around 1 hour).

While the rice is cooking, combine the coconut cream, sugar, salt and pandanus leaf in a large saucepan or small pot and bring to a gentle simmer, stirring until the sugar dissolves. Place the rice flour in a small bowl or cup and add just enough water to make a smooth paste. Add this to the saucepan and cook until the cream thickens slightly (around 3 minutes), then remove from the heat.

When the rice is cooked, remove the pandanus leaf from the coconut cream. Heat the cream back to simmering point then pour half of it into a bowl and set aside. Scoop the rice into the saucepan with the remaining cream and combine. The aim is for the rice to be moistened but not swimming, and sweet to taste; add more cream if needed.

To serve, spoon the rice into serving bowls and place the mango cheeks on the side. Drizzle with the remaining coconut cream and garnish with mint sprigs and Fried Shallots.

Pears poached in palm sugar, cinnamon, cardamom and star anise

2 cups (400 g) shaved dark palm sugar

Grated rind of 2 oranges

2 cinnamon sticks

6 star anise pods

4 cardamom pods, cracked

1¼ cups (300 ml) water

6 pears, peeled, halved and cored

1 lotus root (see Note)

2 cups (500 ml) vegetable oil, for frying

Confectioner (icing) sugar

Serves 6

Lotus roots have quite a mild flavor and can be used in savory or sweet dishes. When cut thinly, fried and dusted in confectioners' sugar, they are like sweet crisps.

Place the palm sugar, orange rind, cinnamon, star anise, cardamom and water in a small pot and bring to a boil. Add the pears—if they are not completely covered, add more water. Weight them down in the liquid with a small plate and simmer gently until tender (the time this takes will depend on the variety and ripeness of the pears).

Remove the pears and return the pan to the heat. Simmer the syrup until reduced and slightly thickened. Remove from the heat and set aside.

Peel the lotus root. Using a sharp knife slice the root into thin slices (if you prefer long slices, slice the root on an angle). Place the slices between sheets of paper towels to absorb any moisture. Heat the oil in a wok to 350°F (180°C) and fry the lotus slices in batches until crisp and golden. Drain on paper towels. Allow to cool then dust with confectioners' (icing) sugar.

To serve, strain the syrup (reserving the aromatics) and return the syrup to the saucepan. Add the pears and gently reheat. Place two pear halves in each serving bowl and pour over the syrup. Garnish with some of the reserved aromatics and a slice or two of lotus root. Accompany with cream or ice cream if desired.

Note You will only need 6–12 slices of lotus root for the garnish, but if you prefer, slice up the whole root and serve the others on the side.

Coconut ginger granitas with lychee and mango salsa

Coconut ginger granitas
4 young coconuts
4 oz (125 g) young ginger
Scant 1 cup (185 g) sugar
1/3 cup + 1 tablespoon (100 ml) water

Raspberry jam
1¼ cups (250 g) sugar
2/3 cup (150 ml) water
8 oz (250 g) raspberries, fresh or frozen, well drained
3 red bird's-eye chilies, deseeded and finely chopped

Lychee and mango salsa
18 lychees, peeled, pitted and coarsely diced
2 mangoes, flesh diced
½ cup (20 g) Vietnamese mint leaves, finely shredded
3 kaffir lime leaves, finely shredded

Serves 6

For the coconut juice, buy the freshest young coconuts you can find—ones that sound like they have the most liquid inside. You should get around ¾ cup (200 ml) of juice per coconut. Raspberry Jam is a hot and sweet combination you can serve with all kinds of tropical fruits.

Coconut ginger granitas
Pierce the coconuts with a metal skewer and drain out the juice—measure out 2½ cups (625 ml) and strain. Reserve the flesh of the coconuts for salads and other recipes.

Wet a large square of muslin cloth and wring it out. Lay the cloth inside a large bowl so that it comes up and over the sides and finely grate the ginger into the cloth. Form a ball around the ginger and squeeze out as much juice as possible—you should get around 1/8 cup (30 ml).

Combine the sugar and water in a saucepan and heat until the sugar dissolves. Set aside to cool. Once cool, stir in the coconut and ginger juices and pour the liquid into a shallow dish or container and place in the freezer. Use a fork to scrape and mix the ice every 45 minutes until it becomes a frozen ice slush—you will need to do this four or five times in total. It is best to serve the granita the day it is made.

Raspberry jam
Combine the sugar and water in a saucepan and heat, stirring, until the sugar dissolves. Simmer until it begins to turn light brown then immediately add the raspberries and chilies. Cook for 10 minutes or until the raspberries and chilies are soft and the liquid has reached a jam-like consistency. Remove from the heat and allow to cool a little. Puree in a blender then push the jam through a sieve to remove the raspberry seeds and chilies.

To serve
Give the Granita another scrape to refresh it. Combine the ingredients for the Lychee and Mango Salsa and divide between serving bowls. Top with scoops of Coconut Ginger Granitas and Raspberry Jam.

Lime tarts with caramelized chili rock sugar

1 cup (200 g) unsalted butter, softened
¾ cup (100 g) confectioner (icing) sugar
1 vanilla pod (optional)
2 egg yolks
1⅔ cups (250 g) all-purpose (plain) flour
Pinch of salt
1 portion Chili Rock Sugar (page 11)

Filling
2⅔ cups (325 g) superfine (caster) sugar
1¼ cups (300 ml) heavy cream
9 eggs
6 limes, grated rind of 3 and all juiced

Serves 6

Chinese raw rock sugar crystals are an unrefined crystal sugar that has great depth of flavor without being overly sweet. I use it a lot in my savory cooking, but it also makes a great brulée topping. If you don't have small tart tins, make this as a large tart to share.

Make the Chili Rock Sugar by following the recipe on page 11

Cream the butter and sugar until pale and smooth. Split the vanilla pod in half lengthwise (if using) and scrape out the seeds with the tip of a knife. Add the seeds and the egg yolks to the butter and sugar and stir through. Sift in the flour and salt and combine until the pastry comes together in a ball. (You could follow this process using a food processor if you prefer.) Knead the pastry for a few minutes until smooth. Wrap in plastic wrap and refrigerate for 30 minutes.

Preheat the oven to 325°F (160°C). Knead the pastry briefly on a floured surface to soften it. Form it into a sausage and divide into six even pieces. Roll each piece into a circle around ¹⁄₁₆ in (2 mm) thick. Press the pieces into six greased, 3½ in (9 cm) individual tart tins and trim the edges. Cover each tart case with foil or baking paper and fill with rice or baking weights. Bake for 10–12 minutes or until the pastry is golden, removing the foil and rice towards the end. Keep the oven running while you prepare the Filling.

Filling
In a mixing bowl whisk together the sugar and cream until the sugar has dissolved. Whisk in the eggs, lime juice and rind and pour the liquid into the tart cases. Bake in the oven for around 15 minutes or until the Filling has just set. Allow the tarts to cool before removing them from the tins.

To serve
Preheat your broiler grill to its highest temperature. Sprinkle the tarts evenly with the Chili Rock Sugar and place them under the grill until the sugar caramelizes. Remove from the grill and leave the tarts to cool for a few minutes until the sugar sets hard. Alternatively, you can caramelize the tops with a gas blowtorch.

Ginger tapioca pudding
with lychees

2 cups (300 g) dried tapioca pearls
2 large pieces (4 oz/125 g) young ginger
1 cup (250 ml) sweetened condensed milk
6 fresh or canned lychees
6 sprigs mint

Serves 6

Use young ginger in this dessert as it is milder and juicier than older, woodier ginger. It is also more likely to give a beautiful pink tinge to the tapioca. Alternatively, use galangal for a more piquant flavor.

Fill a pot with water and bring to a boil. Add the dried tapioca pearls, stirring at first to make sure they don't stick. Simmer until they are almost completely transparent with just a small speck of white left in the middle (around 10 minutes). Drain and refresh under cold water.

Wet a large square of muslin cloth and wring it out. Lay the cloth inside a large bowl so that it comes up and over the sides and grate the ginger into the cloth. Form a ball around the ginger and squeeze out as much juice as possible—you should get around $1/8$ cup (30 ml).

Divide the ginger juice and tapioca between six small serving bowls and stir to combine. Gently warm the condensed milk in a saucepan and pour it over the tapioca. Stir briefly then allow the pudding to cool (the mixture will set as it cools). Chill in the refrigerator until ready to serve.

Garnish with the peeled lychees and mint sprigs.

Papaya coconut custard
with toasted sesame seeds

8 egg yolks
2 cups (500 ml) coconut cream
¾ cup (150 g) shaved dark palm sugar
1¼ cups (200 g) papaya flesh, diced
½ tablespoon sesame seeds, lightly roasted

Serves 6

Instead of papaya you can use any tropical fruits, such as mango, pineapple or banana.

In a mixing bowl whisk together the egg yolks, coconut cream and palm sugar until the sugar dissolves.

Divide the diced papaya between six small heatproof serving bowls. Strain the custard over the fruit, completely covering it. Cover the bowls with plastic wrap and insert into a steamer (or several steamers). Steam until the custard set (around 10 minutes).

Serve the custard either warm or chilled, scattered with the sesame seeds.

Caramelized ginger rice pudding with tropical fruit topping

8 egg yolks

1¼ cups (150 g) superfine (caster) sugar

1¼ cups (300 ml) thickened cream

1¼ cups (300 ml) pure cream

1 in (2½ cm) piece young ginger, finely chopped

2 cups (200 g) cooked Jasmine Rice (page 24)

½ cup (100 g) brown sugar

Tropical fruit topping

½ cup (100 g) diced pineapple

½ cup (80 g) diced papaya

½ cup (80 g) diced mango

Serves 6

I have used pineapple, papaya and mango in this topping, but you may use any combination of tropical fruits.

Make the Jasmine Rice by following the recipe on page 24.

Combine the egg yolks and caster sugar in a mixing bowl and whisk until the sugar dissolves. Add the thickened and pure cream, ginger and Jasmine Rice.

Preheat the oven to 300°F (150°C). Spoon the rice custard into six ramekins or heatproof dishes and place them in a deep baking tray lined with a dish towel (this keeps the dishes from moving around). Pour boiling water into the tray to come between half and two-thirds of the way up the sides of the dishes. Cover the tray loosely with a sheet of foil and place in the oven to bake for 20 minutes or until the custard are just set. Cool and refrigerate the custard until ready to serve.

To serve, combine the pineapple, papaya and mango and set aside. Preheat your broiler grill to its highest temperature and sprinkle the pudding evenly with brown sugar. Place them under the grill until the sugar caramelizes, then set aside to cool for a few minutes until the sugar sets hard. Alternatively, you can caramelize the tops with a gas blowtorch. Top the pudding with a spoonful of the Tropical Fruit Topping and serve immediately.

Lime and lemongrass parfait with palm sugar wafers

I love the combination of lime and lemongrass in desserts. To make the dish truly dazzling, serve it with Raspberry Jam (page 226).

Parfait

2½ cups (300 g) superfine (caster) sugar

6 eggs, plus 3 egg yolks

3 cups (750 ml) heavy cream

3 kaffir lime leaves, finely sliced into thin shreds

Grated rind of 2 limes

2 stalks lemongrass, tender inner part of bottom third only, finely chopped

Wafers

⅔ cup (150 g) unsalted butter, softened

¾ cup (150 g) shaved palm sugar

1¼ cups (170 g) all-purpose flour, sifted

½ cup (125 ml) golden syrup

Serves 6

Parfait

Place the sugar, eggs and yolks in a mixing bowl and set it over a pot of simmering water. Whisk the mixture until it thickens enough to form ribbons (around 10 minutes). Place the bowl on a work surface and keep whisking occasionally until it cools completely.

In a separate bowl lightly whip the cream until soft peaks form, then fold the cream, kaffir lime leaves, lime rind and lemongrass into the egg mixture using a spatula or wooden spoon. Pour into a loaf tin lined with greaseproof paper and freeze for at least 3 hours (preferably overnight).

Wafers

Cream the butter and palm sugar until pale and fluffy. Fold in the flour and then the golden syrup. Refrigerate the dough for 30 minutes.

Preheat the oven to 275°F (140°C). Lay a large sheet of greaseproof paper on a work surface and place the dough on top. Cover with a matching sheet of greaseproof paper and roll the dough out with a rolling pin until it is roughly $1/16$ in (2 mm) thick. Transfer the paper and dough to a baking sheet and cook for around 8 minutes or until the Wafer has browned and is starting to bubble. Set aside to cool. Once cool, remove the paper and break the Wafers into desired pieces.

(You can make these Wafers a day in advance if required and just before serving, heat them for 15 seconds in a 400°F (200°C) oven to make them crisp again.)

To serve

Turn the Parfait out of the mold, cut into slices and serve accompanied with the Wafers.

Special ingredients and kitchen equipment

Asian celery
A close relative of common celery but darker green and more pungent. Substitute common celery or Italian parsley.

Banana leaves
These large, dark green leaves can be used to wrap fish and meats before grilling them on the barbecue, or can be cut into squares and used as serving plates. They are sold rolled in bundles.

Bean curd skins
Large, light brown papery sheets that are softened in water and used to wrap fillings. Bean curd parcels are commonly served at dim sum. Available in packets at Asian grocers.

Betel leaves
Pronounced 'beetle' leaves, these dark green, glossy leaves around the size of the palm of your hand are crisp and almost neutral in flavor. A fantastic textural addition to salads or to use as a garnish, and in Thailand they are used to wrap ingredients for snacks.

Black beans, dried and salted
A Chinese fermented soy bean product. Vacuum-sealed, dried black beans are not as salty as the black beans in brine and they hold together better when cooked. They need to be gently rinsed before use.

Black Chinese vinegar
A Chinese vinegar usually made from glutinous rice. Chinkiang or Pun Chun are good varieties.

Bonito flakes
The dried shavings of the bonito fish are used to flavor Japanese soups. They have a smoked fish flavor and are fine enough to not need straining. In Japan they serve 'dancing bonito'—flakes that jump and wiggle around when sprinkled directly on a dish.

Candlenuts
A popular ingredient in Indonesian and Malaysian cooking. Candlenuts are pounded into curry pastes and can act as a thickener. They are similar in appearance to macadamia nuts, and macadamias are a good substitute.

Chilies
I use a range of chilies in my cooking: fresh red or green bird's-eye chilies for intense chili heat, fresh finger-length chilies for milder heat, and dried red finger-length chilies in slow-cooked dishes, red curry paste and dishes like fried rice—they are usually soaked in warm water before use. To deseed fresh chili slices if required, swirl them around in a bowl of water to dislodge the seeds, then dry them in a salad spinner if you have one, which helps to remove any remaining seeds.

Coconuts, mature
Mature coconuts are used for their flesh (which is also used to make coconut milk and cream and dried coconut products such as desiccated and threaded coconut). When buying mature coconuts, find a supplier that has a high turnover and buy the ones that feel heaviest. Crack them by banging them several times with a hammer or the blunt side of a cleaver, then prise the flesh from the shell in large chunks with a screwdriver or a small sharp knife (an oyster knife is ideal). Shave into thin strips with a vegetable peeler to add crunch to

salads and other dishes.

Coconuts, young
Young coconuts are used for coconut juice and flesh. They are sold with their white fibrous covering carved into a cylinder with a pointed top. When buying them, select the ones that sound the juiciest. To open them, pierce with a skewer and drain the juice then cut off the top with a sharp knife or cleaver. You should be able to scoop out the flesh with a spoon. While the flesh is soft, it doesn't break up easily and is fantastic cut into very fine strands and added to salads. Both young and mature coconuts should yield about 2 cups of meat.

Coconut milk and cream
While you can make your own coconut milk from grated fresh mature coconut, it is often more convenient to use the canned variety. Always buy unsweetened coconut milk and cream.

Cucumber oil
The rich, elegant flavor of cucumber oil goes well with Asian food. It is extracted from cucumber seeds and is available from gourmet food stores.

Dashi
A Japanese soup-base made from dried shavings of bonito fish and kombu seaweed. It is available as an instant powder in sachets or containers and has a delicate, smoky flavor. See also *Bonito flakes* and *Kombu*.

Dried Chinese sausages (*Lup cheong*)
These small, mildly spiced Chinese pork sausages are sold dried.

Dumpling skins
See Wonton skins

Fermented fish paste
Much less common than fish sauce, this pungent paste can be found in jars at Asian grocers.

Fish sauce
One of the classic ingredients in the Thai repertoire. The Squid brand is one of the best—light and not too salty.

Galangal
Galangal is from the same family as ginger. It has a pinkish color and a slight perfume, and its piquant flavor is essential in curry pastes.

Garlic chives
These long, green stems are sold in bunches. Cut them into batons and toss them through stir-fries and other dishes to give a mild garlic flavor and add crunch. Green onions or asparagus can be used as substitutes.

Glass noodles
Thin transparent noodles also known as bean thread or cellophane noodles. They are made from mung beans and are sold dried.

Glutinous rice, white and black
Glutinous rice, for making sticky rice, needs to be soaked before cooking. Steaming is the best cooking technique. This rice is eaten in much smaller quantities than jasmine rice—it is often shaped into rice balls or wrapped in small parcels. Black glutinous rice is a wholegrain and therefore needs a longer cooking time. It can be difficult finding authentic

black rice in Australia. Thailand and Bali produce excellent black rice, which becomes a reddish-brown color when cooked and has a beautiful fragrance and nuttiness. Black glutinous rice is famously used in black sticky rice pudding.

Green peppercorns, fresh
Commonly used in Southeast Asian cooking and a major ingredient in jungle curries. They are sold on the stem and are available at markets or Asian grocers over winter/spring. Substitute green peppercorns in brine if necessary, though they lack vitality.

Hoisin sauce
A richly flavored sauce made of fermented soy beans and spices. Good in marinades for pork and duck and traditionally served with Peking duck.

Kaffir lime leaves
These glossy green leaves with a fresh citrus flavor are essential in Southeast Asian cooking. Use them whole, taking them out before serving as you would a bay leaf, or slice them into fine shreds.

Kombu
A thick seaweed sold as dark dried strips that need to be chopped with a sharp knife or cleaver. Kombu is used to flavor soups, where it is discarded once is has softened, although it can also be finely cut and added to salads and other dishes.

Lemongrass
With kaffir lime leaves, lemongrass is one of the most common fresh ingredients in Southeast Asian cuisine. To flavor a soup or stock,

bruise the stalks with a mallet or the side of a cleaver and throw them in whole (or cut into a few convenient pieces). To use them in curry pastes and salads, discard the tough green end (you should be left with roughly the bottom third) and slice as finely as possible.

Liquorice roots, dried
Dried liquorice roots are sold in packets at Asian grocers.

Lotus roots and leaves
Outside the food world the lotus plant is known for its beautiful flower found in ponds all over Asia. In the kitchen it is very versatile—as well as the roots and leaves you can also eat the seeds. The root is shaped like a sweet potato and is a pale cream color. Inside are hollow compartments that form a beautiful pattern when the root is cut crosswise. It has a subtle flavor that works well in sweet and savory dishes. Lotus roots are available frozen but I avoid buying them that way. Lotus leaves are used in Chinese cooking for wrapping ingredients such as rice— the parcels are steamed and the leaves impart a tea-like flavor. They are sold dried and need to be softened in water.

Lychees
Fresh lychees are available in summer. They are small reddish-brown fruit with a rough outer skin. Inside is very sweet white flesh and a large seed that is discarded.

Maltose syrup
A thick light-brown syrup used in Chinese roast duck to make the skin crisp. Available at Asian grocers.

Mandarin orange peel, dried
A classic Chinese ingredient, used in master stock. Available in packets at Asian grocers.

Mirin
A Japanese rice wine that, unlike sake, is mostly used in cooking. It is pale yellow in color and sweeter than sake.

Miso
A Japanese paste made of fermented soy beans that is used mainly as a base for soup. There are many different varieties but I prefer shiro (white) miso, which has a sweet, mild flavor.

Mushrooms
Shiitake or black Chinese mushrooms are the most common form of Asian mushroom and are available both fresh and dried. Dried shiitake are great for infusing soups and stocks and have a slightly stronger flavor, while fresh shiitake are used in quick dishes like stir-fries. They are small and brown and have a firm texture and rich flavor. *Oyster* mushrooms, or abalone mushrooms, are pale and fan-shaped with brownish-grey backs. *Enoki* mushrooms have long, slender stems and tiny heads and are a white or tan color. Fresh oyster and enoki mushroom are now widely available. *Wood ear* mushrooms are small, dark, petal-shaped mushrooms that grow in clumps. They can be difficult to find; look in gourmet greengrocers and Asian grocers. You can buy them frozen or dried, but I use them fresh.

Oyster sauce
A thick, sweet Chinese sauce flavored with oyster extract. I prefer the Lee Kum Kee brand.

Palm sugar
Palm sugar is a product of the sugar palm tree and is either light or dark. Light palm sugar, which is a pale tan color, usually comes in round cakes as it is set in coconut shells, while dark palm sugar, a dark brown color, is cylindrical as it set inside bamboo. Dark palm sugar is less refined and has a rich molasses-like flavor, which makes it great for syrups and desserts.

Pandanus leaves and essence
Called the "vanilla of the east", the long, spear-shaped pandanus leaf belongs to the screwpine tree (a member of the Pandanus family). Leaves are tied in knots and dropped into curries, soups and rice dishes, where they impart a distinctive vanilla-like flavor. The leaves and essence are also used in desserts for the flavor as well as their bright green color.

Pat Chun sweetened vinegar
Made from rice wine, spices and caramel and sometimes referred to as "Chinese Worcestershire". Available from Asian grocers.

Plum sauce
A traditional accompaniment to Peking duck. I use the plain variety.

Pomelos
Giant citrus fruit that grow up to the size of a soccer ball. The flesh inside can be pink or yellow; it is quite fibrous and dry and has a sour note (although is sweeter than a grapefruit). Peeled and cut into segments, it is a great addition to Thai salads. Use pink grapefruit as a substitute.

Raw rock sugar crystals

An unrefined sugar that has much more flavor than regular white sugar. It has a yellow tinge and slightly earthy character. It is great in desserts and also combines well with Shao Xing rice wine and soy sauce, and is an essential ingredient in Chinese master stock. When you need it in a powdered form, grind it with a mortar and pestle. Available at Asian grocers.

Red bean paste

A thick, burgundy paste made from adzuki beans. You can buy it in cans sweetened or unsweetened (for sweet or savory dishes). I prefer the sweetened Japanese variety and the unsweetened Korean variety.

Red dates, dried

Also known as jujubes, Chinese red dates are small and shrivelled with a deep red color. They team well with spices such as star anise and cinnamon and complement duck and chicken. Sold in packets at Asian grocers.

Rice noodle sheets

Used for Chinese rice-noodle rolls, but they can also be cut into noodles. Available in the refrigerated section of Asian grocers.

Rice vermicelli, dried

Dried rice vermicelli, also known as *mifen* or *beehoon*, are very fine rice threads that must be plunged into hot water to soften before use.

Rice wine vinegar

Japan makes the best quality rice-wine vinegar—the brand we use at ezard is Mitsukan. It has a clean, crisp flavor and is perfect for pickles and dressings.

Rose apples

Rose apples are pear-shaped and usually have rose-colored skin. They are popular in snacks and salads in Indonesia, Malaysia and Thailand and their firm flesh makes them suited for cooking in curries and other dishes. When used this way, they are similar to a choko. Look for them at Asian greengrocers around autumn.

Sake

A clear-colored Japanese rice wine. This is Japan's most famous alcohol, often drunk warm, but it is also good in cooking. The more expensive, the better the quality.

Scallops, dried

Dried scallops have a stronger, sweeter and more intense flavor than fresh scallops, which makes them fantastic in soups and sauces. Look for the Japanese variety—these are not as salty as Chinese dried scallops and are about double the size (they are roughly the same size as large fresh scallops). They can be harder to find—look in Asian grocers or even in Chinese medicine shops in Chinatown, where they are often displayed in large jars.

Shallots, Asian

These small relatives of the onion are essential in Southeast Asian food—whether pounded into curry pastes or fried as a garnish. Their flesh is actually purple, not red.

Shao Xing rice wine

Shao Xing rice wine, or Chinese rice wine, is one of my favorite ingredients to cook with. It originates from northern China and is slightly earthy and rustic in character. You can buy drinking-quality Shao Xing, which you can serve warm like sake, or Shao Xing suitable for cooking. It comes in various vintages: 1 year old, 7 years old or 14 years old; 1-year-old Shao Xing, which is what you'll find in Asian grocers, is fine for cooking.

Shichimi pepper powder

Also known as shichimi-togarashi or Japanese seven-spice. It can include different ingredients, but generally always includes chili, sesame seeds, citrus peel (usually mandarin or tangerine), a variety of pepper and nori seaweed. A popular condiment to serve with soups and other dishes.

Shrimp, dried

Dried shrimp come in packets at Asian grocers. They are miniature and light orange and can be used as they are, or softened in water, or roasted. Roasted dried shrimp have a terrific smoky, salty flavor. They are often used in Thai salads and relishes.

Shrimp paste, dried

Dried shrimp paste is known in Malaysia as *belachan*. Roast it to bring out its full flavor (page 9). You can buy it in jars or blocks, but the firm block variety is more authentic and has a stronger fragrance.

Sichuan pepper

Sichuan pepper isn't a true pepper but the berry of the Chinese prickly ash tree. It has a reddish-brown color and gives a tingling sensation on the tongue. Dry-roasting the peppercorns in a wok before grinding them brings out their flavor when used as a seasoning.

Silk melon
Silk melon looks like a light-colored zucchini. It is also known as luffa melon and has a ridged skin that is peeled off. It has a slightly earthy and muddy flavor and its texture is similar to squash (the yellow pattypan variety).

Soy sauce
I use two types of soy in my cooking—sweet soy and soy. Sweet soy is an Indonesian soy known as *kecap manis*—it is naturally brewed, thick and syrupy, usually sweetened with molasses. I use the ABC brand. There are two kinds of soy I prefer. Naturally brewed Taiwanese soy such as the Kim Ve Wong brand is the least salty of all the soys, so it is suited to salads and other dishes where you don't want saltiness to dominate. Japanese soys (such as tamari or shoyu) are other very good soy sauces that I use when I want a slightly stronger flavor. I avoid Chinese soy sauces as they are often harsh and brewed with chemicals.

Tamarind
Tamarind pulp is extracted from the pods of tamarind trees. It is dried and compressed into dark, sticky blocks. Soak it in varying amounts of water—more if you want a subtly flavored liquid, less if you want a pungent paste. Tamarind has a sour flavor and is great in curries, soups and salads. At ezard we are sometimes lucky enough to get hold of fresh tamarind pods from Queensland—the flavor is unbeatable!

Tapioca pearls, dried
These small white balls made from cassava flour are used in desserts and become translucent when cooked.

Taro
A large potato-like swamp vegetable that grows in the tropics. It has a creamy, starchy texture and sometimes purple flecks inside its rough brown skin. Taros weigh around 2 lbs (1 kg) and are available from Asian grocers.

Thai basil
Thai basil looks much like regular basil but with purple stems. It has a peppery, aniseed flavor. Sometimes, when the flavor of Thai basil seems too strong, I like to combine it with torn betel leaves. If you can find holy basil, which isn't quite as strong as Thai basil, use that instead.

Turmeric
Fresh turmeric is a very underrated spice. It is a rhizome, like ginger and galangal, but is smaller and less knobbly. Bright orange on the outside and inside, it imparts a vibrant yellow color to whatever it is cooked with. The difference between fresh and dried turmeric is considerable—the mustard-like pungency of fresh turmeric is great in curries and other dishes and it is so authentic to Southeast Asian cooking that there really isn't a substitute. Rather than using dried turmeric in its place, I would suggest leaving turmeric out of the recipe; however, I do use dried turmeric in curry powder.

Wakame seaweed flakes, dried
A Japanese seaweed that is sold dried in packets. It is rehydrated in water and sliced, and often tossed through noodle salads or put in miso soup. Wakame has a silky texture and quite a neutral vegetable flavor.

Wasabi paste
A pungent Japanese condiment made from the wasabi root and usually served with sushi and sashimi. Difficult to get hold of fresh, pre-made wasabi paste comes in tubes and you can also buy it as a powder.

Wonton skins
Thin, square sheets of yellow dough for making Chinese wontons. Like dumpling skins, they are available from the refrigerated section of Asian grocers.

Yellow bean paste
A thick paste (more brown than yellow) made from soy beans. It is sold in jars and has a sweet/salty flavor that is good as a condiment or mixed with other ingredients in a sauce.

Wok

The wok is the most essential item in my kitchen, used for everything from stir-fries to deep-frying and dry-frying to steaming. For deep-frying, two handy tools to have with the wok are a wok spider (a mesh basket on a wooden handle, for removing items from the oil) and a slotted spoon, for removing smaller items. For stir-frying and dry-frying, wok spoons are great for stirring and serving.

Non-stick woks are not recommended as stir-frying and other ways of cooking in a wok are intended to be quite vigorous and the surface will be quickly scratched away. Buy a regular mild-steel wok and season it before use: first, rub the inside all over with a little cooking oil and gently heat the wok for 10–15 minutes. Wipe it thoroughly with paper towels—the paper will come away black. Continue the process of oiling, heating and wiping the wok until the paper wipes clean. After each use, wash your wok in hot water without soap and dry immediately.

Mortar and pestle

Every kitchen should have a mortar and pestle. The heavy granite versions available from Asian grocers are best. They are great for grinding spices, making curry pastes and even for Thai salads. The bigger the mortar and pestle the better—you have more weight in the pestle (the pounding tool), which makes pounding easier, and you can fit more into the mortar.

It is possible to make curry pastes in a food processor, but the texture will be different as a processor will chop the ingredients rather than pound and blend them. Beginning a paste with a mortar and pestle (pounding to a coarse slurry) and then finishing to a smooth paste in a food processor is a good compromise and is the method we use at ezard.

While a mortar and pestle is also essential for grinding spices, a spice grinder is a great thing to have on hand for grinding large quantities.

Steamer

I use bamboo steamers, which are available from Asian grocers in just about every imaginable size—large ones for steaming whole fish or large pieces of pork belly, to smaller ones for dumplings. At ezard we use them over woks, and have large woks to fit large baskets, but you could also use a pot with the same rim size. They are stackable, which can be handy for steaming many dumplings at once (though not a good idea for rice or heavier items) or for keeping things warm. We use the perforated steel inserts that are available in each basket size, but if you don't have these, line the basket with a sheet of greaseproof paper, or lightly oil the slats. When steaming, the water in the wok or pot should be at a gentle simmer.

Claypot

Claypot cooking has been around since ancient times. Claypots are the Asian equivalent of the casserole dish, with a handle and a lid. They are porous, so with each use they should be soaked in water for 20 minutes prior to cooking. To prevent them cracking, it is best to start in a cool oven, and when the dish is cooked, turn off the oven and allow it to cool a little before removing. Claypots are available from Asian grocers. Alternatively, you can use a casserole dish with a lid.

Cleaver

A cleaver is essential for cutting up duck and chicken Chinese style (through the bone) as well as splitting crabs and coconuts—anything where a bit of heft is required.

Slicer and shredder

While you can get away with using a sharp knife, a slicing and shredding tool like the Japanese version made by Benriner will make life a lot easier. This is a plastic mandoline with different fittings for slicing and shredding to different thicknesses. They are fantastic for shredding things such as green mango and green papaya.

Electric rice cooker

While you can cook rice without one, using the absorption method in a saucepan or pot on the stovetop, electric rice cookers make cooking and serving rice so much easier. The rice is always fluffy and cooked to perfection, and it also keeps warm until you're ready to serve.

Complete list of recipes

Dedication

This book is dedicated to the hawker markets and dim sum houses I have traveled to over the last few years. From Hong Kong and the back streets of Thailand, where I have dined in many fantastic restaurants, to the outdoor eateries of Malaysia and north to China, where I have sat with some of the great chefs of the East.

Acknowledgments

There are so many people I would like to thank, not only for their input but also for their passion, loyalty and friendship. All of them have touched this project in their own way and deserve significant acknowledgment for helping me write *Lotus*.

Special thanks goes to my good friend and protégé Dane Clouston. Dane has now helped me with the framework and writing of two cookbooks, all the while keeping up his tireless commitment behind the stove as Head Chef at Opia, our restaurant in Hong Kong.

I wish to thank my ezard kitchen staff: Alex Delly, who assisted me enormously with the organisation of the photo shoot; my right-hand-man Ben Cooper, who helped with many of the final touches; and of course my loyal and trusting kitchen brigade: Dylan Roberts, Scott Huggins, Lee Wright, Gerard Timmermans, Simon Polkinghorne, Sean McCarthy, Travis Cropely, Rachel Johnston and Liana Crothers, many of whom helped me test these recipes.

Heartfelt thanks to Tina Rees and Veronica Finarelli for their assistance and support while I was working on *Lotus*. These two really saw my dark side in front of the computer late at night finishing this book, so thank you for putting up with me during that time.

Thanks to my front-of-house team, headed up by Jane Semple. They are Adam Cash, Zoe Clements, Marcus Stokkel, Gudiya Riddell, Samantha Friend, Amy Schneider, Tim Brljacic,

Anna Benton, Elizabeth Reid and Olga Grzbyborska.

Pamela Bakes is a great friend and always there for me. Thank you Pam, for your creative spirit, your energy and enthusiasm for everything I do. And in particular for helping me with the writing of this book.

The team at JIA in Hong Kong have showed unwavering faith in my food. If not for them, there would be no *Lotus*. JIA gave me the drive and encouragement to follow my instincts and create recipes and menus with confidence. Special thanks to Yenn Wong and Barry Polson, the driving force. Thanks also to Matt Lawdorn, Jason Cohen, Marina Bullivant and the both the kitchen and front-of-house teams of Y's and Opia.

This is the second book I have published with Hardie Grant Books and I would like to thank Associate Publisher Mary Small and Editor Rachel Pitts. Thanks also to Ryan Guppy for the exquisite design of the book, to Greg Elms for the beautiful photographs, and to Sara Backhouse for styling them.

Many of my suppliers are my very closest friends. Thank you for your ongoing commitment to providing the quality that inspires me every day. You allow me to push and blur the boundaries of Australian and Asian cuisines.

And lastly, to my wife Tina: for all your love, encouragement, passion and support for what I do, I thank you. You are my world.

Cook's notes

Unless otherwise specified:

Eggs are free-range and weigh around 60 g (2 oz).

Milk is full cream.

Cream is either pure (45 per cent butterfat) or thickened (35 per cent butterfat).

Sugar is white sugar, palm sugar or yellow rock sugar. White sugar is the regular granulated variety and palm sugar is light palm sugar.

Garlic cloves, ginger, galangal, onions turmeric and shallots are peeled.

Chicken is organic and free-range wherever possible.

Sea salt is the flaked variety.

Coconut milk and cream are unsweetened.

Coconuts are mature.

Olive oil is pure.

Tablespoons hold 20 ml liquid.

All conversions to imperial measurements are approximate.

See also *Special ingredients and kitchen equipment*, page 232.